PROPORTIONALISM AND THE
NATURAL LAW TRADITION

Pinckaers - 2 articles
Kaczor -

How do nominalism + nominalists lead to proportionalism?

proportionalism → absolutism, conscience at middle ground, allowed dissent according to absolutism instead of conscience

Christopher Kaczor

PROPORTIONALISM AND THE

NATURAL LAW TRADITION

The Catholic University of America Press
Washington, D.C.

Copyright ©2002
The Catholic University of America Press
Reprinted in paperback 2010
All rights reserved

The paper used in this publication meets the minimum requirements of
American National Standards for Information Science—Permanence of Paper
for Printed Library materials, ANSI Z39.48-1984.

∞

LIBRARY OF CONGRESS CATALOGING-IN-PUBLICATION DATA
Kaczor, Christopher Robert, 1969–
    Proportionalism and the natural law tradition / Christopher Kaczor.
        p. cm.
    Includes bibliographical references and index.
    ISBN 0-8132-1093-3 (alk. paper)
    ISBN-13: 978-0-8132-1867-0 (pbk)
    1. Christian ethics—Catholic authors.   2. Proportionality (Ethics).
3. Natural law.   I. Title.
BJ1249 .K36 2002
241'.042—dc21

To My Parents
with love, honor, and respect
beyond the power of words

CONTENTS

༃

Acknowledgments, ix

Introduction   1

I. The Plausibility of Proportionalism   9

II. How Double-Effect Reasoning   23
Became Proportionalism

III. Human Action and Contemporary   45
Questions

IV. Defining the Object of the Human Act   91

V. Proportionate Reason as the First   119
Principle of Practical Reasoning

VI. Doing Evil to Achieve Good?   141

VII. Exceptionless Norms in the   171
Catholic Tradition

Conclusion   205

Bibliography, 211

Index, 225

Don't neglect; On exam

ACKNOWLEDGMENTS

Many people read this manuscript or portions of it at different stages of development and offered important contributions to it. Their suggestions, though not always accepted, characteristically led to greater understanding of the debate and often to significant reconsideration of the issues. Though errors and weaknesses undoubtedly remain, they have saved me from a great many failings. Deserving particular recognition are Randy Smith, Michael Gorman, John O'Callaghan, Maura Ryan, John Finnis, Stephen Brock, Robert Gahl, Jean Porter, Martin Tracey, Andreas Speer, Albert Zimmerman, Todd Salzman, Paul Weithman, Fred Fredosso, David Solomon, David O'Connor, Andreas Speer, Peter Knauer, Thomas Hibbs, Joseph Boyle, James Walter, John R. Bowlin, David Arius, Jr., and James Hanink. For their time, effort, and helpful advice I thank them warmly. Especially fruitful in writing this book was the opportunity to study proportionalism at the University of Notre Dame with the late Richard McCormick, S.J. His class on Method in Moral Theology as well as written and oral response to my work was tremendously helpful. Above all, I thank Ralph McInerny for the support, example, and encouragement he has given me for such a long time and in so many ways. Knowing him is one of the great gifts of my life.

I also wish to thank the editors of the following journals for their permission to republish in this book the following articles: "Double-Effect Reasoning: From Jean Pierre Gury to Peter Knauer," *Theological Studies* 59 pp. 297–316, "Distinguishing Intention from Foresight" *International Philosophical Quarterly* vol. XLI, No.1, 161, pp. 77–89, and "Moral Absolutism and Ectopic Pregnancy" *Journal of Medicine and Philosophy,* volume 26, number 1. Copyright © by The Journal of Medicine and Philosophy, Inc. Special thanks to Susan Needham of The Catholic University of America Press, whose keen eyes expelled a legion of errors, and to Tom Ellis for constructing the index and proofreading the manuscript.

In addition to summer research grants at Loyola Marymount University, this book was also aided by the Alexander von Humbolt Foundation which supported this project with a 1996–1997 Federal Chancellor (Bundeskanzler) Fellowship that allowed me a chance to more fully incorporate German contributions to the debate while working at the Thomas-Institut at the University of Cologne. The von Humbolt Foundation also supported the presentation of portions of the manuscript to audiences at Queens' College, Cambridge University, the Pontifical Gregorian University, the International Theological Institute in Austria, the Catholic University of Leuven, and at Lady Margaret Hall, Oxford University. Also helpful were questions raised at presentations of sections of the work, at the U.S. Naval Academy, Loyola University–New Orleans, the University of Notre Dame, Loyola Marymount University, and Stanford University.

INTRODUCTION

On the anniversary of Hiroshima and the Feast of the Transfiguration in 1993, John Paul II signed the encyclical *Veritatis splendor*. A world divided about moral absolutes found reflection in a Church itself divided about moral absolutes, indeed about the very meaning of the phrase. Reactions to the encyclical, from within the Church, reflected the deep divisions that have arisen between so-called "proportionalists" and "traditionalists."

Although there are authors who genuinely fall under these descriptions, the labels can also be misleading. The most prominent traditionalists, for example Germain Grisez, Joseph Boyle, and John Finnis, reject "traditional" doctrines of both fundamental ethics, such as the commensurability of goods, and of applied ethics, such as the impermissibility of craniotomy. These authors and their colleagues have done strikingly creative and original work on the principle of double effect, the basis of moral obligation, and the nature of human flourishing. As John Langan notes, these authors have revised "many standard positions on the hierarchical order of goods, on the connection between nature and morality, and on the relevance of consequences to determining moral rightness."[1] They hardly reflect the static associations of the word "traditionalist." Nor is it accurate to say that advocates of proportionalism, sometimes called revisionists, are

---

1. John Langan, "Catholic Moral Rationalism and the Philosophical Bases of Moral Theology," *Theological Studies* 50 (1989) 43.

entirely untraditional. While they have revised aspects of received teaching, they do indeed carry on a tradition of moral
analysis, and part of the work of this book is to identify this tradition more precisely. Appeals to the letter and spirit of Thomas
Aquinas are not at all atypical of those who call themselves proportionalists or revisionists.

The labels "traditionalist" and "proportionalist" can also mis-
lead insofar as they suggest two unified groups concerned merely
with each other, when in fact neither group is entirely unified.
It is clear that the so-called traditionalists disagree among themselves about many significant matters, and the same thing
may be said about proportionalists. The proportionalism of Garth
Hallet, for example, differs from the proportionalism of Peter
Knauer, and this in turn differs from the proportionalism of
Richard McCormick.

However, there are in fact certain commonalities that suggest
speaking of proportionalism is not entirely ambiguous. A wide
range of proportionalists, though perhaps not every one, would
agree with this definition of proportionalism given by James Walter in the *Encyclopedia of Catholicism,* edited by Richard McBrien:

A type of analysis for determining the objective moral rightness and
wrongness of actions in conflict situations and procedure for establishing
exceptions to behavioral norms. It began in the mid-1960s as a revision
of both the principle of double effect and the doctrine of intrinsic moral
evil. "Proportionate reason" is the moral principle used to determine concretely and objectively the rightness or wrongness of acts and various exceptions to behavioral norms. Proportionalists argue that no judgment of
moral rightness or wrongness of acts can be made without considering all
circumstances of the action. Because the human act is a structural unity,
no aspect of the act can be morally appraised apart from all the other
components. Consideration of the agent's intention, all foreseeable consequences, institutional obligations, and a proportion between the premoral values and disvalues are necessary before making moral judgment.

The proponents make a distinction between moral and premoral val-
ues/disvalues. Moral values and disvalues describe the qualities of persons as they confront situations, e.g., just or unjust. Premoral evils or disvalues refer to the harms, lacks, deprivations, etc., that occur in, or as a
result of, human agency, e.g., death. Premoral values refer to those conditioned goods that we pursue for human and non-human well-being,

application of the principle of proportionate reason. The principle contains two elements. First, the word "reason" means a premoral, i.e., a conditioned, and thus not absolute, value that an agent seeks to promote in the whole act. Second, the term "proportionate" refers to a proper relation that must exist between the premoral disvalue(s) contained in, or caused by, the means and the end or a proper relation between the end and the premoral disvalue(s) in the consequences of the act.

In making exceptions to negative behavioral norms, e.g., no killing, proportionate reason is used to discern if the premoral disvalue contained in, or caused by, the means (killing) stands in due proportion to the premoral value in the act (self-defense). If a proportionate reason is present, the norm as stated does not apply to this act under its terms of reference. Exceptions to behavioral norms that prohibit premoral evil, then, are made on the basis of the presence of a proportionate reason.

Proportionalists claim that the distinction between direct and indirect in the principle of double effect is not always morally decisive. The distinction can be merely descriptive in that it only indicates what agents are doing, what they are aiming at, and with what means.[2]

This lengthy definition does not definitively capture all the variations and different formulations of proportionalist theory, but it does give a good overview that summarizes a number of authors' views. Individual versions of proportionalism may be made more intelligible in light of this general understanding.

Though there is widespread agreement among proportionalists in rejecting traditional understandings of intrinsically evil acts, there are indeed significant differences among revisionist theologians. In early writings, both Curran and McCormick disagreed, not only with each other but also with Bruno Schüller, as to whether and why judicial execution of an innocent person is wrong. McCormick and Daniel Maguire differ on whether or not there is ever a proportionate reason for "direct" killing (euthanasia) in terminal cases.[3] Similar differences could be pointed out among other prominent writers who differ in approaches taken, terminology used, and conclusions drawn.

2. James J. Walter, "Proportionalism," *The HarperCollins Encyclopedia of Catholicism*, ed. Richard McBrien (San Francisco: Harper, 1995) 1058.

3. Richard McCormick, "Commentary on the Commentaries," in *Doing Evil to Achieve Good: Moral Choice in Conflict Situations*, ed. Richard McCormick and Paul Ramsey (Chicago: Loyola University Press, 1978) 215.

All revisionists do agree, of this one can be confident, that the use of contraception may be morally licit. In fact, there is a strong sociological link between proportionalism and this position. As Edward Vacek notes:

> An argument could be made that *Humanae Vitae* has fueled the development of P[roportionalism] in Catholic thought, and that the birth control debate has been so drawn-out and intense precisely because it is really a debate over a style of moral reasoning and a vision of what it means to be human, not to mention over what God is doing in the world—therefore over much larger matters than the use of a pill.[4]

Vacek is absolutely correct that *Humanae vitae* led to a greater questioning of traditional formulations of many matters.[5] If one surveys the literature that began what is now called "proportionalism,"[6] one will find a recurring pattern: first basic principles are laid down and defended, and then it is invariably shown that these principles justify the use of contraception.

Although proportionalism arose contemporaneously with and in response to the Catholic Church's teaching on contraception, and sociologically the topics seem to go hand in hand, the two issues are logically quite distinct. Although every proportionalist agrees that the use of contraception can be morally licit, several prominent critics of proportionalism, for example Paul Ramsey, Stanley Hauerwas, William Frankena, Jean Porter, and Alan Donagan nevertheless agree with them that the use of contraception is not always intrinsically evil. In fact, it is logically possible to accept proportionalism and still hold that all acts of contraception are wrong.[7] To question or reject proportionalism is not thereby to accept the Catholic Church's teaching on birth

4. Edward Vacek, "Proportionalism: One View of the Debate," *Proportionalism For and Against*, ed. Christopher Kaczor (Milwaukee: Marquette University Press, 2000) 412–13.

5. See too, Bernard Hoose, *Proportionalism: The American Debate and Its European Roots* (Washington, D.C.: Georgetown University Press, 1987) 37.

6. See, for instance, *Moral Norms and Catholic Tradition*, ed. Charles E. Curran and Richard A. McCormick (New York: Paulist Press, 1979), and *Proportionalism For and Against*, ed. Kaczor.

7. See Christopher Kaczor, "Proportionalism and the Pill: How Developments in Theory Lead to Contradictions to Practice," *The Thomist* 63 (1999) 269–81. Reprinted in *Proportionalism For and Against*, ed. Kaczor, 467–77.

regulation, though it is an understandable confusion to conflate the two issues. Nevertheless, the genesis of proportionalism cannot be understood apart from this issue.

Other logically distinct issues have become inseparably associated with this revolution, including Karl Rahner's fundamental freedom (not to be confused with the fundamental option), disputes about infallibility and the ordinary magisterium, the role of the theologian and public dissent, and Scripture's relationship to moral theology. Is this discussion then properly theological and left to those working within this context and this context alone?

The answer given by advocates of proportionalism and many of its critics is, no. One does not need to presuppose reliance on divine revelation or authoritative interpretation of revelation in order to access the plausibility of proportionalism. The debate in question rather belongs to what was once called "philosophical theology" or "natural theology." Although both the natural law tradition (at least as instantiated by Aquinas) and proportionalism can readily be related to the realm of revealed theology or mysteries of faith, it nonetheless seems that one can settle certain debates between these two schools within the realm of natural theology or moral philosophy. In the words of Timothy O'Connell, "[I]n a certain sense, moral theology is not theology at all. It is moral philosophy, pursued by persons who are believers."[8] Again, as those familiar with the work on proportionalism done by the authors named earlier know, one's beliefs about the specificity of Christian ethics are often related to but logically independent of the discussion of proportionalism.

It is not surprising that ethicists turn to the sources of Christian wisdom in their search for answers to difficult contemporary questions. Indeed both traditionalists and proportionalists characteristically ground their moral theories more or less directly in the work of Thomas Aquinas. He is their lodestar, so the relationship of Aquinas to proportionalism is no mere antiquarian concern.

8. Timothy E. O'Connell, *Principles for a Catholic Morality* (New York: Seabury Press, 1978) 40.

In an effort to emphasize their continuity with this Thomistic tradition, some have tried to downplay the innovation and controversial character of proportionalism. For instance, one scholar writes: "To discuss concrete moral norms is not to discuss a 'conception of morality.' It is much more modest. [Proportionalists] are but dialoguing with their own tradition on a relatively narrow issue."[9] This surely does not capture the central focus these issues have attracted. Elsewhere Richard McCormick more accurately writes: "I do not believe 'revolution' is too strong a word for the developments that have occurred in moral theology in the last 30 years."[10] Nor was McCormick the first one to recognize the radical character of the changes taking place. He notes: "In 1970, Germain Grisez wrote of Knauer that he 'is carrying through a revolution in principle while pretending only a clarification of traditional ideas.' Grisez was, I believe, right. That 'revolution in principle' gradually led to a vast literature that huddles under the umbrella-term 'proportionalism.'"[11]

"Vast" is exactly the right word. The explosion of literature that this subject has generated suggests not an insignificant adjustment or a resolution to a marginal question, but something very important indeed. The Catholic Church stands as almost a solitary proponent of the existence of moral absolutes in the modern world. No other church or political body in the West has been as visible in opposition to the prevailing melange of emotivism, pragmatism, positivism, and intuitionism dominant in the public square. Hence, the attempt to undermine traditional understandings of moral absolutes from within the Catholic Church itself is significant for the present "culture wars" in Western societies today.

Proportionalism has both theoretical and practical import. It

9. Richard McCormick, *Notes on Moral Theology, 1981 through 1984.* (Washington D.C.: University Press of America, 1984) 114.

10. Richard McCormick, "Moral Theology 1940–1989: An Overview," *Theological Studies* 50 (1989) 6–7. For remarks seemingly minimizing the importance or the significance of the changes, see McCormick, *Notes on Moral Theology, 1981 through 1984,* 69.

11. McCormick, "Moral Theology 1940–1989," 9.

has a tremendous influence, if only implicitly, on the day-to-day lives of millions of people. Unlike many academic moral theories, proportionalism has been translated into practice through the education of priests and other religious educators who serve as teachers on the local and pastoral level. Contemporary training in Catholic moral theology is dominated by one school: proportionalism. No less an authority on the subject than Richard Mc-Cormick writes: "So-called proportionalists include some of the best known names in moral theology throughout the world. . . . My acquaintance with the literature leads me to believe that most theologians share similar perspectives."[12] The sociological influence of this "revised natural law theory" as it is sometimes called should not be underestimated.

The importance of this subject is reflected in part by the inflated, indeed abrasive, rhetoric used in the debate. For instance, one proportionalist author describes those in sympathy with him as sensible, revered, remarkable, insightful, and interesting. On the other hand, those who disagree with his point of view are confused, guilty of elementary philosophical mistakes, one delivering an "analytic howler," and another volunteering to be an "Inquisitor."[13] Opponents of proportionalism are described as the "*immobilisti*"[14] who crush the faithful under unchanging principles[15] in the course of waging war with ongoing police action.[16]

Of course, inflammatory rhetoric comes from those holding the opposite perspective as well. Proportionalists, we learn from one author, are "superficial utilitarians whose Christian principles are for sale."[17] According to others, they promote "deviant

---

12. Ibid., 10, 19.
13. Richard McCormick, "Some Early Reactions to *Veritatis splendor*," *Theological Studies* 55 (1994) 483, 487, 489, 493, 494, 495, 496.
14. Richard McCormick, "Moral Theology 1940–1989," 21.
15. Kathleen Talvacchia and Mary Elizabeth Walsh, "The *Splendor of Truth*: A Feminist Critique," in *Veritatis Splendor: American Responses*, ed. by Michael E. Allsopp and John J. O'Keefe (Kansas City: Sheed and Ward, 1995) 308.
16. Clifford Stevens, "A Matter of Credibility," in *Veritatis Splendor: American Responses*, ed. Allsopp and O'Keefe, 77.
17. Gustav Ermecke, as cited by Richard McCormick in *Notes on Moral Theology, 1965 through 1980* (Washington, D.C.: University Press of America, 1981) 809.

moral theology"[18] and "utilitarian laxism."[19] Some would seem to liken proportionalists to the probabilists of the sixteenth and seventeenth centuries, whom Pascal scalded with his *Provincial Letters*. Indeed, "it was not without reason that one moralist became known as the Lamb of God because he took away so many of the sins of the world."[20]

To paraphrase Richard McCormick, merely to cite such polemic is to condemn it, but clearly the hyperbolic language used reflects that it is issues of great importance and not mere quibbles and slight adjustments at the margins that are at stake. Proportionalism poses and answers questions of signal importance about the fundamentals of ethics, faith's relationship to reason, the nature of the human person, and this person's relationship to God. When proportionalism is considered sociologically, philosophically, and theologically, it is clear that we are certainly dealing not with a marginal, insignificant revision of natural law theory but rather with a revolutionary one. Richard McCormick points out the relevant issue at hand: "Is the revolution justified?" This book tries to situate and evaluate this revolution in the history of the natural law tradition, the tradition especially as exemplified by Thomas Aquinas. I will begin by setting forth the case for proportionalism as it is understood by its advocates (chapter I) and will continue by arguing that proportionalism developed out of a manualist account of double effect reasoning (chapter II). Finally I will, for the rest of the book, analyze, situate, and evaluate the revision of (or, perhaps better, revolution in) the natural law tradition known as "proportionalism."

18. Richard R. Roach, "Medicine and Killing: The Catholic View," *Journal of Medicine and Philosophy* 4 (1979) 383–97, as cited by McCormick in *Notes on Moral Theology, 1981 through 1984*, 2.

19. Diaro Composta, "Il consequenzialismo: Uno nuova corrente della 'Nuova Morale,'" *Divinitas* 25 (1981) 127–56, as cited by McCormick in *Notes on Moral Theology, 1981 through 1984*, 57.

20. John Mahoney, *The Making of Moral Theology* (Oxford: Oxford University Press, 1990) 138.

I. THE PLAUSIBILITY OF PROPORTIONALISM

This chapter describes proportionalism as it is understood by its proponents, while the chapters that follow will situate and critically evaluate proportionalism within the scope of the natural law tradition. Usually advocates of proportionalism emphasize their continuity with this tradition, especially with Aquinas himself. On their view, it would be a misunderstanding of both Thomistic ethics and proportionalism to presuppose that one had to choose one or the other. However, it would not be controversial to say that proportionalism seems to be asking and answering different questions than those that most interested Thomas Aquinas. By incorporating aspects of contemporary moral theory, proportionalists, or revisionists, employ many distinctions that are at best implicit in medieval texts. In part, this is due to the proportionalist appropriation of some strains of analytic philosophy, which were common in the first half of the twentieth century. Through the work of Bruno Schüller, the distinction between rightness and goodness and the distinction between teleology and deontology entered the debate. To understand proportionalism one must have some understanding of these terms.

Some describe goodness as a disposition or striving to do and know what is right, and rightness as action in accordance with nature or reason. "Acting from love *(agape)* is morally good," writes Bruno Schüller:

Doing what on the whole is impartially beneficial to all persons concerned is morally right. Therefore, an action may be morally bad because performed from pure selfishness, but nonetheless be morally right on account of its beneficial consequences.[1]

Josef Fuchs offers this example of how to parse the distinction between goodness and rightness in a practical case:

Perhaps someone makes a great contribution to the well-being of humankind but is only motivated in his activity by egotism for instance, in order to be honored. He has done the morally *right* thing, for he has created premoral human goods or values; but he is not morally *good*.[2]

What is common to all the ways in which the distinction is made is this: Goodness and badness refer to persons in their motivations and in their striving or failing to strive to do what is right; rightness and wrongness refer to acts. How do we determine what is right and what is wrong?

Here a second important distinction comes into play. Most proportionalists again follow Bruno Schüller, who borrowed from the work of C. D. Broad, in considering that there are two major answers to the question of how norms are grounded, namely the "deontological" and "teleological" approaches.[3] For advocates of proportionalism, the key questions are: How do we formulate moral norms? On what basis do we make exceptions to norms? The answers to these questions in turn depend upon what sort of normative approach is adopted: deontological, teleological, or a combination of the two often called "moderate teleology."

Schüller writes: "A theological or philosophical discipline aims to provide an original understanding of the validity of the moral norms according to which an action is to be assessed,

1. Bruno Schüller, "The Double Effect in Catholic Thought: A Reevaluation," in *Doing Evil to Achieve Good*, ed. McCormick and Ramsey, 183.

2. Josef Fuchs, *Christian Ethics in a Secular Arena*, trans. Bernard Hoose and Brian McNeil (Washington D.C.: Georgetown University Press, 1984) 81, emphasis in the original.

3. The best study of Schüller's appropriation of Broad, as well as of the use of these two terms in proportionalist literature, is undoubtedly Todd Salzman's *Deontology and Teleology: An Investigation of the Normative Debate in Roman Catholic Moral Theology* (Leuven: Leuven University Press, 1995).

whether by a judge, accuser, or defender."[4] Actions, on this account, may be morally evaluated from the third-party perspective (judge, accuser) as well as the first-party perspective (defender). On this view, questions of perspective are insignificant. Schüller proposes a method whereby first one determines what form of ethical reasoning to adopt (deontological or teleological) and then formulates norms in light of this fundamental ethical reasoning; finally, the act is judged right or wrong by its accordance with the norm (or lack thereof).[5]

What is the difference between deontology and teleology? Todd Salzman, speaking in the most broad and basic terms, suggests:

Where concepts of obligation (such as right, duty, ought, and their opposites) take precedence and the concepts of value (good, merit, and their opposites) are identified in terms of them, the theory is deontological. When, however, the reverse is the case and the concepts of value take priority, then the theory is teleological.[6]

Although these concepts have taken on a very different meaning than they originally had for Broad,[7] in the discussion about proportionalism, teleology and deontology represent two approaches to the question of intrinsically evil acts. The deontologist, in a common view, accepts the existence of intrinsically evil acts; the teleologist rejects any such possibility. (Philosophers use the terms differently, insofar as many have a "deontological" yet non-absolutist theory, such as Ross.) Another way of parsing the distinction is to hold that the teleologist, in the vein of Garth Hallet or Richard McCormick, determines the rightness of an act

4. Bruno Schüller, *Wholly Human: Essays on the Theory and Language of Morality*, trans. Peter Heinegg (Washington, D.C.: Georgetown University Press, 1986) 128.

5. Salzman, *Deontology and Teleology*, 177. Others have proposed, in contrast, that it is not whether an act violates a norm that makes an act right or wrong, but rather whether an act is or is not in accordance with certain paradigmatic cases. James Keenan suggests this approach. See his "The Function of the Principle of Double Effect," *Theological Studies* 54 (1993) 294–315. Todd Salzman argues that both movements, from judgments about specific actions to the formulation of norms and vice versa, should be employed. See *Deontology and Teleology*, 177.

6. Salzman, *Deontology and Teleology*, 50.

7. A persuasive case for this assertion is made by Salzman in *Deontology and Teleology*.

by whether or not it brings about the greater good or the lesser evil.

Most proportionalists would describe themselves as neither teleologists nor deontologists in a strict sense. Charles Curran offers an explanation of the differences between the extremes of pure deontology and pure teleology, while positioning proportionalism as the golden mean. He writes:

> One position is clearly deontological. Some actions are always wrong, no matter what the consequences. A second position is truly consequentialist, utilitarian, or strictly teleological, and derives norms and the morality of actions solely on the basis of consequences. . . . However, it is evident that there also exists a third position mediating between the two and called by different names, including teleology, and *prima facie* obligationalism. This position rejects deontology but also disagrees with strict consequentialists or utilitarians. In disagreement with strict consequentialists or utilitarians, this middle position maintains the following three points: (1) moral obligations arise from elements other than consequences, e.g., promises, previous acts of gratitude, or evil; (2) the good is not separate from the right; (3) the way in which the good or evil is obtained by the agent and not just the end result is a moral consideration.[8]

For Curran, proportionalism or *prima facie* obligationalism is the mean between the extremes of deontology and strict consequentialism. His view differs from a deontological position in which a given action may be wrong regardless of consequences, but it also differs from a strict consequentialism that would derive the rightness or wrongness of an act from the consequences alone without regard to what sort of act brought about the consequences.[9] The accent, for the most part, in proportionalism has been on the rejection of the deontological approach and not on the differences between "moderate" and "strict" teleology. Why

---

8. Charles Curran, *Directions in Fundamental Moral Theology* (Notre Dame: University of Notre Dame Press, 1985) 21.

9. From a philosophical perspective, Curran's analysis is confused. One can be a deontologist without being a strict absolutist, that is, without holding that there are some acts that may never be done regardless of the consequences. Charles Fried, Bernard Williams, W. D. Ross among others are deontologists, but not absolutists. Likewise, no consequentialist would hold that the way in which the end is achieved is not a moral consideration, as if stealing and working were morally equivalent ways of making money.

do advocates of proportionalism reject a deontological position? Many reasons have been given and some of the most prominent will be presented here. *Reasons to reject Deont.*

First, it is held that the deontological position requires a certain narrowing of horizons. According to a deontological theory, one can come to judgment about an act's wrongness before taking into account all the concrete circumstances of the act. According to a teleological theory, such judgments cannot be made without full knowledge of the particulars of a given situation. Todd Salzman puts the point this way:

> These two theories, deontology and teleology, are often juxtaposed on the basis that the former does not take into consideration the consequences of acts while the latter only takes consequences into account. The fundamental difference between the two theories, however, is in the consequences and the characteristics of those consequences which each theory sees as relevant. For the deontologist, it is a limited evaluation of the consequences and only one or a few characteristics of those consequences. For the teleologist, it is the intrinsic goodness or badness of those consequences.[10]

Teleological reasoning takes all aspects of the act into account, while deontology focuses on only one or a few characteristics of the action. Objectivity, reason, and truth require that one take everything into account when making a judgment, and therefore teleology has a decisive advantage over deontology.

In addition, proportionalists argue that the Catholic tradition is for the most part teleological in its approach to norms. Garth Hallet notes that the tradition held that goods were commensurable and that it further showed a preference for the greater good:

> Countless instances of value-balancing, by the most varied authors on the most varied topics, betray a preference for the greater value. Such preferences can be discerned in traditional reasons for . . . disobedience to laws or those in authority, for capital punishment, for dispensation from Sunday observance, for legitimately breaking a promise, for exceptions to positive precepts such as paying a debt.[11]

10 Salzman, *Deontology and Teleology* 66–67.
11. Garth Hallet, *Greater Good: The Case for Proportionalism* (Washington D.C.: Georgetown University Press, 1995) 42–43.

Adult members of the Catholic community are obliged to participate in the Eucharist each week, but this norm does not oblige those who are ill or seriously inconvenienced by attending. On Good Friday, the faithful are obliged to fast, but once again, if one is ill, the norm does not obtain. In like manner, one should try not to break a promise to have dinner with a friend, but if your services are needed to save an accident victim's life, then one may licitly break the promise.[12] Richard McCormick notes similar exceptions to norms regarding secret-keeping, integral confession, the obligation to say the divine office, and the duty of fraternal correction.[13]

In fact, every norm in the Catholic tradition is teleologically parsed, save for norms governing two areas: acts contrary to nature, such as speaking a falsehood and various sexual acts that exclude openness to procreation, and acts lacking due authorization, namely the "direct" or intentional killing of innocent human persons. These acts alone are deemed "intrinsically evil." Aside from intrinsically evil acts, the tradition is entirely teleological.

Even norms forbidding "intrinsically evil" acts have been narrowed in scope in light of teleological considerations. Consider for instance the norm forbidding lying. No proportionalist would question that lying is always wrong, provided that "lying" is understood in a truly teleological way, i.e., "speaking a falsehood without a proportionate reason." Realizing that non-moral values can be in conflict with one another (e.g. the good of speaking the truth versus the good of preserving innocent life from attack), the tradition gave a more and more restrictive interpretation of this norm.[14] Augustine in *De mendacio* and *Contra mendacium* condemned speaking an untruth with the intention of deception even to save innocent life. On McCormick's rendering of the Augustinian position: "We are required to tell the truth even if that

---

12. Richard McCormick, *Notes on Moral Theology, 1981 through 1984*, 56.
13. Ibid., 68.
14. See, for instance chapter 10 of Albert R. Jonsen and Stephen Toulmin's *The Abuse of Casuistry: A History of Moral Reasoning* (Berkeley: University of California Press, 1990).

means that telling the truth could result in exposing a victim to a possible assailant, thereby causing a greater evil than speaking a falsehood would have caused."[15] Other Catholic authors, relaxing the Augustinian norm, sanctioned the use of ambiguous language in such situations. St. Athanasius reportedly told soldiers who were inquiring about his own whereabouts: "He is not far off." This concession allowed the clever, but not the slow-witted, to protect innocent human life. Some later writers held that "mental reservations" were permitted, that is, one may utter an ambiguous statement, but qualify it mentally in such a way that the statement is true. These authors would allow one to answer aloud, "Yes, I did see him, but he was a few miles away from here," adding mentally, "a few days ago." Finally, more modern authors, recognizing that the killer has no right to the truth, would permit one to say, "The man isn't here. I haven't seen him." At this point, the norm became, for practical purposes, fully teleological. Proportionalists simply recognize and develop a tradition of restrictive interpretation to its logical conclusion:[16] one can speak a falsehood, but only for a proportionate reason.

The reason for this restrictive interpretation of the norm forbidding falsehood is clear. Falsehood is a premoral evil, not a moral evil. It does not have to be avoided in every case. The premoral evil of leading one into falsehood is always relevant although not definitive for moral judgment, as are other premoral evils such as sickness, pain, and violence. In order to avoid one premoral evil, we may have to cause, sometimes even intentionally, another evil. We spank the child pedagogically so as to help induce virtue. The tradition justified causing certain physical, ontic, or premoral evils as long as one had a commensurate reason, while other physical, ontic, or premoral evils were not subject to the same justification. Peter Knauer writes:

Many moralists content themselves in their argument with a pure proof of physical evil. They confuse the physical and the moral sense of con-

15. Salzman, *Deontology and Teleology*, 164–65.
16. For a short history supporting these theses, see L. I. Ugorji, *The Principle of Double Effect: A Critical Appraisal of Its Traditional Understanding and Its Modern Reinterpretation* (Frankfurt am Main: Peter Lang, 1993) 124–33.

trariness to nature. This is as though the killing of an aggressor in case of necessity were identified with killing in a moral sense. It is, to be sure, true that contrariness to nature in a moral sense has a relation to physical evil which can be defined in a physical sense as contrary to nature; but moral evil comes about only through permission or causing of physical evil without commensurate reason.[17]

Killing and speaking a falsehood are premoral evils. Tradition allowed that death could be caused for commensurate reason, but not a sterile marriage act or saying an untruth, for these acts were said to be against nature. The proportionalist approach does not single out certain premoral evils as somehow special cases, but treats all cases of causing premoral evil, e.g. killing and telling falsehoods, in like fashion, with consistency. Josef Fuchs suggests that giving answers to moral questions presupposes a sufficient knowledge of all relevant elements in a situation, in order to come to a well-founded judgment on moral rightness and wrongness:

Moral theology has always recognized that. It has not therefore tried to answer such questions generally with the aprioristic designation "intrinsic evil." But it has acted differently with regard to the good of human life, to marriage, and to human sexuality.[18]

Proportionalism, therefore, is a corrective to an inconsistent analysis, an analysis that singled out acts "against nature" and acts "in which the agent lacked authorization," from the otherwise overwhelmingly teleological tradition of moral judgment. Properly speaking, one is not "lying" when one has a proportionate reason for speaking a falsehood, just as the dentist cannot be said to be "torturing" when he or she has a proportionate reason for causing pain.

Likewise human life, though a central value, is nevertheless a premoral one. The norm "Thou shall not kill" is not absolute. In fact, tradition has allowed a number of exceptions to this norm.[19]

17. Peter Knauer, "The Hermeneutic Function of the Principle of Double Effect," in *Moral Norms and Catholic Tradition*, ed. Curran and McCormick, 33; reprinted in *Proportionalism For and Against*, ed. Kaczor, 25–59.
18. Fuchs, *Christian Ethics*, 86.
19. James Gaffney, "The Pope on Proportionalism," in *Veritatis Splendor: American Responses*, ed. Allsopp and O'Keefe, 63.

Even when treating such an important value as human life, a value that all other values presuppose, the norms in this area are parsed teleologically.[20] The norm forbidding killing does not forbid all killing of human beings, but only the *direct* killing of the *innocent.* These qualifiers are added to make room for killings in war, self-defense, and capital punishment. Like lying, over time the norm forbidding murder has been narrowed in light of teleological considerations to "one may not kill the innocent." Even the norm forbidding killing the innocent, however, is narrowed still further by the addition, "one may not *directly intend* to kill the innocent." Thus, the removal of a cancerous uterus, even if the woman happens to be pregnant, is licit, even though the fetus will die as a result of this removal. The death of the unborn child would be foreseen but not intended. The norm governing murder became narrowed to include only the taking of innocent life intentionally.

Why must one never directly or intentionally kill the innocent? After all, in Scripture, Abraham was ordered to kill the innocent Isaac. Along with suicide, direct killing of the innocent "is thought of as morally unlawful," writes Schüller, "because performed without the required authorization."[21] McCormick echoes the same point: "The killing 'distanced from' in the tradition (direct, of innocents) was seen as intrinsically evil but *precisely because of a lack of right* given to human beings by God to take life in this way. It was seen as arrogation of God's right of dominion."[22] In fact, since the argument from contrariness to nature supposes that God's will is inscribed in natural inclinations, the basis for intrinsically evil acts in both cases is the same.

Proportionalists point out that the justification used in both cases precisely begs the question as to what extent God has given

20. Richard McCormick, *Notes on Moral Theology 1981 through 1984,* 4; "Notes on Moral Theology: 1985," *Theological Studies* 47 (1986), n.60.

21. Bruno Schüller, "Double Effect: A Reevaluation," 169.

22. Richard McCormick, "A Commentary on the Commentaries," 217, emphasis in the original. This argument is also affirmed by Charles Curran, "Veritatis Splendor: A Revisionist Perspective," in *Veritatis Splendor: American Responses,* ed. Allsopp and O'Keefe, 232.

us dominion over natural processes and human life.[23] Further-more, it confuses extrinsic and intrinsic morality. Extrinsic evil refers to an evil that is so termed because it is contrary to the positive dictates of law. For example, driving on the left side of a two-way street is an extrinsic evil in the United States because it is a violation of positive law. In England, just the opposite is the case. Intrinsic evil refers to some lack caused by the nature of the thing and not by the proclamation of some authority. A divine command theory of morality holds that right and wrong consist in whatever God wills as right and wrong, but such a voluntaris-tic theory is not in accord with the traditional Catholic ethics.[24] God commands us to avoid some choice because it is evil; some-thing is not evil because God commands us to avoid it. If one re-jects divine command theory, it is illegitimate to claim something is evil *because* God commands as if what God commands could be independent of God's wisdom.[25]

Since the arguments for intrinsically evil acts, both those "against nature" and those "wrong because of a defect in the agent," have been found wanting, the tradition becomes thor-oughly and, at last, consistently teleological. This teleological ori-entation eliminates the error present in the tradition of defining the "object of the human act" sometimes in a narrow, physical sense and other times in a broader sense that includes important circumstances.[26] As Richard McCormick notes, "an action cannot be judged morally wrong simply by looking at the material hap-pening, or at its object, in a very narrow and restricted sense."[27] Charles Curran, among others, describes the tendency to de-

23. John Giles Milhaven, "Moral Absolutes in Thomas Aquinas," in *Absolutes in Moral Theology*, ed. Charles Curran (Washington, D.C.: Corpus Books, 1968) 154–85; also see his *Toward a New Catholic Morality* (New York: Doubleday, 1972) 136–67, 228–36; Richard McCormick, *Notes on Moral Theology 1981 through 1984*, 4; Joseph Fuchs, *Christian Ethics*, 79.

24. Taking into account those who tend toward voluntarism such as Abelard, Scotus, and Ockham, such a statement could be qualified in many ways but seems to hold true for the most part.

25. Fuchs, *Christian Ethics*, 9.

26. B. Andrew Lustig, "*Veritatis Splendor*: Some Implications for Bioethics," in *Veritatis Splendor: American Responses*, ed. Allsopp and O'Keefe, 257.

27. Richard McCormick, "*Veritatis Splendor* and Moral Theology," *America* 169.13 (October 30, 1993) 10.

scribe the object of the act in such physical terms as "physicalism."[28] In the words of Josef Fuchs, "The basic idea of 'intrinsically evil' seems to be that an action described in its physical reality (for example, killing or masturbation), is said to be morally 'intrinsically evil,' so that these actions cannot be rendered morally right by any further specific elements."[29] When the concept of intrinsically evil acts is found wanting, one is no longer tempted to understand the object of the act in the narrow physical sense.

Once the object of the act is defined in this less physicalistic sense, one can eliminate the arbitrary expanding and contracting of the object present in the tradition. Consider a situation in which a woman fires a gun, killing a man. Given merely this physical description, traditional analyses would not be able to evaluate this act in a moral sense. Why? Because the intention of the agent is not yet known. Her action could be murder if the man were an innocent passer-by. On the other hand, the action could be an act of self-defense if the man were attempting to rape her. Or, in still another case, the woman may be an executioner following a legal command given by the judge and jury to punish a criminal guilty of heinous crimes. Advocates of proportionalism suggest that the difference between these cases is the presence or absence of a commensurate or proportionate reason *(debita proportio, ratio commensurata)* for effecting the pre-moral evil of killing.[30] In the case of murder, such a reason is absent. In the case of self-defense, a commensurate reason is present. In the third case, scholars disagree about whether or not a commensurate reason is present. All three situations have this in common: until we know more about the intentions of the agent and the circumstances which determine whether or not a proportionate reason is present, final moral judgment on what con-

28. Charles Curran, *"Veritatis Splendor:* A Revisionist Perspective," 238; See also John F. Dedek, "Intrinsically Evil Acts: The Emergence of a Doctrine," *Recherches de Théologie ancienne et medieval* 50 (1983) passim; Ronald R. Burke, "Papal Authority and the Sovereignty of Reason," in *Veritatis Splendor: American Responses,* ed. Allsopp and O'Keefe, 134.

29. Fuchs, *Christian Ethics,* 74.

30. The concept of premoral evil plays a central role in proportionalist analysis. More needs to be said later about the relationship of this concept to Thomas.

stitutes the object of the act is impossible. In the words of Mc-
Cormick, "One can speak of intrinsic evil only in instances where
the action is fully and exhaustively defined with all of its morally
relevant elements (with its object, circumstances, goals, consequences)."[31]

Some would object to this project on biblical grounds. Doesn't
McCormick's analysis contradict Scripture, specifically Paul's rejection of the idea that we should "do evil that good may come"
(Rom. 3:8)? Some proportionalists claim that Paul's discourse,
like all the rest of Scripture, provides only *parenesis,* and not normative guidelines;[32] he is exhorting, not providing absolute rules.
Others suggest that Paul is laying down an absolute prohibition,
but it is only that *moral evil* should not be done that good may
come.[33] In the words of Garth Hallet, "No proportionalist would
disagree with Paul's reply or its evident justification: wrongdoing
is wrong, sinning is sinful."[34] Here, Paul refers not to *premoral* evil
(killing, speaking falsehoods, causing pain) but to moral evil (for
example, leading another into sin). Proportionalism consistently
affirms norms forbidding murder, lying, and other terms for action that contain both factual element (killing, falsehood) and an
element of negative moral description (without a proportionate
reason, unjustly).[35] Thus, theft is taking the property of another
against his or her reasonable will; lying is deceiving someone
who has a right to the truth;[36] murder is unjust killing, adultery is
unjust sexual relations, etc. Thus, proportionalism retains excep-

---

31. Richard McCormick, *Notes on Moral Theology, 1981 through 1984,* 110.

32. Bruno Schüller, "Die Quellen der Moralität: Zur systematischen Ortung
eines alten Lehrstücks der Moraltheologie," *Theologie und Philosophie* 59 (1984)
545. Translations from German or Latin are mine unless otherwise noted. For a
proportionalist rejecting this approach, see Charles Curran, *Toward an American
Catholic Moral Theology* (Notre Dame: University of Notre Dame Press, 1987)
57–59. Proportionalists accepting this distinction include Salzman, *Deontology and
Teleology,* 132 n.5, et passim.

33. Garth Hallet, *Greater Good,* 44–45.

34. Ibid.

35. Charles Curran, "*Veritatis Splendor:* A Revisionist Perspective," 236, 238;
McCormick, *Notes on Moral Theology, 1981 through 1984,* 64.

36. "Lüge sei die Täuschung eines andern, der ein *Recht* auf die Wahrheit
habe." Wolbert, "Die 'in sich schlecten' Handlungen und der Konsequentialis-
mus," in *Moraltheolgie im Abseits?* ed. Dietmar Mieth (Freiburg/Basel/Vienna:
Herder, 1994) 108.

tionless norms, intrinsically evil acts, and the ban on morally evil means, defined in this formal way.

On the other hand, if Paul's remarks are understood as forbidding the intentional causing of premoral evil for the sake of good, the tradition and common sense would have to be radically mistaken. Tradition allowed, for example, the deception of another to protect the secrets of the confessional, the amputation of a limb to preserve the health of the body, the death of the criminal to preserve the common good of society, the death of the assailant in cases of self-defense, and the pain of a spanking for disciplining a child. Paul was not excluding premoral evils in Romans 3:8.

Furthermore, according to proportionalism, in addition to making tradition consistent, this revision allows the tradition to become more in accord with common sense. Consider the case of an ectopic pregnancy. It can happen that a fertilized egg implants not in the uterus but in the fallopian tube. As the zygote develops, the tube will begin to bleed and, without intervention, eventually both mother and child will die.[37] This case puzzled moralists for some time in the early twentieth century, until in the 1920s it was suggested that since the tube was pathological, it would be removed by double-effect reasoning (DER).[38] The child is within the tube; however, the surgeon does not intend the newly conceived human being's death but rather foresees it as a side effect of removing the tube that threatens the woman's life. Although such an action was licit by the DER of the manualists, the result is that the child *and* the tube are lost. Tradition allowed the removal of the tube with the child within (salpingectomy), but not the removal of only the child (salpingostomy) leaving the

37. I speak of "child" here in part since it is often presupposed by those in the debate that the zygote deserves the same respect as any other human being. If the zygote is considered mere tissue, the *moral* problem ceases to be one.

38. For a brief, fascinating account of the history of this case, see James Keenan, "The Function of the Principle of Double Effect," 303–4. See also Christopher Kaczor, "Is the 'Medical Management' of Ectopic Pregnancy by the Administration of Methotrexate Morally Acceptable?" in *Issues for a Catholic Bioethic*, ed. Luke Gormally (London: Linacre Center, 1999) 353–58, and "Moral Absolutism and Ectopic Pregnancy," *Journal of Medicine and Philosophy* 26.1 (2001) 61–74.

tube intact. Proportionalists, first of all Peter Knauer, pointed out that if one removes the tube with the human embryo in it, both the embryo's life and one-half of the potential fertility of the woman are lost. Why not just remove the embryo (salingostomy) and save the only good that can be saved—the woman's fertility?[39] McCormick brings forward another example of the common sense that underlies proportionalism; that if abortion is the only way to save one life, the only other choice in such a situation would be to choose the greater evil, clearly an absurdity.[40] McCormick's suggestion follows from a general maxim. In conflict situations, and every situation is in some sense a conflict situation, we should avoid the greater evil. He writes: "This statement [we should avoid the greater evil] is, it would seem, beyond debate; for the only alternative is that in conflict situations we should choose the greater evil, which is patently absurd."[41]

To summarize, not just the consistency of the tradition, but the dictates of reason itself demand that we adopt a teleological approach. Many view proportionalism not only as utterly consistent with the spirit of previous moral teaching but as a rational correction and improvement of the approach one finds in the manuals.

Although much has been written since then, this approach first began with Peter Knauer's 1965 article on double-effect reasoning and goes by the name "proportionalism." Knauer's version of proportionalism, though accepted by few proportionalists, paved the way for the move from double-effect reasoning to the teleological approach, teleology here understood in a particularly new way. It is this shift, from Thomas's account of self-defense to the principle of double effect, ending in proportionalism which is the subject of the next chapter.

39. C. E. Curran, "Moral Absolutes and Medical Ethics," in *Absolutes in Moral Theology?* ed. Charles E. Curran (Washington, D.C.: 1968) 113, cited in Bernard Hoose, *Proportionalism: The American Debate and Its European Roots* (Washington, D.C.: Georgetown University Press, 1987) 6; James Keenan, "The Function of the Principle of Double Effect," 310.

40. Richard McCormick, "Notes on Moral Theology: 1984," *Theological Studies* 46 (1985) 59.

41. Richard McCormick, "Ambiguity in Moral Choice," 38.

II. HOW DOUBLE-EFFECT REASONING

BECAME PROPORTIONALISM

꧁꧂

It is now commonplace to affirm the historicity of ethical discourse. The evaluation of acts with more than one morally significant effect has a history also, and it is that history which clarifies the origin of proportionalism. Double-effect reasoning has undergone a number of changes over time. One of these changes is that earlier formulations did not appear under the heading "the principle of double effect." This relative neologism is in fact a bit misleading. Most authors in the history of the tradition stemming from Thomas Aquinas have written not about a *single* principle, but rather about a number of criteria governing acts with more than one significant effect. Furthermore, it is not clear that all authors understood these criteria as foundational *principles*. Rather, the criteria seem to have arisen from applications of more fundamental principles to particular cases. To avoid these misunderstandings, Thomas Cavanaugh therefore has spoken of "double-effect reasoning."[1]

The history of double-effect reasoning (DER) has been shaped in its most important aspects by Thomas Aquinas's thirteenth-century *Summa theologiae*, in particular its treatment of self-defense. This text from the *Summa* is cited by Jean Pierre Gury in his own treatment of DER in the often reprinted and in-

---

1. Thomas Cavanaugh, "The Intended/Foreseen Distinction's Ethical Relevance," *Philosophical Papers* 25. 3 (1996) 179–88.

fluential *Compendium theologiae moralis.* Although Gury cites Thomas as his authority, it is clear that in fact the Jesuit has distanced himself from Thomas in a number of ways. When these differences between Thomas and Gury are more clearly defined, one is in a position to better contextualize and appreciate the accounts of double-effect reasoning given by Peter Knauer, Louis Janssens, and other proportionalists. Thomas, Gury, and Knauer, and their respective contemporaries, in fact represent three rival approaches to double-effect reasoning supported by distinctive presuppositions and conceptions of the moral life.

Double-Effect Reasoning According to Aquinas: The Case of Self-Defense

Scholars often cite *Summa theologiae* II-II, question 64, article 7—Aquinas's treatment of killing in self-defense—as the origin of double-effect reasoning. This article does not come in the *Prima secundae,* in which Thomas explores and develops a theology of the fundamental principles of morality. Rather, the *locus classicus* of double-effect reasoning comes in the *Secunda secundae.* Here, Thomas undertakes an exploration of certain *applications* of the fundamental principles—*"singula in speciali"* as he says in the preface to the *Secunda secundae.* This observation does not exclude the possibility of the introduction of principles in the *Secunda secundae,* but insofar as the principles underlying the treatment in 64.7 can be traced to the *Prima secundae,* the hypothesis of a novel introduction is superfluous.

In the immediate context of 64.7, Thomas follows Aristotle by introducing a distinction between two kinds of justice: distributive and commutative.[2] Acts of distributing the goods of the community, Thomas notes, belong to those who exercise authority in the community.[3] Distributive justice governs the distribution of rewards and punishments. In the first two questions treating commutative justice, questions 61 and 62, Thomas writes about restitution and respect of persons. Question 64.7, however, falls

2. *Summa theologiae,* II-II, 61, 1; hereafter abbreviated *ST.*
3. See, *ST* II-II, 61, 1 ad 3.

within *commutative* justice, the justice that pertains to the relationship of individuals *qua* individuals to one another. Thomas holds that the legitimate head of the community may kill on the community's behalf, but no individual *qua* individual may intend to kill. These presuppositions contextualize the problem of killing in self-defense for Thomas.

It is within this context that one finds the *locus classicus* often adduced by scholars as Thomas's own treatment of double-effect reasoning:

Nothing prevents that there be two effects of one act: of which the one is in the intention, but the other is outside the intention *(praeter intentionem)*. However moral acts take their species from that which is intended, not however from that which is outside the intention, since it is *per accidens*, as is clear from things said before. Therefore, from the act of one defending himself, a two-fold effect is able to follow: one the preservation of his own life, the other however the death of the aggressor *(invadentis)*. Therefore, an act of this type, from the fact that the preservation of one's own life is intended, does not have the character of the illicit *(rationem illiciti)*, since it is natural to anyone to preserve himself in his being insofar as he is able. Nevertheless, it can happen that some act proceeding from a good intention be rendered illicit, if it is not proportioned to the end *(proportionatus fini)*. Therefore, if someone for the sake of defending his life uses more force than is necessary, it will be illicit. If however he repels the violence moderately, it will be a licit defense. For according to rights *(secundum iura)*, it is licit to repel force with force with the moderation of a blameless defense. Nor is it necessary for salvation that a man forgo an act of moderate defense so that he might avoid the death of another, since man is held *(tenetur)* to provide more for his own life than for the life of another. But since it is not licit to kill a man, except for the public authority acting for the common good, as is clear from what was said above, it is illicit that a man intend to kill a man, so that he might defend himself, save for him who has public authority, who intends to kill a man for his own defense referring this to the public good, as is clear in the case of a soldier fighting against the enemy, and an officer of the law fighting against thieves. Although even these too would sin, if they were moved by private animosity *(privata libidine)*.[4]

One can read Thomas's analysis of self-defense as an application of principles enunciated in the *Prima secundae*, question 18. First, the remote end or intention must not be evil (I-II, 18, 4 ad 3);

4. *ST* II-II, 64, 7.

secondly, the proximate end intended, the object, must not be evil (I-II, 18, 2); and finally, the circumstances must be fitting (I-II, 18, 3 & 10, and I-II, 6, 3).

First, Thomas establishes that in cases of legitimate self-defense the remote intention is not evil: "an act of this type, from the fact that the preservation of one's own life is intended, does not have the character of the illicit *(rationem illiciti)*." Next, he argues that the proximate intention or object is not evil: "it is lawful to repel force by force." Finally, he suggests circumstances which, if present, would vitiate the act, namely, that the means taken in self-defense are not proportioned to the end *(illicitus reddi, si non sit proportionatus fini)*. Thomas immediately exemplifies what he means by the phrase "proportioned to the end" noting that "if someone for the sake of defending his life uses *more force than is necessary* [to achieve the end of self-defense] it will be illicit." In other words, the violence used must be the least amount possible that can secure the end of self-defense, since greater violence would be more force than necessary to achieve the end. The least violence possible may often be no violence, such as self-defense by evasion, argument, or flight. If violence is the only possible defense, this violence need not be deadly. One who uses more violence than necessary does not take care to avoid the evil effects of an act that, though not intended, can and should be avoided. The action of self-defense in terms of its three elements (intention, object, and circumstances) is licit and lawful, but not for the private person obligatory, for "suffering injury to oneself is able to pertain to perfection when it is undertaken for the well-being of others."[5] Characteristically, the "greater good" would be not to defend oneself at the risk of another's well-being. Thus, in *Secunda secundae*, question 64, article 7, Thomas applies the principles laid down in the *Prima secundae* to determine whether any human action is good to the case of self-defense.

---

5. *ST* II-II, 188, 3, ad 1. See too, *ST* II-II, 40, 1, ad 1.

Double-Effect Reasoning According to Gury

Those who do not consider Thomas to be the origin of DER invariably cite the French Jesuit Jean Pierre Gury (1801–1866). Considered by some modern scholars "the leading Jesuit casuist of the nineteenth century,"[6] Gury, if not the most sagacious moralist of the period, was at least among the most widely distributed and influential.

Gury's version of double-effect reasoning is introduced early in his *Compendium theologiae moralis* in the very first section, *De actibus humanis*. Gury divides this section into three parts: (1) the Notion of Human Acts, (2) the Principles of Human Acts, and (3) the Morality of Human Acts. Double-effect reasoning is addressed in part two.

Following a discussion of the conditions under which indirectly voluntary effects, i.e., effects foreseen and voluntarily but not intentionally brought about by the agent (i.e., voluntary in cause, indirectly voluntary effects), become imputed to an agent, Gury offers his formulation of the conditions of double-effect reasoning:

It is permitted to posit a good or indifferent cause, from which a two-fold effect follows, one good, but the other bad, if there is present a proportionately grave reason *(causa proportionate gravis)*, the end of the agent is honest, and the good effect follows from that [good or indifferent] cause not from a mediating bad one.[7]

The first criterion of DER for Gury is that the cause put in place, posited, or set into motion must be good or indifferent. From this good or indifferent cause comes a two-fold effect. Obviously, it is licit to posit something good or indifferent from which good follows, so the remaining qualifications refer to the evil effect. These qualifications include that the end of the agent is good. The agent should intend not the evil effect but the good effect that follows from the action. "The agent," he writes, "ought not to intend the evil effect, since in that case the evil effect would

---

6. Jonsen and Toulmin, *The Abuse of Casuistry*, 155.
7. Jean P. Gury, *Compendium theologiae moralis* (Rome, 1874) vol. 1, c.2, n.9, 5.

be in the will voluntarily."[8] He adds as another criterion that
there must be a proportionately grave reason: "[T]here must be a
proportionately serious reason for actuating the cause, so that
the author of the action would not be obliged by any virtue, e.g.,
from justice or charity, to omit the action."[9] Gury, though not in
the manner of Aquinas, connects his analysis at least nominally
to the virtues. For Gury, however, the actual emphasis of moral
analysis is undertaken almost entirely in terms of law. Gury, like
Thomas, holds that self-defense by private persons is licit, i.e. allowed but not required, although those who are essential to the
common good or who would die in mortal sin are required to
defend themselves.[10]

Later authors in the manualist tradition severed even this
nominal link to virtues and understood this fourth condition as
exclusively the weighing or balancing of various goods and evils.
Joseph Mausbach and Gustav Ermecke, for instance, understand
proportionate reason as "a positive, personal or general value or
welfare, which outweighs the negative evil consequence."[11] Gerald Kelly puts it this way: "The good effect is sufficiently important to balance or outweigh the harmful effect."[12] This shift in
meaning, to the emphasis on weighing or balancing effects, is
not as evident in Gury's formulation, and comes quite late in the
tradition. However, the shift became very important for proportionalism.

Finally, Gury notes that "the good effect follows from that
cause, not from a mediating bad one."[13] Paramount is the causal
relationship between the effects. Gury explains:

If the cause directly and without intermediary (immediate) produces the
evil effect and if the good effect comes about only by means of the evil

---

8. Ibid., 1.8   9. Ibid.
10. Ibid.
11. Joseph Mausbach and Gustav Ermecke, *Katholische Moraltheologie* (Münster, 1954) 258, as quoted in L. I. Ugorji, *The Principle of Double Effect: A Critical Appraisal of Its Traditional Understanding and Its Modern Reinterpretation.* (Frankfurt am
Main: Peter Lang, 1993) 33.
12. Gerald A. Kelly, *Medico-Moral Problems* (St. Louis: Catholic Hospital Association, 1958) 12, as cited in Ugorji, *The Principle of Double Effect,* 33.
13. Gury, *Compendium theologiae moralis* 1.5.

effect, then the good is sought by means of evil. And it is never lawful to do evil, no matter how slight, in order that good may come of it. For according to the biblical maxim adduced by the Apostle in Rom. 3.8: Evil should not be done that good may follow.[14]

The good effect must come from the good or indifferent cause, not from the bad effect. Since these causal relations and the positing of effects can be observed by third parties watching an agent, Gury's formulation is notably "objective," facilitating judgment of acts. Not only the causal links, but the chronological relationship of effects to cause becomes important for writers following Gury. Joseph Mausbach and Gustav Ermecke write: "The good effect should proceed from the cause as immediately as the evil effect. If the evil effect proceeds first and the good effect follows from it, the act will be forbidden, since a good end does not sanctify an evil means."[15] E. F. Regatillo and M. Zalba likewise emphasize that the "good effect should at least be equally immediate as the evil effect, in the sense that it is not obtained by means of the evil, lest the evil effect be really intended 'in se' as a means."[16] Elsewhere Benedict Merkelbach writes: "The effect which is evil must follow as immediately from the cause as the good one."[17] Similarly, Joseph Sullivan writes: "The good effect must proceed equally immediately with the death as a result of the action."[18] Thus, the chronological order in which the effects appear gained an importance unseen in earlier episodes of the tradition.

Reminder: novelty is not in itself a departure from the tradition.

14. Ibid., 1.8.

15. Mausbach and Ermecke, *Katholische Moraltheologie*, vol. 1, 258, as quoted in Ugorji, *The Principle of Double Effect*, 33.

16. E. F. Regatillo and M. Zalba, *Theologiae Moralis Summa*, vol. 1, (Madrid: Editorial Catolica, 1952) 211; as quoted and translated by Ugorji, *The Principle of Double Effect* 33.

17. Benedict Merkelbach, *Summa Theologiae Moralis*, vol. 1 (Paris: Desclée de Brouwer, 1949) 166–67; as cited in Brian Thomas Mullady, *The Meaning of the Term 'Moral' in St. Thomas Aquinas* (Vatican City: Libreria Editrice Vaticana, 1986) 30. Unlike many others, Merkelbach adds, following earlier tradition: "By that is meant that the good effect may not be obtained by means of the evil effect."

18. Joseph Sullivan, *Special Ethics* (Worcester, Mass.: Holy Cross College Press, 1931) 31.

Double-Effect Reasoning According to Knauer

1979   In his seminal article "The Hermeneutic Function of the Principle of Double Effect," which began the movement now called "proportionalism," Peter Knauer places double-effect reasoning at the very heart of moral analysis. The article begins: "The principle of double effect leads a marginal existence in the handbooks of moral theology and appears to be useful only in making possible a species of hairsplitting. It is in reality, *the fundamental principle of all morality.*"[19] Why is this the fundamental principle? Knauer answers in this article: "Every human act brings evil effects with it. The choice of a value always means concretely that there is denial of another value which must be given as a price in exchange."[20] The agent's inability to realize *all the values* that he could potentially realize is the evil effect, what is also called "ontic evil." Josef Fuchs, Louis Janssens, Richard McCormick, and Bruno Schüller, among many others, eventually took up Knauer's analysis. Since every act is necessarily an omission of goods that could have been realized, the non-realization of these goods is a premoral evil. Each and every act, then, is governed by double-effect reasoning.

What are the conditions of double-effect reasoning, on Knauer's account? He reinterprets the four conditions coming from Gury in an almost entirely new way.

The principle demands first that the act may not be morally bad. In place of this condition, one may merely demand that the act must seek a premoral good, which anyhow in every act is the case and for this reason

---

19. Knauer, "Hermenutic Function," 1–39 at 1, emphasis in the original.

20. Ibid., 16. In later articles, Knauer's position is more accurately summarized by the idea that moral evil is present only due to the causing of some non-moral evil. As DER governs judgments about whether a given evil brought about is justified or not, DER governs the whole of the moral life. "It is, indeed, quite difficult to imagine an act could be morally evil without the allowance or the causation of some harm, or at least without one thinking that some harm might be caused (even hatred of God is only really hatred of God if it consists in the will to bring about harm in God's creation)." "A Good End Does not Justify an Evil Means—Even in a Teleological Ethics," in *Personalist Morals: Essays in Honor of Professor Louis Janssens,* ed. Joseph Selling (Leuven: Leuven University Press, 1988) 71–85, at 72.

requires no special mention. As a second condition, it was stipulated that *Reduction* the evil effect, which is caused *(verursacht)* or allowed in it, should not be *to 4th* intended in itself. The third condition can also be traced back to the sec- *condition* ond, that the bad effect should not be willed as a means to attainment of the good. Now it can be seen that the bad effect in fact would be always intended, when it is not—so claims the fourth condition—excused through a "serious" reason. Therefore it seems that the second and third conditions lead back again to the fourth. Since the first condition, as said, merits no special mention, the fourth condition alone remains.[21]

The purpose of double-effect reasoning is to determine whether or not an act is ethically permitted. If the act is morally wrong, it is no longer an open question whether or not it is permitted. The question at hand is whether an act, though having bad effects, is nevertheless permitted. Hence the first condition falls away as superfluous. In addition, once the distinction between premoral and moral evil is made, the first condition drops out as begging the question.[22] The second condition, that the evil not be intend-ed in itself, and the third, that evil not be intended as a means, both obviously depend upon some account of intention. It is Knauer's account of intention that allows him to reduce the sec- *New DEP* ond and third conditions to the fourth: proportionate or com-mensurate reason. Double-effect reasoning has become, for the first time in the tradition, a single principle: "Today the principle of double effect is most briefly formulated as follows: One may permit the evil effect of this act only if this is not intended in it-self but is indirect and justified by a commensurate reason."[23] Not only have the four conditions been reduced in meaning to one,[24] but as we shall see, "intention" here has a new meaning as well, a meaning defined in terms of proportionate reason. It is this emphasis on the fourth condition that led William May to coin the terms "proportionalist" and "proportionalism."

21. Knauer, "Fundamentalethik: Teleologische als Deontologische Normenbe-gründung," *Theologie und Philosophie* 55 (1980) 321–60, at 330.
22. Ibid., 325–26.
23. Knauer, "Hermeneutic Function," 20.
24. According to Knauer in "Good End," 82–83, an act defined as evil may not be used as a means to another end, nor may a good act be used as a means to an evil act. In this way, the usual conditions of DER may be more closely re-tained.

Knauer offered an innovative account of intention. According to Knauer, the Catholic tradition often mistakes physical categories for moral ones,[25] for example, when the causal or temporal relationship of effects is taken as morally important, as was apparent in the accounts of double-effect reasoning given by Mausbach, Ermecke, Regatillo, and Zalba briefly alluded to above. Knauer suggests that the usual explanation of the direct/ indirect or intended/foreseen distinction was in physical or chronological terms. Knauer himself retains the distinction between intended (direct) and foreseen (indirect) but interprets the pair in terms of proportionate reason.

The purely physical series of events is irrelevant to the moral qualification of good or bad. One and the same means can in one aspect be a value or lead to the realization of a value and simultaneously be a physical evil in another respect. If there is a commensurate reason for the permitting or causing of the evil, the means is effectively willed only in its good aspect. The effect or, more exactly, the aspect which is physically evil, remains morally outside of what is intended.[26]

For Knauer, what one *psychologically* intends is different from what one *morally* intends. If the agent has a proportionate reason, the evil caused, even if used as a means, though psychologically intended, remains outside of the agent's moral intention. The moral intention here is not defined in terms of the agent's practical reasoning, the means chosen to achieve various chosen ends. This phenomenon is merely psychological intention. Instead, the presence or absence of commensurate reason will determine what one morally chooses, what one intends morally.

Other proportionalists, perhaps stimulated by Knauer, explain the lack of importance of the distinction between intended and foreseen in other terms. For example, in a response to Joseph Boyle's argument that one cannot intend to kill a child in utero without setting oneself against the good of life, Richard McCormick writes that Boyle's reasoning "asserts what is to be proven: that there is a fundamentally different moral attitude in-

25. Knauer, "Hermeneutic Function," 20.
26. Ibid.

volved when abortion is directly intended and where it is only permitted though fully foreseen."[27] Earlier, Bruno Schüller concluded similarly that although there is a descriptive difference between intended and foreseen consequences, there is no moral difference when the distinction is used with reference to premoral, ontic, or non-moral goods and evils. Hence, the distinction is morally relevant only with respect to intending the sin of another person (a *moral* evil).[28] Garth Hallet, in his book *Greater Good*, suggests further that, also with respect to moral goods and evils, the distinction between intending and foreseeing is of no moral import.[29]

The fundamental moral category, then, is proportionate reason. What is proportionate or commensurate reason? Knauer writes: "Unintelligent and therefore immoral acts are in the last analysis self-contradictions and consist in the unmeasured desire taking the fruit from the tree before it is ripe."[30] A morally evil act is one in which "there is a long-run contradiction in reality between the value sought and the way of achieving it."[31] For example, killing done to preserve life (self-defense, just war) does not represent a contradiction of act and end as, in contrast, killing to take money does. In surgery that removes a limb to save a life, although the mutilation is psychologically intended, it is not morally intended, for the preservation of life is a commensurate reason for damaging the body.[32]

How do we know when doing evil to achieve good is not commensurate? Knauer's answer: counter-productivity. When the way in which a good is sought is counterproductive "in the long run and on the whole" *(auf die Dauer und im ganzen)*, the act

---

27. McCormick, "Notes on Moral Theology: 1984," 59.

28. Schüller, "Double Effect: A Reevaluation," 184.

29. Garth Hallet, *Greater Good*, 109.

30. Knauer, "Hermeneutic Function," 13.

31. Ibid., 23.

32. In "Hermeneutic Function" Knauer writes: "[I]t is not true, for example, that a medically necessary amputation is willed in the moral sense as a removal of an organ. What is willed is only the removal of what is an obstacle to health in its entirety. That this obstacle is identical with the hitherto useful member of the body is accidental for moral judgment *(existimatio moralis)*, because a commensurate reason justifies the acceptance of the loss" (21–22).

lacks proportionate reason. To use Knauer's example, to study intensely without the required rest, nourishment, and relaxation undermines the attaining of knowledge. The very good sought, knowledge, is undermined by the disproportionate way in which the good is sought.

In contrast, most authors known as proportionalists understand proportionate reason and counter-productivity itself as imposing a duty to maximize value or minimize disvalue.[33] This version of "proportionate reason" has greater organic unity with the weighing of goods and evil present in the late manuals. Exemplary and influential are the words of Janssens: "[W]herever ontic evil *can* be lessened *it must be* lessened. . . . If we do not care to eliminate ontic evil *to the best of our ability,* we neglect our duty to ensure a truly human life in a truly human world for each and every human being."[34] On this account, an important, but perhaps not the only, aspect of proportionate reason is the maximizing of non-moral goods and/or the minimizing of non-moral evils.[35]

From Gury's Reading of Aquinas to the Proportionalism of Knauer

After considering these three versions of double-effect reasoning, we might ask: What is their relationship? Knauer suggests that there might be discrepancy between Thomas's account of double-effect reasoning and the account prominent in the work of various neoscholastics.[36] Similarly, Janssens notes: "The

33. Knauer himself does not interpret proportionate reason in terms of greater or lesser goods as leading to rigorism and presupposing the commensurability of goods (see his "Fundamentalethik," 328), though he says elsewhere, "Evil may be accepted in exchange if, in relation to the whole, the *smallest* possible evil is exchanged for the *highest* possible gain" ("Hermeneutic Function," 6, emphasis added).

34. Janssens, "Ontic Evil and Moral Evil," In *Moral Norms and Catholic Tradition,* ed. Curran and McCormick, 81. See also Janssens, "Norms and Priorities in a Love Ethics," *Louvain Studies* 6 (1976–77) 207–38 at 222–23.

35. Janssens sometimes also works with a structural understanding of proportionate reason.

36. Knauer, "Hermeneutic Function," 6.

principles which govern [the moral evaluation of acts with several effects] were formulated in the sixteenth century and are not conformable with the thought of St. Thomas."[37] There are reasons for supporting the contentions of Knauer and Janssens that the neoscholastics differed from Thomas with respect to DER, as in so many other matters. Although Gury cites Thomas as the authoritative justification for his position, careful reading suggests significant differences between double-effect reasoning as proposed in Gury's *Compendium* and double-effect reasoning as found the *Summa*. Both Knauer and Janssens suggest furthermore that proportionalism is a recovery of Thomas and rejection of the neoscholastic account.

In fact, however, proportionalism can be better understood as an extension of the trends that differentiate neoscholastics from Thomas and not as a recovery of Thomas. Just as manualists like Gury reworked Thomas's account of double-effect reasoning, so too proportionalists like Knauer reworked the scholastic account by extending and emphasizing the differences that had already developed between Thomas and various neoscholastics. These accounts of DER differ in at least three ways.

The first difference among these authors is the importance placed on double-effect reasoning. Thomas's treatment of double-effect reasoning comes as the 178th of 304 moral questions treated in the *Secunda pars* of the *Summa*, midway through the *Secunda secundae* at question 64. He has already treated many other "moral" topics not only in the *Secunda secundae* but also in the *Prima secundae*. To mention only a sampling of topics, Thomas treats the nature of human action, virtues, vices, sins, and grace in the *Prima secundae* and faith, hope, love, prudence, and justice in the *Secunda secundae* before treating what we have called double-effect reasoning. In addition, Thomas's twofold conception of justice is central to his treatment of self-defense. According to Thomas's understanding of commutative justice, private persons may not intentionally kill one another. Such a killing would be in itself evil; thus any defense by private persons must not aim at

37. Janssens, "Ontic Evil and Moral Evil," 41.

the death of the attacker but only at stopping the attacker. Because it presupposes so many principles laid down in the *Prima secundae*, Thomas's analysis of self-defense should be understood as an application of the principles of judging human action given in the *Prima secundae*.

On the other hand, Gury in his 1874 *Compendium* situates his formulation of the criteria for double-effect reasoning at the very beginning of his work, in the explication of the foundations of his moral system. Gury, like many neoscholastics, organizes his "fundamental moral theology" around three elements: human action, conscience, and law. Double-effect reasoning arises in the first of these three basic elements, which is not so much a treatment of human action *per se* as an account of the conditions and aspects of voluntary acts. Gury's treatment of double-effect reasoning comes in a very early and fundamental section of his work, in the second of more than a hundred chapters of his *Compendium theologiae moralis*. In this, he follows St. Alphonsus's 1748 *Theologia moralis*, Tamburini's 1755 manual, Busembaum's 1848 manual, but not the authority he cites—Thomas Aquinas.[38] As opposed to Thomas, whose treatment comes later as an application of basic principles laid down much earlier, the placement of the topic in the *Compendium* leads one to believe that Gury understands double-effect reasoning to be so indispensable to the proper understanding of the human act that its role must be made clear at the outset of the discussion.[39] The origin of this innovation, according to Joseph T. Mangan, is Domingo de Santa Teresa's 1647 *Cursus theologicus.* Mangan's often-cited article "An Historical Analysis of the Principle of Double-Effect" suggests that theologians after *Cursus theologicus* "began discussing the

DER
as first
denoted

---

38. See Joseph Mangan, "A Historical Analysis of the Principle of Double Effect," *Theological Studies* 10 (1949) 41–61.

39. Double-effect reasoning appears later in the tradition in discussions of voluntariness, imputability, or culpability of agents. For Thomas, the question is not one of imputability or excusability but of justifiability. In this, Thomas and the proportionalists side together against neoscholastics. For a discussion of whether double-effect reasoning should be understood as justifying or as excusing, see Joseph Boyle, "Toward Understanding the Principle of Double Effect," *Ethics* 90 (1980) 527–38.

principle more and more in their sections of general moral theology, and then in their sections of particular moral problems they referred back to the more general treatment."[40] Double-effect reasoning became not merely an application of fundamental principles of morality, but rather a fundamental moral principle. In the words of Mangan, "It is only beginning with the various editions of Gury's admirable and repeatedly edited *Compendium theologiae moralis* in the nineteenth century that the moral theologians universally gave an adequate, thorough explanation of the principle of double-effect as a general principle applicable to the whole field of moral theology."[41]

We find this increasing emphasis and importance placed on double-effect reasoning from Thomas to Gury culminating in the work of Knauer.[42] DER becomes absolutely central for Knauer: "The principle of double effect is, in reality, the fundamental principle of all morality."[43] In other forms of proportionalism, DER is just as central. If every act brings about premoral evil, and DER determines whether or not the bringing about of premoral evil is justified, then DER determines whether or not each and every act is justified. Thus, double-effect reasoning changes from being a particular application of fundamental principles in Thomas, to being one of a number of fundamental principles in Gury, to being the single fundamental principle of all morality in Knauer and other proportionalists.

The second difference between Thomas, Gury, and Knauer is the role and meaning of intention. There are a number of contrasts between Thomas's concept of intention and the understanding of intention in later authors. Thomas speaks of intending ends, Gury of positing causes. *Ponere*, the word used in Gury's Latin, is ambiguous as to the intentional status of the agent. In other words, one could posit or set in motion some

---

40. Mangan, "The Principle of Double Effect," 56.
41. Ibid., 59.
42. See also Daniel C. Maguire, *The Moral Choice* (Garden City, N.Y.: Doubleday, 1978) 164, as cited by McCormick, *Notes on Moral Theology, 1981 through 1984*, 67.
43. Knauer, "Hermeneutic Function," 1.

cause either intentionally or unintentionally. Unlike the *Summa*, Gury's initial formulation does not explicitly mention the moral difference between intended and foreseen consequences. Gury did in fact acknowledge the moral importance of the distinction, mentioning it later in his explanation of the criteria of double effect reasoning. However by altering Thomas's formulation from *intending* a good or indifferent end to *positing* or *setting in motion* an effect, the importance of the intention/foresight distinction is under-emphasized. This under-emphasis on the difference between the intended and the foreseen effects of an act may have come about because the rationale for the distinction's importance no longer obtained. Gury's focus on questions about voluntariness and his lack of interest in other aspects of human action put him in a position in which he lacked the resources available to Thomas for giving the intended/foreseen distinction moral importance.

Knauer returns to the language of "intention," but the meaning of the term is no longer the same as in Thomas. In Thomas, the agent's intention is determined by the means and ends chosen by the agent in practical deliberation. Knauer, on the other hand, draws a distinction between *moral* intention (governed by proportionate reason) and *psychological* intention (that is, intention in something like Thomas's sense). As long as one has a proportionate reason for allowing the evil, one's *moral* intention is just, even if one *psychologically* intends an evil means. This allows him to reduce the other conditions of double effect reasoning, as found in Gury and his neoscholastic inheritors, to the condition of proportionate reason.

Recall Gury's DER criteria: The first is that the cause posited itself be good or indifferent. However, one cannot determine what sort of act has taken place morally without reference to intention; hence, if proportionate reason governs intention, it governs also the first criterion. The next criterion following proportionate reason is that the end of the agent is honest or upright, but once again intention is needed to determine the moral nature of this end. The final condition, that the good effect follows from that cause and not from a mediating bad one, also depends upon an account of what it is to intend as a means. Hence, in Knauer's new understanding of intention, the language of intention found in Thomas is retained but its meaning is displaced. What Knauer calls moral intention, parsed in terms of proportionate reason, becomes the central moral category replacing psychological intention governed by means/end relationships conceived through the practical deliberations of the agent. Like Knauer, Schüller, Fuchs, Janssens, and others suggest that the distinction between intention and foresight lacks moral importance with respect to premoral evils. Thus, while Gury merely did not highlight the importance of the intention/foresight distinction in Thomas's sense of the term, Knauer positively denies it. In sum, on the matter of the importance of psychological intention, Knauer emphasizes the tendencies that distinguished Gury's position from Thomas's.

Finally, the meaning of "proportion" has changed over time among the authors here surveyed. As Brian V. Johnstone has suggested, an important question to ask is "[W]hat is compared with what in the assessment of proportion?"[44] For Thomas, the means used in self-defense must be proportioned to the end of self-defense. Thomas reformulates a position found in his Franciscan predecessor at the University of Paris, Alexander of Hales, who suggested that killing in self-defense was licit only as a last resort. If pushing away the attacker is adequate for self-defense, one may not slash the attacker with a knife. However unclear the application may be in the concrete, what is clear is that the proportion has to do with the relationship between the means (e.g. running, pushing, slashing) and the end (self-defense). Thomas then speaks of what Johnstone calls "act/end proportion."[45]

Later in the tradition "proportion" is used to indicate the relationship between good and bad effects. If the good effects outweigh the bad, one has proportionate reason for allowing the bad effects. For Aquinas, on the other hand, the moral legitimacy of potentially lethal self-defense does not rely upon the good effects

---

44. Brian V. Johnstone, "The Meaning of Proportionate Reason in Contemporary Moral Theology," *The Thomist* 49 (1985) 229.
45. Ibid., 229–31.

outweighing the evil effects of the act. First, it is better not to use violent force than to use it, other things being equal. For Thomas, who holds as his highest ideal the non-violent example of Christ in the Gospels, the greater good would be to avoid defending oneself with violence at the risk of taking another's life.[46] Medieval Dominicans both before Thomas, like Albert the Great,[47] and after Thomas, like Pierre de Scala,[48] hold similar positions: the avoidance of the use of potentially deadly force is to be preferred to such defense, even at the risk of one's life. Hence, were one required to choose the "greater good" one would be required, in most cases, not to defend oneself at the risk of an attacker's life.

Secondly, for Thomas, one has the right to defend oneself even if this defense will end up with a net result of evil *outweighing* the good, understood in terms of non-moral values. Although preserving five lives is a greater good than preserving a single life, other things being equal, for Thomas the private agent has the prerogative of risking the lives of five or five hundred attackers to save his own. The prerogative of self-defense arising from the natural inclination to self-preservation would not appear to be weakened by the number of attackers, as it must if one justifies the prerogative by the weighing of goods.[49] Nor does this prerogative presuppose that one has taken "everything" into account. For instance, there is no reason to suppose that a woman without children cannot use potentially lethal means of self-

46. Thomas, *Super Evangelium Matthaei*, c.26 (Paris edition, 1876) 634.
47. Albertus, *Super Matthaeum* (Münster: Aschendorff, 1998) c. XXVI 52, 627–28.
48. Dominican Pierre de Scala, Bishop of Verona from 1291 to 1295, is the author of sections of a commentary on Matthew which appears amidst Thomas's commentary, *Super Evangelium Matthaei*, c.5, 326.
49. Perhaps, however, one could respond that an innocent life is more valuable than an attacker's life, hence an innocent person can defend himself or herself against many attackers. Even if it is granted, that innocent lives are more "valuable" than non-innocent lives, it would seem the non-innocent lives still count in the calculations. If one justifies self-defense on the basis of the balancing of goods, then one more urgently threatened by numerous attackers has weaker prerogative for self-defense than one under less serious attack. It seems counterintuitive to hold that the more need one has to defend oneself the less right one has to defend oneself.

defense against a man with children, for the interests of his progeny need not be taken into account. In justifying an act, the act/end proportion of Thomas does not have to do with seeking a present good in a way not detrimental to the long-term good or the balancing of goods and evils against one another.

What is compared with what in the assessment of proportion in Gury? For Gury, proportionate reason obtains if "the author of the action would not be obliged by any virtue, e.g., from justice or charity, to omit the action."[50] What sort of proportion is present? Gury continues, "For natural equity obliges us to avoid evil and prevent harm from coming to our neighbor when we can do so without proportionately serious loss to ourselves."[51] We are dealing then with the relationship between two effects of action or what has been called by Johnstone "effect/effect proportion." One must balance then the possible harm to oneself against the possible harm coming to one's neighbor, though it seems that for Gury one has no obligation to chose the "greater good" impersonally considered at one's own grave disadvantage.

Later authors in the scholastic tradition understand proportionate reason as exclusively the weighing or balancing of various goods and evils without the personal prerogative present in Gury's account. Joseph Mausbach and Gustav Ermecke, for instance, speak of "a positive, personal or general value or welfare, which outweighs the negative evil consequence."[52] Gerald Kelly similarly speaks of effect/effect proportion: "The good effect is sufficiently important to balance or outweigh the harmful effect."[53] This shift in meaning away from Gury's formulation, toward the emphasis on weighing or balancing effects, comes quite late in the tradition but became very important for proportionalism, whose authors also invoke effect/effect proportion.[54]

What is being compared with what in the assessment of pro-

50. Gury, *Compendium theologiae moralis*, 8.
51. Ibid.
52. Mausbach and Ermecke, *Katholische Moraltheologie*, vol. 1, 258, as quoted in Ugorji, *The Principle of Double Effect*, 33.
53. Kelly, *Medico-Moral Problems*, 12, as cited in Ugorji, *The Principle of Double Effect*, 33.
54. Johnstone, "The Meaning of Proportionate Reason," 229–31.

portion according to Knauer and other proportionalists? The answer is less clear for Knauer insofar as he rejects an account of proportionate reason as the maximizing of non-morally good or the minimizing non-morally evil effects so clear in effect/effect proportion. Disproportion, on his account, consists in a certain counter-productivity between an act and its end. The value sought by an act is in the end undermined by the way in which the act seeks the value in question. Clearly this sense of act/end proportion is not the same as that of Aquinas, who, in speaking of "proportion," meant that the defender should use only that force needed to stop the attack. On the other hand, it does not seem to be the same as the effect/effect proportion of the manuals.

However, the examples that Knauer gives to illustrate counter-productivity seem to reintroduce the idea that one effect or outcome of an act is being compared with another. He notes that a student who studies for such a long stretch may defeat by his or her straining the end sought by studying—the attainment of knowledge. Here, he compares the short-term gain of extremely intense study to the long-term gain (or loss) in the attainment of knowledge. In other words, we know disproportion by comparing the short-term and long-term effects of an action. Elsewhere Knauer explains counter-productivity by the following example. "That people die in traffic accidents may be tolerated only because the total abolition of traffic would lead to still more deaths, for example, by starvation."[55] One compares, in this example, the number of deaths brought about in traffic accidents to the number of deaths brought about through an abolition of traffic. Consider, too, Knauer's example of an insurance company that seeks to induce customers not to procure any medical prescriptions for a quarter year. Soon the company discovers, through comparison of the amount saved to the amount spent on more severe illnesses brought about by lack of treatment, that this strategy costs more than it saves. The judgment that the act is counter-productive presumably depends upon the comparison of capital saved

55. Knauer, "Good End," 76.

to capital expended.[56] When the total of negative effects is compared with the total of positive effects, the negative effects predominate and the act is deemed counter-productive. Although there is no obligation to maximize goods, there is an obligation to minimize damages. Though couched in similar language to Thomas's act/end proportion, Knauer's analysis of various cases makes clear that he in fact offers another version of effect/effect proportion.[57]

Insofar as they advocate choosing the "lesser evil" or "greater good," most proportionalists clearly invoke effect/effect proportion, for judgments of "greater" or "lesser" depend at least in part on the various effects of an act. Proportionate reason is, on this account, maximizing goods and minimizing evils which are to be "weighed" against one another. Thus, we see both in Knauer and other proportionalists an extension of the late neoscholastic tradition of effect/effect proportion and not a recovery of the act/end proportion found in Thomas.

In summary, it can be said that Thomas and Gury offer very different formulations of double-effect reasoning, while Knauer offers still a third alternative. Double-effect reasoning appears in the *Secunda secundae* as an application of fundamental principles laid down in the *Prima secundae*. Gury, on the other hand, treats double-effect reasoning as a topic necessary and primary to fundamental moral theology. Knauer takes one step further, suggesting that double-effect reasoning "is the fundamental principle of all morality." Thomas differs from both Gury and Knauer in explicitly underscoring the importance of the distinction between intended and foreseen effects in terms of means and ends chosen. Though Gury accepts the moral importance of the intention/foresight (I/F) distinction, he alters Thomas's language, while nevertheless invoking him, by speaking of "positing" causes. Knauer argues that the distinction between the intended and foreseen consequences (in the psychological sense meant by Aquinas) is of no moral import. Finally, Gury alters the meaning

---

56. Ibid.
57. Cf. Johnstone, "The Meaning of Proportionate Reason," 244–45.

and purpose of "proportion" from its meaning and use in Thomas. With Gury and the scholastics who followed him, there is a shift from act/end proportion to effect/effect proportion. Likewise, Knauer and the proportionalists who follow him invoke effect/effect, and not act/end, proportion.

How can one trace the motivations for these changes and determine what made some alternatives more compelling than others? Whose version of double-effect reasoning is to be preferred? The answers given to these questions depend upon one's answers to many other questions—for instance, questions about the constitution of the human act and the specification of human acts. Proportionalism, at least in most forms, proposes a method by which judgments may be made about human acts. Particularly Louis Janssens, in his lengthy study entitled "Ontic Evil and Moral Evil," must be credited among proportionalists with recognizing the importance of human action (and not mere acts of a human being) as regards the issues treated here. If the human person, as a distinctly *human* agent, and not only a passive recipient of effects, is to have a central place in moral judgment, then human action must have a central place. It is to that subject that we now turn.

III. HUMAN ACTION AND
CONTEMPORARY QUESTIONS

⚜

Although Aquinas, Gury, and Knauer would all agree that one can defend oneself even at the risk of the attacker's life, the principles, methods, and arguments used by these authors and their like-minded contemporaries lead to different conclusions on a variety of other issues. This is not to deny numerous similarities among them, such as a conviction that the human end is union with God, this union's connection with love of God and neighbor, love's connection with doing good for the neighbor, a respect for the philosophical and theological tradition, and finally a belief in the centrality and dignity of the human person. It is by common touchstones such as these that a moral theory succeeds or fails in the Catholic tradition.

Although the secondary literature often gives a misleading impression, most central to Thomas's account of the moral life is not natural law, conscience, commandments, or even, as many modern interpreters contend, virtue, but rather human action.[1] The *Prima secundae* begins in its prologue with a quotation from St. John Damascene, "Man *(homo)* is made in the image of God." Just as God acts freely, so also the image of God, having free choice, is the source of his or her own works, having dominion

---

1. The contemporary shift in interpretation is summarized and evaluated well by Jean Porter's "Recent Studies in Aquinas's Virtue Ethic," *Journal of Religious Ethics* 26.1 (Spring 1998) 191–215.

over personal acts. Thomas begins the *Prima secundae* with a consideration of the end of human life and then considers how someone might attain this end.

For Thomas, the end of all human striving is, of course, union with God, and this end is achieved, on the part of the human agent aided by grace, not through mere instinct or exterior forces but through human action. God's providence does not direct human beings to their end as it directs animals and inanimate objects, but rather God's providence works in the lives of men and women through their reason and will.

This insight leads Thomas to draw attention to the difference between two kinds of action properly attributed to human beings. In the response of the first article of the *Prima secundae,* Thomas draws the distinction, so important in Thomistic ethics, between acts of a human being *(actus hominis)* and human acts *(actus humani).* Human action proceeds from that in the human person which is distinctly human, namely, reason and will. Hence, distinctly *human* acts are those that proceed from reason and will, such as shooting a free throw, telling a joke, or pondering a theorem.

On the other hand, acts of a human being are acts properly attributed to the human person, but not insofar as he or she is a human person. Certain activities that can be properly attributed to a person nevertheless do not proceed from the reason and will of a person. As Konrad Adenauer reworked the *Grundgesetz* following the Second World War, his heart beat, his digestive system processed food, and his hair grew. However, insofar as these processes were not under his control via acts of reason and will, these activities were not human actions, but acts of a human being. One can morally evaluate Adenauer's establishment of the political foundations of post-war Germany, while other activities rightly attributed to him, like digestion, are not subject to moral analysis. These activities can be subject to other forms of analysis; digestion can go well or badly depending on a number of factors. However, in this example the evaluation is not moral but medicinal.

It can happen that the very same activity viewed externally is sometimes a human act and other times not. When a person breathes helium to alter her voice, *this* breathing is a human act. Other times, such as during sleep, her breathing is an act of a human. If a baby knocks a live hairdryer into the bathtub lethally shocking its innocent occupant, she is not considered a murderer. Although the child initiated the causal chain of events that led to the death of the one bathing, this action did not proceed from deliberate reason and will, and so is not subject to moral analysis.

Confronted with the many atrocities that occurred while the Roman Empire crumbled, Augustine insisted that virtues, such as chastity, cannot be undermined by anyone but the agent him or herself. That good in which we find happiness, Augustine argues,

should be a good which the unwilling cannot lose. Of course, no one is able to have confidence in such a good, which he senses can be taken from him, even if he wished to retain and embrace it. However, who lacking confidence in the good which he enjoys, in such a fear of loss, is able to be happy?[2]

Thus, for example, the woman raped by the invader retains her chastity nonetheless. For Augustine, "There cannot be sin, if there is not voluntariness."[3] In Thomas's language, the intercourse, on her part, was not a human act. Thus, a married woman forced to have intercourse with a man not her husband does not in any way violate chastity or justice. She has committed no act of adultery. As Thomas says, "moral acts are the same as human acts,"[4] both must involve reason and will. The distinction, though, between acts of a human and human acts is not always a distinction that can be made on the basis of viewing exterior events. Crying may be a spontaneous reaction or an artful manipulation.

Another key distinction for Thomas's account of human action is that between the natural and moral orders of an action. Agents who perform acts identical according to the natural order

---

2. Augustine, *De moribus ecclesiae catholicae*, 5; see also, *De libro arbitrio*.
3. Augustine, *De vera religione*, cap. 14.
4. *ST* I-II, 1, 3.

(in genere naturae) may not be performing the same act in a moral order *(in genere moris)*. In both *King Lear* and *Romeo and Juliet,* Shakespeare depicts scenes in which someone ingests poison and subsequently dies. The moral meaning of the scenes is, however, entirely different. Although Regan ingested poison, since she (arguably) did not ingest it *as poison,* her act is not suicide. Rather her sister Goneril has responsibility for Regan's death. On the other hand, since Romeo knew and chose to drink a cup of poison precisely insofar as this drinking was a means for bringing about his own death, his act is properly described as committing suicide. Physically the two acts share an exterior resemblance, but morally the acts are of an entirely different nature or species.

Although there has been much discussion about the structure of the *Summa theologiae* as a complete work and the relationship between its three parts,[5] the order that governs the *Prima secundae* is not difficult to discern. Thomas makes the distinction between human acts and acts of a human being the organizational framework of the *Prima secundae.* Following questions 1–5 the treatment of beatitude, an end to be obtained by human action, Thomas treats the human act itself in questions 6–17. Questions 18–21 consider the goodness and badness of human acts. The rest of the *Prima secundae* can be divided between a treatment of the interior (qq. 22–89) and exterior (qq. 90–114) principles of human action. Interior principles of human action are those by which we move toward or away from God by influences within ourselves. Exterior principles of human action are those by which we are moved toward or away from God by influences outside of ourselves, such as the devil and God acting by means of grace and law. Questions 22–48 treat the various passions of the soul, e.g., love, hatred, desire, delight, sadness, hope, desperation, fear, boldness, and anger. These passions are common to

5. See, for example M.-D. Chenu, "Le plan de la *Somme théologique* de saint Thomas," *Revue Thomiste* 47 (1939) 93–107; E. Schillebeeckx, *De Sacramentele Heilseconomie* (Anvers, 1952), and the summary presented by Jean-Pierre Torrell in *Saint Thomas Aquinas: The Person and His Work* (Washington D.C.: The Catholic University of America Press, 1996) 150–56.

both human beings and other animals, and hence are not subject to moral evaluation save insofar as they can be either commanded or inhibited by a human act.[6] The objects of these passions also are of vital importance, for they distinguish the moral virtues from one another.[7] After treating the nature of habits (qq. 49–54), Thomas undertakes a discussion of both good habits, the virtues, and those things which are connected with these good habits[8]—namely, the gifts of the Holy Spirit, beatitudes, and fruits of the Holy Spirit (qq. 55–67)—or opposed to good habits —namely, vices and sins which give rise to these bad habits (qq. 71–89). The virtues make it possible to perform good human action with ease and enjoyment. Having treated the interior principles of human action, Thomas turns to the exterior principles of human action by which God moves human beings to the good, these being law (qq. 90–108) and grace (qq. 109–14).[9] These exterior principles correspond to the nature of the human act as knowing and willing. Law aids the intellect by informing it about what is good and evil. Grace aids the will by enabling it to choose the good and illumines the intellect to know the good. Insofar as the *Secunda secundae* presupposes the *Prima secundae*, one can suggest that the whole of the *Secunda pars* presupposes the importance of, and is actually structured around, human action. This emphasis was not retained, however, through all episodes of the tradition.

Why did Thomas place such importance on the distinction between human acts and acts of human beings, and then, if the act is indeed voluntary, between the natural species of an act and its moral species? Indeed, for Thomas, why does the moral character of the agent make a difference to human action? An historical answer can be found in part by considering the two most important non-scriptural sources of Thomas's work, Augustine of

---

6. *ST* I-II, 24, 1
7. *ST* I-II, 60, 5. See too, *ST* I-II, 59, preface; *ST* I-II, 60, 4.
8. Prologue, *ST* I-II, 55.
9. "Consequenter considerandum est de principiis exterioribus actuum. . . . Principium autem exterius movens ad bonum est Deus, qui et nos instruit per legem, et juvat per gratiam. Unde primo de lege, sedundo de gratia dicendum est." *ST* I-II, 90, prologue.

Hippo and Aristotle. From Augustine, Thomas took the lesson that exterior human actions cannot always be judged by simple observation as morally good or evil, that is, conducive to happiness or not. In the opening chapters of *De civitate dei*, Augustine notes how the Romans had many virtues, such as industriousness and temperance, which made Rome a great empire. It was these virtues, and not sacrifices to gods, that made *"Roma aeterna."* The Romans had virtues of a kind but were motivated only by lust for glory and praise.[10] Likewise, the Manichees described in the *Confessions* possessed only a simulacrum of the authentic virtue of chastity.[11] These "virtues," on Augustine's account, were not rightly ordered to true happiness, that is union with God, and therefore are considered virtues only in an attenuated sense. In *De moribus ecclesiae catholicae*, Augustine shows the proper ordering of the virtues through the transformation of all the cardinal virtues that occurs when they are connected with the love of God. These considerations arise from and reinforce Augustine's emphasis on the necessity of charity for genuine virtue.

Thomas's other major non-scriptural authority likewise finds grounds to support this distinction. According to Aristotle, human beings by their very nature act for the sake of ends, and their ultimate end is *eudaimonia*. There is a distinction among these ends, between activities that are ends themselves and ends that are apart from the activities that produce them. Philosophers and common opinion have proposed many candidates for the nature of the end in which happiness consists, including political power, riches, and honor. Rejecting these possibilities, Aristotle has a different answer. In the very first paragraph of the *Nicomachean Ethics*, he writes:

Every art and every inquiry, and similarly, every action and every intention is thought to aim at some good; hence men have expressed themselves well in declaring the good to be that at which all things aim. But there appears to be a difference among ends; for some are activities, others are products apart from [the activities that produce them]. Whenever

10. For a brief summary, see John Mahoney, *The Making of Moral Theology*, 85–88.

11. Augustine, *Confessions*, 6, 7.

there are ends apart from actions [which produce them], the products are by nature better than the corresponding activities.[12]

Happiness, Aristotle holds, consists in activity in accord with virtue. Thus, the end for Aristotle is nothing exterior that could be bestowed on an agent, like riches, power, honor, or anything that could be produced and evaluated as a "product" apart from human action.

In Thomas's commentary on Aristotle's *Nicomachean Ethics,* he suggests that order can be related to reason in four distinct ways leading to the differentiation of various sciences.[13] Reason sometimes does not create but simply contemplates the order of a thing *(res).* An astronomer or the geometrician does not, on Thomas's account, create the order that reason contemplates, but rather in learning receives this order. This relationship between reason and order he calls natural philosophy. Reason establishes a second order among its own considerations of concepts and signs of concepts. Logic, the second order, considers the order of parts of verbal expression to one another and the order of principles to their conclusions. A third relationship of reason to order is that proper to the moral science, an order reason can establish in the will. This is the sphere of what later philosophers have called "intransitive" human activity (*actio* in Thomas's terminology), that is, activity that does not necessarily bring about change in external affairs. Thomas further divides this relationship of reason to order into individual ethics, household ethics, and politics. Finally, reason can introduce order into external things, as when a carpenter makes the rough wood of a tree into a chest or a cabin. This is the transitive sphere of activity, the introduction of change into external states of affairs, *factio* in Thomas's Latin.

12. Aristotle, *Nicomachean Ethics,* trans. Hippocrates G. Apostle (Grinnell: The Peripatetic Press, 1984) 1109a1–6; see also, *ST* I-II, 1, 3, ad 3.

13. "Ordo autem quadrupliciter ad rationem comparatur: est enim quidam ordo quem ratio non facit, sed solum considerat, sicut est ordo rerum naturalium; alius autem est ordo quem ratio considerando facit in proprio actu, puta cum ordinat conceptus suos ad invicem et signa conceptuum, quae sunt voces significativae; tertius autem est order quem ratio considerando facit in operationibus voluntatis; quartus autem est ordo quem ratio considerando facit in exterioribus rebus quarum ipsa est causa, sicut in arca et domo." *Sententia libri ethicorum,* prefatio.

Each human act, then, is primarily, in terms of its evaluation, an intransitive act. At the beginning of the second book of the *Summa contra gentiles*, Thomas draws the distinction between *actio* and *factio*. God's willing, knowing, and loving, the *actiones Dei*, Thomas considers in book one of the *Summa contra gentiles*. In book two of that work, he turns his attention to the *factiones* of God such as the creation of the earth, sky, and creatures. The same distinction may be drawn with respect to human actions as well. Precisely as moral, they should be considered as *actio* not *factio*, i.e., a "doing" considered precisely as self-determining activity, rather than as a "making" that is the shaping of what is outside the person's will and mind.[14] A ballerina's *actio*, determines, in part, what kind of person she is. Her choice to begin, and her ongoing participation in the dance, together constitute an *actio*. She is by an act of self-determination making herself into a certain kind of person. On the other hand, the ballerina's activity as understood and appreciated by the audience is a *factio*. The audience can watch and appreciate her skill, jumping ability, precision of movement, and so on. *Factio* but not *actio* can be fully assessed from the third-person perspective.

In *Summa theologiae* I-II, 3, 2, Thomas asks, "Whether happiness is operation?"[15] In this, Thomas accords with Aristotle and in fact cites him as the authority in the *sed contra*, concluding, "happiness is operation in accord with perfect virtue." This operation is an *action*, not a *factio*, and as such it is not necessarily productive of effects in the world.[16] Thomas notes this in both the *Sententia libri ethicorum* and the *Summa theologiae*. In the article cited above, to the third objection, Aquinas replies:

Just as it is said in the ninth book of the Metaphysics, action is two-fold. One proceeds from the agent into exterior material, just as burning and

---

14. See *ST* I-II, 74, 1. I am indebted here to John Finnis's *Aquinas: Moral, Political, and Legal Theory* (Oxford: Oxford University, 1998). The point is put in a more phenomenological way in James G. Hanink, "Karol Wojtyla: Personalism, Intransitivity, and Character," *Communio: International Catholic Review* 23 (Summer 1996) 244–51.

15. Utrum beatitudo sit operatio?

16. See *Summa contra Gentiles* (hereafter *ScG*), II, 1, for an explication of this distinction. See too *ST* I-II, 55, 2 ad 3; *ST* I-II, 74, 1.

cutting. And such an operation is not able to be happiness, for such an operation is not an act and a perfection of the agent, but rather of the one undergoing change, as we have said. The other action remains in the agent himself, as sensing, understanding, and wanting. And action of this kind is a perfection and the act of an agent. And such an operation is able to be happiness.[17]

This immanent activity referred to by Thomas as the "*actio manens in ipso agente*" constitutes happiness for the agent. Not just any *actio* is our happiness, but rather only the *actio* in which we know the highest object, God. Thomas's account is profoundly, but not exclusively, interior. He does not begin his moral description of acts with an analysis of exterior effects produced by the agent. He begins rather with the acting person and what the person seeks. It is not that exterior effects of action have no place, but their place in Thomas's account is carefully subsumed under the aegis of human action. Thomas does not reduce action to external effects, but neither does he suggest that action is merely internal desires, wishes, or acts. As Stephen Brock has suggested, for Thomas *usus* is the hinge linking the exterior and interior elements of the act, both of which contribute to a full understanding and evaluation of the moral act.[18]

According to some scholars, this balanced approach to human action became obscured in the tradition that followed Thomas. John Mahoney's *The Making of Moral Theology* contrasts Thomas's approach with the tendency to begin with the exterior effects and work back toward the agent. He notes that Aquinas

approaches morality from within the subject rather than presenting it to him from the outside.... For this way of viewing the moral life proceeds by a capitalizing of personal resources, or in more Aristotelian terms, by the fulfillment of one's human potentialities toward happiness, or Aquinas's beatitude.... The emphasis moves away from the series of more or less connected acts and objective stepping-stones along which one must move to the agent performing the acts, or to be more accurate, to the person becoming more, or less, himself in and through his actions.

17. *ST* I-II, 3, 2, ad 3.
18. For a very helpful account of the relationship between these elements of action, see Stephen Brock, *Action and Conduct: Thomas Aquinas and the Theory of Action* (Edinburgh: T&T Clark, 1998).

Morality is ultimately in this view not about actions but about the acting subject. It is this approach, of course, which makes more sense of the whole approach to morality by way of the moral virtues, which are not to be seen simply as moral skills enabling one to more easily follow the moral road map, and choose and perform the right actions. They are perfections and liberations of the person, who not only acts virtuously, but actually is, or is becoming, really judicious, fair-minded, self-controlled, and courageous.[19]

In Mahoney's estimation, this subject-centered morality, which begins with the acting person and judges actions from this first-person perspective, was lost in the development of a neo-scholasticism which focused more and more on the evaluation of acts without reference to the agent by taking the third person perspective of judge.

Human Action as Knowing Willing

Certain forms of proportionalism insist that we cannot evaluate an exterior action without reference to the agent's intention. This brings us to consider the acting person and his or her desires, knowledge, intentions, and so forth, in acting. This consideration, the consideration of distinctly human activity, is of "human action" in contrast to "acts of a human being." There are a number of very good, if sometimes conflicting, accounts of Aquinas on this topic.[20] Here, an effort will be made to see the import of Thomas's account for proportionalism.

Thomas takes a great deal of care to clarify what he means by human action. Since proportionalism, according to Richard McCormick, makes, "no claims to be establishing a model of the human act,"[21] we can, without begging questions, rely on Thomas's account, an account often appealed to by Louis Janssens.[22]

19. Mahoney, *The Making of Moral Theology*, 220–21.

20. See, for example, Ralph McInerny, *Aquinas on Human Action: A Theory of Practice* (Washington, D.C.: The Catholic University of America Press, 1992); Alan Donagan, "Thomas Aquinas on Human Action," in *The Cambridge History of Later Medieval Philosophy*, ed. Norman Kretzmann, Anthony Kenny, Jan Pinborg, and Eleanor Stump (Cambridge: Cambridge University Press, 1982) 642–54.

21. McCormick, *Notes on Moral Theology, 1981 through 1984*, 61.

22. Janssens, "Ontic Evil and Moral Evil."

Though question 18 about the goodness and badness of human action attracts more attention, questions 6–17, describing human action, are indispensable to a proper understanding of Thomas's account of the moral life, for it is human action and not virtues, natural law, or divine laws around which the *Prima secundae* is structured. Human action, for Thomas, involves six (or, if there exists a plurality of means, eight) interlocking acts of knowing and willing beginning with understanding *(intellectus)* and proceeding through willing *(voluntas)*, intention *(intentio)*, [deliberation *(consilium)*, consent *(consensus)*,][23] choice *(electio)*, command *(imperium)*, and use *(usus)*.[24] It is this structure to which we shall now turn, and its importance should not be underestimated, as the eleven lengthy questions dedicated to the subject in the *Summa theologiae* would seem to indicate.[25] Indeed, attention to this structure leads to further insight into the vexing questions occasioned by proportionalism.

Human action begins with understanding *(intellectus)*.[26] We cannot want or bring about what we do not prospectively know or conceive of. This knowledge is not of that which *already* exists, but that which *could* exist. This understanding is not retrospective, but prospective, not hindsight, but foresight.[27]

23. Deliberation and consent do not obtain in each and every human action but only in those in which a number of means are available.

24. The order in which I set out these acts is itself subject to some controversy. Ralph McInerny, John Finnis, Alan Donagan, Daniel Westburgh, and Servais Pinckaers, offer accounts of the human act whose order and content differ in various respects. Here, I am not concerned with sorting out rival Thomistic exegeses of I-II, 6–17. The argument vis-à-vis proportionalism does not depend upon adopting one of these readings of Thomas in place of another. Readers interested in this debate should see not only the work of scholars referred to above, but also J. A. Oesterle, *Ethics: The Introduction to Moral Science* (Englewood Cliffs, N.J.: Prentice Hall, 1957), 85; and Vernon Bourke, *Ethics: A Textbook in Moral Philosophy* (New York: Macmillan, 1966).

25. Daniel Westberg suggests that there was no long history of treatment of the "psychological process of action" before Aquinas who nonetheless drew upon Maximus the Confessor, Nemesius, and John Damascene. See *Right Practical Reason: Aristotle, Action, and Prudence in Aquinas* (Clarendon Press: Oxford: 1994) 126–29.

26. *ST* I-II, 9, 1. See also, *ST* I-II, 17, 1; I-II, 82, 4; *De veritate* q.14, a.1 and 2, *De malo* q.4, a.2.

27. *Pace*, Michael Bratman, *Intention, Plans, and Practical Reason* (Cambridge: Harvard University Press, 1987) 115. Doubting success is not disbelieving something is possible.

Human actions begin with knowledge of what *could* take place—for example, the building of the atomic bomb. Having been told by Einstein and other scientists that building such a weapon was a possibility, President Roosevelt considered whether or not this possibility was attractive. It could be of great use in the war, and of devastating effect if developed by the enemy first; hence at this point we may speak of an act of willing *(voluntas)*. The agent recognizes not only that the end can be *(esse)*, but also desires this end as good *(sub ratione boni)*. At times, the process of human action proceeds no further. An agent can simply recognize some possibility but take no further interest in it.

In the case under consideration, though, the President considered such a possibility a good. "Such a weapon would be able to end the war much more quickly. . . ." In some renderings of Thomas's account of human action, this stage is named as delight (fruitio). Delight, in this technical sense, is fully compatible with an emotional revulsion. The delight is the rational apprehension of and attraction to some goal, even if the goal is only a means to some other end attractive in itself. If our attraction to, or "entertaining" of, the project does not end at this stage, but rather leads to the point where we move to realize the end in question, then we may speak of intention *(intentio)*. Roosevelt, of course, decided to build the bomb. He formed an intention to accomplish this end. How? This stage of human action corresponds to deliberation *(consilium)*. If one is to attempt to develop such a technological wonder as the atomic bomb, there are many options as to how to go about it. One could hold international symposia and bring all the world's experts together to exchange information and collaborate on the project, as now takes place in the quest for a cure for AIDS. Since Roosevelt's desire for the bomb grew out of the international turmoil of wartime and secrecy accompanying military operation, the President ruled out this option at once, giving consent *(consensus)* to one of the other means available, namely secret research undertaken by the best scientists available and underwritten by government support. Next, he made the choice *(electio)* that this indeed was the route to be taken. In order to carry out this choice, Roosevelt exercised various

presidential privileges and issued directives to various government and military officials to carry out the plans. Thomas desig-
nates these the stages of human action as command *(imperium)*
and use *(usus)*.

Usus is the very nexus in which the interior desires and reasoning of the agent come together with the (sometimes) exterior
movements toward the desired and reasoned-about effects.[28] As
Stephen Brock writes: "Use reaches beyond the proportion of the
will to its object. It belongs within the order of the object's actual
realization."[29] In order to avoid confusion, the whole series from
understanding *(intellectus)* through use *(usus)* shall be called "human action." The various elements making up a human action
individually taken, i.e., choice, intention, etc., we shall call "human acts."

Lest the Roosevelt example lead one astray, it should be noted that these interlocking stages or elements of human action do
not necessarily correspond to conscious decisions made by
agents. It is not as if a violinist must deliberate concerning all
seven or even nine stages in order for her action to be properly
called human. Rather, as Donagan and others have pointed out,[30]
these steps need not be, though they could be, consciously deliberate stages of human action. At times, the elements of a human
action are chronologically simultaneous or nearly simultaneous.
Sometimes, then, it is only when an agent is interrupted in human action or when the action requires time in execution that
the stages of which Thomas speaks may indeed be explicitly recognized by the agent.

The progression of the stages indicates a greater and greater
commitment of the person. An agent who recognizes that he or
she could, in a certain case, steal *(intellectus)* is not as committed
to that act as one who is also attracted to theft *(frui)*, "entertaining" so to speak the thought of achieving the end. The person

28. See, for example, Stephen Brock, "The Use of *Usus* in Aquinas' Psychology of Action," in *Moral and Political Philosophy in the Middle Ages: Proceedings of the
Ninth International Congress of Medieval Philosophy* ed. B. Carlos Bazán, Eduardo Andujar, and Leonard G. Sbrocchi. (Ottawa: Legas, 1992) 654–64.

29. Stephen Brock, *Action and Conduct*, 179.

30. Alan Donagan, "Thomas Aquinas on Human Action," 654.

who sets his or her heart on stealing *(intentio)*, but does not in the end actually choose the means to achieve this end *(electio)* is again less committed to the theft than an agent who deliberates and actually follows through with the theft *(usus)*. Thomas writes: "Consider someone who wants to do something good or evil in end, and on account of some impediment stops; another however continues the motion of the will until the work is complete. It is clear, that the will of this kind is more firmly in good or evil, and in this respect worse or better."[31] In other words, Thomas's stages of human action help to evaluate the extent to which an agent is committed to an end, be it good, bad, or indifferent.

Intention

The term "intention" is far from unambiguous. It may be helpful to be guided by Thomas and those who followed him in developing an understanding of intention within the context of human action. Thomas writes:

Intention, just as the name sounds, indicates to tend into something *(in aliud tendere)*. Both the action of the mover and the movement of the moveable *(motus mobilis)* tend into something. But the motion of the moveable tending into something issues from the action of the mover. Hence, intention first and primarily pertains to that which moves to an end. Hence we say that the architect, and everyone who commands, moves others by his direction *(imperium)* to that toward which he tends. The will moves all the other powers of the soul to an end, as was previously shown; hence it is manifest, that intention properly is an act of the will.[32]

Intention is that which moves the agent to action. Thomas's example of the architect in I-II, 12, 1 helps illustrate the way in which intention relates also to means. The architect moves those under his direction as a means to his end. Likewise in the soul, the will moves the other powers as means to its end. We do not have intention without the choice of means, as Thomas makes

31. *ST* I-II, 20, 4; see also *ST* I-II, 72, 7 ad 1, and *De malo* q.2, a.2, ad 8.
32. *ST* I-II, 12, 1.

explicit later in the same question. Summarizing the acts of the will bearing on the end, he notes that will relates to ends in various ways: absolutely, as one naturally desires health *(voluntas)*; and also as an end to be sought by means *(intentio)*. "And thus, intention regards an end, for we are not said to intend health because we will it, but because we will to attain it through something else."[33] Merely to wish for some end *(vellitas)* or to will some end as a good *(voluntas)* indicates very little commitment, while seeking the end by some means *(intentio)* represents a greater commitment or self-determination of the person in accord with the given end.

In the second article of question 12, Thomas considers whether intention is only of the ultimate end. His response helps clarify the relationship between intention, choice, and two kinds of ends, proximate and remote. He writes:

Intention regards an end inasmuch as it is a terminus of the motion of the will: a terminus can be considered in regards to motion *in two senses*. *In one sense*, the final terminus in which one rests, which is the terminus of all motion. *In another sense*, as some intermediate [terminus], which is the principle of one part of a motion, and an end, or terminus of another; just as in motion which goes from A into C through B, C is the final terminus, B however is a terminus, but not the final one. *And of either of these there is able to be intention*, whence it is always of an end, but nevertheless it need not be that it is always of the final end.[34]

Thus, for Aquinas an agent intends each proximate end. Thomas's reasoning allows us to consider a whole span of human acts in relation to one another of which each proximate end is intended. Roosevelt, in order to achieve the end of building the bomb, had to allocate sufficient resources, both financial and military, to achieve the end. This required that he alert the relevant personnel of his decisions. In order to do so, various papers had to be drawn up to that effect, and these papers in turn lacked validity until signed by the President. According to Thomas's analysis, the President intends all five ends in this series, including the most proximate: signing the papers. In an example

33. *ST* I-II, 12, 1, ad 4.
34. *ST* I-II, 12, 2, emphasis in original.

from his commentary on Aristotle's *Physics*, Thomas shows that often there are many ends related one to another in a human act:

> Moreover [Aristotle] adds that all those things which are intermediate between the first mover and the final end, all are in a certain way ends: just as when a doctor thins the body, and thus health is the end of the slimming; however slimming is effected through purgation; purgation through a potion; one prepares a potion however using some instruments. Hence, all these things are in a certain sense ends; for the thinning is the end of purgation, the purgation of the potion, the potion of the implements, and the implements are the ends in operation or in the acquisition of the implements.[35]

One finds this example of a series of ends ordered to one another under the aegis of a final end reflected in the *Summa* as well: "For intention is not only of the final end, as was said, but also of an intermediate end: someone at the same time intends the proximate and the final end, preparation of medicine and health."[36] Hence, all the means taken for the sake of an end are intended. One can certainly distinguish means as distinct from ends and means as partially constitutive of ends.[37] Intention, however, applies to both sorts of means. Intention can be of both sorts of means, for those means distinct from and those means partially constitutive of the end are both possible objects of the will.

In handling an objection that intention is called "light" by the Lord, and that light pertains to cognition rather than to the will, Thomas further refines his use of the term intention in I-II, 12, 1. "Intention is called *light*, since it is manifest to the one intend-

---

35. *In II Phys.* lect 5.
36. *ST* I-II, 12, 3.
37. Alasdair MacIntyre writes: "More than one commentator [on Aristotle's *Nicomachean Ethics*] has pointed out that what conduces to an end either may be what is more commonly in English called a means, that is, some activity distinct from an end-state, which is causally efficacious in producing that end-state, as the building of a wall may be a means to enjoying shelter from the wind—or it may be a means instead in the sense of a constitutive part, as making the opening moves in a game of chess is a means to the end of playing a game of chess." Alasdair MacIntyre, *Whose Justice? Which Rationality?* (Notre Dame: University of Notre Dame Press, 1989) 132.

ing; and hence works are called *darkness*, since man knows what he intends, but he does not know what follows from his works."[38] Since any action brings with it a multiplicity of effects, but not all effects specify an act as one kind of act or another, intention specifies the kind of act undertaken (even if in a given situation an agent may be morally irresponsible for allowing unintentional effects that could have and should have been prevented).

Important work clarifying the meaning of intention and its relation to effects foreseen by the intellect has been done by Elizabeth Anscombe. Like Aquinas, Anscombe suggests that an agent cannot be ignorant of an intended effect and that this knowledge is had without observation. The intention of the agent, Anscombe points out further, is not merely a prediction about what will come about in the future.[39] An example she gives makes the distinction clear. Imagine a man says, "I am going to fail this exam," and his wife says, "No you will not. You have studied well." If he were to reply, "But it really is a difficult exam and many good students have failed it before me," his response indicates that his prior statement was a prediction. If however he were to say, "I need to fail this exam so that I can postpone graduation, retain my student status, and avoid the draft," then his statement "I am going to fail this exam" is not a prediction but a statement of intention. Intended consequences differ from foreseen consequences, which, it seems, in many cases amount to a prediction about future states of affairs.

Anscombe also points out that the acceptance of the question "Why did you . . . ?" helps differentiate the intended from the foreseen and more broadly from the unintended. That Anscombe's question distinguishes the intended from the unintended may be seen, if one posed to a jogger the question "Why are you killing all those ants in lane 4?" He might reply, "I'd no idea there were ants there; I'll jog in lane two." His response indicates

---

38. *ST* I-II, 12, 1, ad 2. These remarks accord well with what Elizabeth Anscombe notes in *Intention* (New York: Cornell University Press, 1963) that one can be mistaken about what one does, but never about what one intends to do.

39. Anscombe, *Intention*, 2.

that his "killing ants" did not come from reason and will, and therefore was unintentional. The intentional presupposes prospective knowledge.[40]

Anscombe's work helps illuminate and expand Aquinas's own account of intention. These ongoing developments of Aquinas's work have led to two differing views of intention—the "broad" and the "narrow" accounts. These two versions of intention can be exemplified through the court case "R. vs. Desmond, Barrett, and Others" (1868).[41] In this case, Barrett dynamited a prison wall, hoping to free two of his imprisoned Irish Fenian friends. Instead, the explosion killed two guards (a consequence Barrett presumably could have foreseen). The *mens rea* for murder requires the intention to kill or cause grievous bodily injury. The broad view of intention, advocated H. L. A. Hart and Glanville Williams,[42] suggests that the intention to murder is here present, since the killing of the guards, although not intrinsically part of Barrett's plan, could be seen to follow with certainty from the action. Hence, all effects that follow necessarily, or with high probability, or with what has been called "closeness," from an act are included in the intention, along with effects that are "strictly" intended.

The narrow conception of intention advocated by John Finnis, Germain Grisez, Joseph Boyle, and others holds that only those consequences which are means to ends should be considered as intended. Hence, on this view, Barrett intends only blowing up the wall and freeing his friends. The deaths of the guards are foreseen, but not intended (unless, of course, part of Barrett's plan was that several guards be killed by the blast and are thereby unable to capture him and his friends). That the deaths were

40. Of course, as Thomas notes in *ST* I-II, 6, 8, culpable ignorance does not cause absolute involuntariness, for which there can be no culpability, but rather involuntariness in a certain respect.

41. H. L. A. Hart, *Punishment and Responsibility* (Oxford: Clarendon Press, 1968, rev. 1982) 119, as cited in Mark P. Aulisio, "On the Importance of the Intention/Foresight Distinction," *American Catholic Philosophical Quarterly* 70.2 (1996) 189–205, at 202.

42. Glanville Williams, *The Sanctity of Life and the Criminal Law* (London: Faber and Faber, 1958).

foreseen does not mean that Barrett is innocent of their deaths, but he is on this view innocent of *intending* their deaths.[43]

The narrow account of intention has at least two advantages not enjoyed by the wide account. Intention is, for Thomas, an act of will and not reason. Anscombe puts the same point another way. The fundamental sign of intention, says Anscombe, is desire. We cannot therefore be said to intend those effects of our action which, however closely connected with the desired effects, we do not desire. The narrow account also allows us to avoid an ambiguity present in the wide account of intention. Just what should be included in this wide account? Just how "close" must the undesired effects be to be included as intended with the desired? A treatment of this essential topic, indeed how to define the human act itself, will be the subject of the next chapter.

Contemporary Questions

Having given a brief account of human action, intention, and foresight in Aquinas and some modern appropriations and developments of these Thomistic insights, let us now return to proportionalism. Proportionalists generally advocate the goodness/rightness distinction (GRD). However, the GRD should be distinguished from proportionalism itself. There are philosophers and theologians who advocate the GRD who are not proportionalists, and, thus, proportionalism (as a method of making exceptions to norms) should be distinguished from the GRD. For example, Alan Donagan's distinction between first-order and second-order

43. What St. Thomas says in *ST* I-II, 20, 5 seems to favor the broad account of intention: "For when a man foresees that many evils may follow from his action, and yet does not therefore desist therefrom, this shows his will to be all the more inordinate." Although he seems to be saying that the foreseen consequences, when they follow necessarily or for the most part from a given action, enter into the intention of the agent, it may be said that the agent at least intends not to avoid the consequence. But that is not to say that the agent intends the given consequence. What Thomas has in mind here is an action that is evil in kind (or good in kind) from which an agent foresees still other evils (or goods) arising. In such a case, the evil (or good) of the action increases. But the act itself (the object) is not defined as good or evil by this intention not to avoid, for the act itself is already good or evil in itself. Rather this circumstance of the agent foreseeing evil (or good) increases the evil (or goodness) of the action as a whole.

moral judgments tracks neatly onto the GRD, yet Donagan is known as an absolutist of a sort. Likewise, the foremost advocate of the GRD in theological circles, James Keenan, S.J., is not a proportionalist. Early versions of proportionalism did not draw the GRD. Hence, a treatment of the GRD in relation to human action as described falls outside of this investigation.[44]

Debates over the distinction between intention and foresight (I/F) are more directly connected to proportionalism. The I/F distinction should not be confused with the distinction between omission and commission, nor with the distinction between doing and allowing. Although every commission and doing is intentional, some omissions and some allowings are also intentional, while some omissions and some allowings are not intentional. Thus, one ought not to suppose that one merely foresees whatever one allows or omits.

Although the distinction between intention and foresight has received the most attention in connection with Thomas's treatment of self-defense, other places in Thomas's corpus have a more explicit treatment of the distinction that is really presupposed by II-II, 64, 7. For instance, in I-II, 73, 8 ad 3, Thomas notes that although spiritual death is worse than physical death, the one who murders commits a worse act than the one who lures another into fornication, because the murderer intends to inflict injury on the other, while the seducer presumably intends only the pleasurable act and merely foresees that this leads the other into sin.

Thomas writes in *De malo* 2.2 that it is from *the motion of the will* that greater or lesser merit is determined before God. Other

---

44. Most of the standard accounts of proportionalism, including Hallet's and Hoose's, also defend the GRD. For a view advocating the GRD as Thomistic, see James Keenan, *Goodness and Rightness in Thomas Aquinas's Summa theologiae* (Washington, D.C.: Georgetown University Press, 1992). A criticism of this reading is given by Lawrence Dewan, "St. Thomas, James Keenan, and the Will," *Science et Esprit* 47 (May–September 1995) 153–76. Jean Porter gives another criticism of Keenan's interpretation in "Recent Studies in Aquinas's Virtue Ethic," 191–215, at 197–202. For a criticism of the GRD from a strictly philosophical perspective, see J. L. A. Garcia, "The Right and the Good," *Philosophia* 21, nos. 3–4 (April 1992) 235–56; "Motive and Duty," *Idealistic Studies* 20, no. 3 (September 1990) 230–37, and "On High Mindedness," *Proceedings of the ACPA* 47 (1989) 98–107.

things being equal, if John merely considers a wicked plan of action and believes it desirable *(intellectus, voluntas)*, he is less corrupt than Larry who considers it, delights in the possibility, and moves to carry it out *(intellectus, voluntas, intentio)*. John and Larry are both less badly off than Bruce who considers, desires, moves to carry out, plans for, and finally carries out a wicked end *(intellectus, voluntas, intentio, consilium, electio, imperium, usus)*. For Thomas, the greater the motion of the will, the greater the engagement or identification of the person with the end, for either good or ill. Thus, contra Abelard, *ceteris paribus* the person who intends to give alms *(intellectus, voluntas, intentio)* merits less than the one who actually does give alms *(intellectus, voluntas, intentio, consilium, electio, imperium, usus)*.

In concrete cases, numerous factors are characteristically involved in the agent's merit or demerit. Two persons may do the same good deed, but one do so reluctantly and the other with zeal. The intensity of the will makes a difference in the assessment of the agents, as does the end sought by the agents. One person may intend to give $1000 to charity but fail to do so through no fault of his own, while another may carry through with a five dollar contribution. In such case, the wealth of the contributor is also relevant, for the widow's mite merits much more than Bill Gates's million. However, when other circumstances are equal, the agent who follows through with a good act does better than an agent who merely intends but does not follow through even though interrupted through no fault of his own. The basis of this judgment is that differences in following through with intentions and in the execution of the act itself *(usus)* make a difference in moral judgment for Aquinas. To ignore these differences obscures the full reality of human action, which cannot be reduced to any single stage such as intention. The analysis of these examples leads us to conclude that the more acts of willing and knowing involved, the further down the chain of human action toward the execution called *usus* the agent goes, the more significant is the end in forming his or her character. Hence, Thomas writes in ST I-II, 20, 4, that the exterior act adds goodness or malice to the preceding interior act.

Even some of the foremost critics of proportionalism have not fully appreciated or followed Thomas's sophisticated account. Some write as if only choice and intention were of moral significance and as if other aspects of human act were irrelevant to moral analysis. For instance, Germain Grisez's and Joseph Boyle write that the

> definition and moral characterization of killing in the strict sense make no distinction between intent to kill, attempt to kill, and the consummation of the undertaking by successful execution. These distinctions, which are legally significant, are morally irrelevant. If one commits oneself to realizing a certain state of affairs, by the commitment one constitutes oneself as a certain type of person. If one commits oneself to killing a person, one constitutes oneself a murderer. This remains true even if one is prevented from attempting to execute one's purpose—for example, if someone else kills the intended victim first. Even more obviously it remains true if one attempts to execute one's purpose but fails—for example, if one shoots to kill but misses the intended victim.[45]

Although Grisez and Boyle rightly note the self-constituting aspect of choice, an appreciation for Thomas's developed position on this matter is not evident. There are indeed significant moral differences between an intent to kill, a botched attempt to kill, and a successful killing. Recall Thomas's account of the procession of human action from thought *(intellectus)*, wish for the end *(voluntas* or *velle)*, intention of the end *(intentio)*, deliberation about the mean *(consilium)*, choice of means *(electio)*, command *(imperium)* and finally the carrying out the deed *(usus)*. To be even more complete one might add the enjoyment of realizing that one's end has been accomplished *(fruitio)*. Intent to kill can always be abandoned when the moment of execution arrives. Surely, other things being equal, one who carries out an evil intent is worse than one who does not follow through with such an intention. Otherwise, a person who has an evil intention would have no moral reason not to carry out the evil intention. There is also a moral difference between a botched attempt to kill and a successful killing insofar as the agent would be respon-

45. Germain Grisez and Joseph M. Boyle, *Life and Death with Liberty and Justice* (Notre Dame: University of Notre Dame Press, 1979) 393.

sible for the many bad effects following from the latter, but in an unsuccessful attempt, the bad effect of death is missing; hence the responsibility for the effects following this death are also missing. Thomas's account then lends a degree of sophistication and analysis that is captured neither by Grisez and Boyle nor by their proportionalist critics.

Thomas's account leads one to see a morally significant difference between the intended and the foreseen effects of human action. Since the foreseen consequences of an action are understood or foreseen by the intellect *(intellectus)*, while the intended consequences involve not only intellect but also acts of the will *(voluntas, intentio)*, the intended more fully engages the human person.[46] Just as the one who intends an effect and carries out an intention to bring about the given effect is more self-determined by that effect than the one who intends an effect but does not carry out the intention, so also the one who intends an effect is more self-determined by it than the one who merely foresees that an effect will come about but does not intend it as a means or a remote end.[47] The intended pertains to the will of the person, for *intentio* is an act of will. A good or bad will leads to a good or bad character, or in revisionist terms, the goodness or badness of the person. The foreseen pertains to the understanding of the person *(intellectus)* but not to the will of the person *(voluntas*, intentio . . .). The foreseen, in fact, is not an object of *the will* properly at all, but only of the intellect.[48] A person who

46. Nor should Thomas's account of human action be interpreted as "merely" psychological, for it appears not in the discussion of the nature of man in the *Prima pars* but between a treatment of man's final end and good and evil in human action. Given its context, Thomas's account of the steps of human action must have moral and not merely psychological significance.

47. I add *"ceteris paribus"* to cover the indirect voluntary, i.e., a consequences that one can and ought to effect, but does not. Hence, even though the ship's captain intends to take a nap and merely foresees that this will mean the ship will be in danger of sinking, since the captain can and *ex hypothesi* should guide the ship, he is responsible for the danger in which he puts the ship. The "indirectly voluntary" does not help proportionalists however, for their denial has to do with foreseeing and intending the very same end, for instance, abortion; their denial does pertain to the *voluntarium in causa*.

48. As Thomas Cavanaugh pointed out: "[A]n agent's intention reveals the agent's volitional commitment to acting to effect the object apprehended as good

foresees bad consequences coming from her action cannot be said to want that effect, though perhaps she does *not* want the effect *not* to be. Thomas's theodicy presupposes the importance of this distinction by arguing that God never intends sin though he does permit and foresee sin from which, by his omnibenevolence and omnipotence, he wills and is able to bring goodness.[49]

Furthermore, the Christian prohibition of suicide and exaltation of martyrdom hinge on the importance of this distinction. The suicide intends his own death often as means to be freed from a life "not worth living"; the martyr foresees she will die but cannot be said to intend that she die (we cannot, after all, intend the actions of others but only our own).[50] Death, even as a foreseen effect of an act, does not define the human act as *killing* since a human act proceeds from reason and will, and *ex hypothesi* a merely foreseen effect does not proceed from the will desiring the effect as either a means or end *(electio/intentio)*.

What is proportionalism's account of the distinction? There is no one answer to this question. Some versions of proportionalism define the intended and the foreseen in terms of proportionate reason. On Knauer's account, for instance, moral intention differs from psychological intention, and ethics concerns itself with moral, not psychological, intention. When evil is involved in an act, the determination of the moral intention derives from the presence or absence of proportionate reason. One parses moral intention in terms of proportionate reason, i.e., an "evil is not direct [intended] unless it is willed without a commensurate reason."[51] Here, the language of intention is retained but its customary tie to the means-end relationships envisioned by the agent is severed. Proportionate reason and not means-end rela-

---

and realizable. Foresight reveals an agent's intellectual apprehension of what will be. Thus, intention differs from foresight as volitional commitment differs from intellectual apprehension." *Double Effect Reasoning: A Critique and Defense* (Dissertation. University of Notre Dame, 1995) 148.

49. *ST* I, 2, 3, ad 1.

50. Cf. Christopher Kaczor, "Faith and Reason and Physician Assisted Suicide," *Journal of Christian Bioethics* 4.2 (1998) 183–201.

51. Knauer, "Hermeneutic Function," 21.

tionships proposed in the practical reasoning of the agent determine what is intended.

Problematic is the dualism implicit in the strong distinction between psychological and moral intention. The human act, like the human person, is unified. Psychological intention, i.e., what one wants as a means and/or an end, precisely is moral intention insofar as the ends that a person desires determine, reinforce, and express a person's moral character. We do have reason to distinguish physical causality from moral intention, for physical causality can be divorced from the acting person, but what one desires as a means or an end precisely, although perhaps only partially, constitutes one's moral character. That Thomas places the ordering of the "psychology" of human action (I-II 6–17) in the *Prima secundae*, between his treatment of the human end and good and bad human action, and not in the *Prima pars*, suggests that he too believed that this account was relevant to moral evaluation.

Most forms of proportionalism reject Knauer's division between psychological and moral intention. However, they also reject the moral importance of the I/F distinction at least with respect to non-moral goods. On this view, to intend the sin (moral evil) of another differs morally from merely foreseeing the sin of another, but intending the death of a person (premoral evil) does not differ from merely foreseeing the death of another. With respect to moral evils, the I/F distinction is significant, leading to the judgment that it is never permissible to lead another into sin, though it may be permissible to foresee and not prevent another's sin. On the other hand, with respect to non-moral evils, it is the presence or absence of proportionate reason that determines whether or not the act is permissible.

Often the moral significance of the I/F distinction is rejected for a number of reasons. It is argued that the importance of the distinction arises from the existence of intrinsically evil acts. As McCormick argues, "If it can be shown or at least argued that doing the actions in question is not intrinsically evil, or, what is the same, that the special characteristics appealed to are not valid, the need to redouble the intention [i.e. direct intention versus indirect intention/foreseen] disappears."[52] Intrinsically evil acts, i.e. acts *contra naturam* or without proper authorization, do not exist, it is argued; hence the intended foreseen distinction has no moral import.

Even if the arguments undermining intrinsically evil acts are sound, the importance of the I/F distinction could still be germane. The relationship between intrinsically evil acts and the intended/foreseen distinction is not as close as the objection supposes. One could hold, as is the view of perhaps Michael Bratmann, Bernard Williams, Francis Kamm and others, that the distinction has importance and yet at the same time hold that there are no acts of such a nature that they ought never to be done whatever the consequences. Although Joseph Boyle argues in "Who's Entitled to Double Effect" that only moral absolutists have reason to adhere to the I/F distinction, I take Francis Kamm's objection to Boyle in the same 1991 issue of *The Journal of Medicine and Philosophy* to be decisive.[53] Although we may not believe that the intentional infliction of pain is *always* wrong, we can nevertheless hold that the intentional infliction of pain, e.g. by a police officer to get testimony, differs importantly from the pain inflicted unintentionally, say by a dentist.

 On Thomas's account, the importance of the distinction between intention and foresight does not arise from, nor does it presuppose, the existence of intrinsically evil acts. Rather, the distinction's importance arises from the intransitive nature of human action. It is not that the I/F distinction presupposes the existence of intrinsically evil acts, but rather the reverse, that intrinsically evil acts seem to presuppose the importance of the I/F distinction. Without the I/F distinction, there would be cases of *perplexus simpliciter* in which agents could not help but do wrong. For example, a woman with a gravid cancerous uterus would be forced to choose between suicide and killing her own child. Ei-

---

52. McCormick, "A Commentary on the Commentaries," 198.

53. See Joseph Boyle, "Who's Entitled to Double Effect?" *Journal of Medicine and Philosophy* 16 (1991) 475–94, and Francis Kamm, "The Doctrine of Double Effect: Reflections on Theoretical and Practical Issues," *Journal of Medicine and Philosophy* 16.5 (1991) 571–85.

ther she allows the child to come to term, in which case she foresees the deadly cancer will spread, or she removes the uterus,
thereby foreseeing the death of the unviable child. She fully
foresees a death in either case, which allegedly is no different
than fully intending death in either case. If there is no I/F distinction, then there can be cases where innocent of any prior
wrongdoing agents cannot help doing wrong. But if our theory
traps innocent agents in wrongdoing, then perhaps it must be
adjusted.

Secondly, it has been suggested that the importance of teleological reasoning makes superfluous the distinction between intended and foreseen. This leads to a recognition that one may use
a premorally evil means in order to achieve a proportionate good.

If abortion is the only life-saving, life-serving option available (as in the
classical case: allow both to die vs. save the one [the mother] that can be
saved), one would think that the intervention is just the opposite of
"setting oneself against life." Certainly this is what the Belgian bishops
implied when they said that, "the moral principle which ought to govern
the intervention can be formulated as follows: since two lives are at
stake, one will, while doing everything possible to save both, attempt to
save the one rather than allow two to perish."[54]

In conflict situations, we should choose the greater good even if
evil means must be adopted to achieve this good.

Following McCormick, we can suggest that the statement of
the Belgian bishops as given is ambiguous.[55] If one is confronted
with losing one life or losing two lives, other things being equal,
it is of course clear that it is better to lose only one. The well-

54. McCormick, "Notes on Moral Theology: 1984," 59.
55. As Richard McCormick suggests, Notes on Moral Theology, 1965 through
1980, 511. One could understand the statement of the Belgian bishops to mean
that when two lives are at stake, one person's life may be intentionally taken, so
that the other person may live. This interpretation is difficult to reconcile with the
phrase "while doing everything possible to save both" that seems to qualify the
thesis that "one can attempt to save one rather than allow two to perish." If one is
intentionally killing one person to save another, clearly one has not at the same
time done everything possible to save both. How could intentionally killing X be doing everything possible to save X's life? Rather, the formulation of the Belgian
bishops could seem to refer to common opinion regarding removal of a gravid
uterus. Either the mother and the nonviable child will die (if no intervention
takes place) or only the child will die (if the uterus is removed). We remove the

known trolley example is a case in point. A runaway trolley, if directed to the right will kill five people, if directed to the left it will kill only one person. One should, given only these two alternatives, direct the trolley away from the larger number of people. The single death that results is a foreseen but not intended effect of one's action and *ex hypothesi* unavoidable.

The question at hand, however, is not so simple as either to lose one life or to lose two. There is another factor involved. The question is rather: Is it better to save one life, even if one must intentionally kill another to save that life? The question is indeed only a rhetorical one if one has accepted one version of teleological practical reasoning instead of another. If one has already determined that goodness of will consists in willing, with whatever means, better exterior states of affairs, then indeed it is better that one should be killed so others might be saved. At issue here is the form of practical reasoning one adopts. A treatment of this topic will have to be put off, though, until later chapters, which examine the two alternatives present in this debate. For, until various versions of practical reasoning are more fully treated, a judgment from one form of practical reasoning either for or against the I/F distinction should be suspended.

On the other hand, it may be that one's answer to the question of the importance of the distinction between intention and foresight leads a person to one or another form of practical reasoning. In his "Commentary on the Commentaries," McCormick makes this point as follows:

If no persuasive account of this distinction can be elaborated, then one will either modify it or abandon it and accept the consequences of doing so. In this case, the *consequence* appears to be some form of teleology in the understanding of moral norms.[56]

If the intended/foreseen distinction lacks moral import with respect to non-moral goods, then McCormick suggests that good-

---

uterus, doing everything possible to save both (but it is not possible for the child to live), attempting to save one life rather than allow both to perish.

56. McCormick, "A Commentary on the Commentaries" 197, emphasis added.

ness of will consists in willing the best state of affairs teleologically understood. On the other hand, if the distinction does have
moral import, then a good will entails willing good means and
good ends (hence, no abortion).[57] If this way of approaching the
question is correct, then we cannot argue from a teleological
form of practical reasoning to the conclusion that the distinction
at hand lacks moral import. Rather, it is one's answer to the
question about the importance of the distinction that leads to
conclusions about practical reasoning. If the question at hand is
whether the distinction has moral importance, and if it is true
that we are to adopt a form of practical reasoning based in part
upon our answer to this question, then we cannot adopt a proportionalist form of practical reasoning to argue against the distinction, for it is precisely our answer to the question about the
distinction's import that leads to one form of practical reasoning
or another.

Another argument against the importance of the I/F distinction is that the relevant category involved in moral analysis of
conflict situations should not be whether a disvalue is intended
or merely foreseen, but whether or not the disvalue is welcomed
or wanted.[58]

When I want or welcome disvalue, then I reveal a disordered heart.
"When we perform an act that has consequences which we otherwise do
not want, we identify ourselves with those consequences differently
than when we desire those consequences. In that sense we do not align
our heart in favor of their negative value."[59] This is all but identical with
Schüller's analysis, though Vacek comes at the matter phenomenologi-
cally. By that I mean that he probes the consciousness of the disvalues
conjoined to our actions. There is a different consciousness, and hence a
different personal posture ("aligning of heart"), when the disvalue is

57. A revisionist response is that there is a difference between willing premoral evil and willing moral evil as noted by Lisa Cahill in her article "Teleology,
Utilitarianism, and Christian Ethics," *Theological Studies* 42 (1981) 614.

58. Janssens remarks that we should "never *per se* will ontic evil. . . . [I]t is
obvious that we would fall into immorality if we should strive for ontic evil itself
and *for its own sake*, because ontic evil necessarily impedes and precludes the development of man and society. Janssens, "Ontic Evil and Moral Evil," 69.

59. Vacek, "Proportionalism: One View of the Debate," *Theological Studies* 46
(1985) 67. Reprinted in *Proportionalism For and Against*, ed. Kaczor.

welcomed or wanted. When it is not welcomed or wanted, whether merely permitted or intended as a means, the heart remains ordered.[60]

This analysis is connected with the division between goodness and rightness and also with "attitudes of approval or disapproval." A good person manifests attitudes of disapproval when intending non-moral evil as a means. He or she would not choose this evil were it not the only way to achieve an important, indeed proportionate, good. On the other hand, approval of evil—that is, the very wanting of an evil *(in se et propter se)* and not merely as a means *(in se sed non propter se)* to some proportionate end—is a sign of a disordered person. Thus, the morally germane distinction in analysis of situations of conflict is that between attitudes of approval or disapproval and not between intending and merely foreseeing a disvalue.

Questions arise here about the assumptions of the analysis. What does it mean for those with an "attitude of approval" with respect to evil to say that they *want* a disvalue? Does it mean that they *welcome* an evil? As McCormick notes: "The phrase *in se sed non propter se* is, in my opinion, not a vehicle for suggesting that people choose evil qua evil *(propter se).* Clearly they do not."[61] Peter Knauer offers similar suggestions.[62] These insights can be found earlier in Thomas, who writes: "Since the will is of a good, or of an apparent good, the will is never moved to evil, unless that which is not a good appears as good to reason in some respect."[63] Thomas holds that the will always seeks at least an apparent good.[64] God has ordered the human person to the good. We want, whatever we want, under the formality of the good *(sub ratione boni),* even if in reality it is not a good.[65]

---

60. McCormick, "Notes on Moral Theology: 1984," 60.
61. Richard McCormick, *Notes on Moral Theology, 1965 through 1980,* 767.
62. "Im Grunde sucht man ja in überhaupt jeder Handlung unvermeidlich einen vorethischen Wert zu verwirklichen. Man kann nur 'sub ratione boni' überhaupt handeln." Knauer, "Fundamentalethik," 325. The first sentence deserves some qualification, for one could act for an ethical or moral good, and not merely premoral, as when one repents of wrongdoing or strives to improve one's character.
63. *ST* I-II, 78, 2.   64. *ST* I-II, 19, 10, ad 1.
65. The end may not in fact be good, although it may appear that way to an

Wanting evil *per se et propter se* then is not wicked, but impossible. If no one, even the most vile criminal, desires evil itself and for its own sake but rather everyone, even those doing wrong, chooses *sub ratione boni,* then the distinction between those doing evil for its own sake *(per se et propter se)* and those doing evil to achieve some good *(per se sed non propter se)* does not obtain. It makes no sense to suggest that the rightly ordered person chooses evil only for the sake of some good, while the wrongly ordered person chooses evil on its own account, for no one chooses evil on its own account.

But cannot one know that something is a disvalue and still want it? What is sin but knowingly and willing choosing evil? Even in sin however, it is not the evil itself that is willed but rather some good is willed to which the evil is attached. The adulterer wills not the evil of sin but the good of pleasure to which the evil of sin is attached. Willing evil *per se* is impossible for Aquinas because will is always of an apparent or real good.

In some cases, an evil is at the same time good in a certain respect, namely as a means. If wanting evil, as a means, is the sign of a disordered heart, then those who intend evil as a means have disordered hearts. As Anscombe noted, the fundamental sign of intention is desire. One intends precisely that which one *wants,* either as a means or an end. Indeed, if wanting a merely apparent good (i.e., in truth, an evil) is the sign of a disordered heart, then intending an evil is the sign of a disordered heart, even when that evil is intended only as a means and not on account of itself *(in se, sed non propter se).* Aquinas follows Augustine's famous distinction at the beginning of the *De doctrina christiana:* all our "ends" are in some sense "means" save God.[66]

---

agent. For Thomas, it is simply impossible for someone to want or will an evil *qua* evil. For a primary account, see *De veritate* q.24, a.2; *In De div. nom.* 4. 22, no. 581; *ST* I-II, 78, 1, ad 2. How objects move the will, *ST* I-II, 80, 1. For a secondary account, Daniel Westberg, *Right Practical Reason,* 73, 84. There are accounts in the Christian tradition, particularly the Neoplatonic Christian tradition, that hold that agents may desire evil *qua* evil. See Carlos Steel, "Does Evil Have a Cause?" *Review of Metaphysics* 48.2 (1994) 251–73.

66. Of course, Aquinas does not thereby violate the Kantian prohibition

Why is the I/F distinction the subject of such controversy? And why do perhaps the majority of professionals working in Catholic ethics side with the advocates of proportionalism in rejecting the moral importance of the distinction with respect to non-moral evils? There may be an historical explanation. In the manuals, the authentic basis for making this distinction and for seeing its importance had been neglected in the tradition immediately preceding the rise of proportionalism.

The conception of human action at work clearly arises out of the late neoscholasticism of the manuals which like Gury is understood human action as "actuating a cause."[67] Various advocates of proportionalism speak in similar terms, e.g., the "placing," "realiz[ing]," and "Verursachung" of effects.[68] In both neoscholastic manualists and proportionalist authors, "causing" as an analysis of action has simply replaced "intending." An account of intentional human action, the theme that merits some eleven questions in the *Summa* (ten more than written on the natural law!) as in the neoscholasticism of the manuals, is not to be found in proportionalism.[69] Timothy O'Connell's *Principles for a Catholic Morality* is a typical example of the proportionalist under-emphasis on human action.[70] The topic merits only two pages and is immediately followed, following the pattern of Gury's manual, by a much more detailed and lengthy discussion of impediments to

---

against treating humanity simply as a means for kindness to a human person as an image of God expresses a person's love of God.

67. "nec teneatur agens ex alia obligatione, ut ex iustitia, caritate, eam omittere." Gury, *Compendium theologiae moralis*, vol. 1, c.2, n.9, 5.

68. Joseph Selling, "The Problem of Reinterpreting the Principle of Double Effect," *Louvain Studies* 8 (1980) 49.

69. On this point, Louis Janssens, "Ontic Evil and Moral Evil," is the only significant exception. That all other forms of proportionalism do not offer an account suggests that the Janssens reading of 6–17 is not necessary for proportionalism. Readers may also be interested in the exchange between Martin Rhonheimer and Richard McCormick. See Rhonheimer's "Intrinsically Evil Acts and the Moral Viewpoint: Clarifying a Central Teaching of Veritatis Splendor," *The Thomist* 58 (1994) 1–39; McCormick's "Early Reactions to *Veritatis Splendor*," 500–504; and Rhonheimer's, "Intentional Actions and the Meaning of Object: A Reply to Richard McCormick," *The Thomist* 59 (April 1995) 279–311.

70. Timothy O'Connell, *Principles for a Catholic Morality*, 46–47. Since a treatment of the interior aspects of human action is absent, the need for some aspect of interiority is recast in terms of "fundamental freedom," a freedom over which we have neither deliberate control nor conscious awareness (62–66).

human action, the conditions of voluntariness. Thus, as in the case of double-effect reasoning, we find proportionalism emphasizing and extending the differences that had developed between Thomas and various neoscholastics.

The shift that occurred between Aquinas and Gury, from talking about intended acts to talking about posited acts, has its consequences. Some scholastics, such as Vasquez and Logo, simply lacked appreciation of the depths of human action but focused instead on the order of physical causality.[71] Todd Salzman here summarizes the view of not a few authors of this period:

Within the authoritative commentaries on Thomas, it is implicitly understood and accepted that the first five questions of the *Prima secundae* have to do with the "beatific vision," humanity's ultimate end, heaven, to which all human activity is directed. In such a discussion, what particular goal would be served by distinguishing between two types of acts [human acts and acts of a human] which pertain to human beings? It would seem that it would have been more appropriate for Aquinas to "cut and paste" this section to the body of his work, qq. 8–21, which specifically address "moral theology."[72]

This "cutting and pasting" happened in manualist appropriations of Thomas. Gury, for instance, includes a discussion of what he calls "human acts" in his *Compendium* because of the nature of the case and common custom.[73] His relatively sketchy account of human action, especially when compared to Aquinas's detailed treatment, indicates a great concern about determining what constitutes voluntariness, but his interest in human action is basically limited to such questions. In the words of Daniel Westberg, "Interest in the stages of process of action seems to have dropped out of discussion soon after St. Thomas. The results of the success of voluntarism after Scotus are clearly evident in the commentary on the *Summa* by Cajetan."[74] Human action, like a

---

71. See John Connery, *Abortion: The Development of the Roman Catholic Perspective* (Chicago: Loyola University Press, 1977) 131–32 and 188.

72. Salzman, *Deontology and Teleology*, 315.

73. As Charles Curran argues in "The Manual and Casuistry of Aloysius Sabetti," in *The Context of Casuistry*, ed. James Keenan with Thomas Shannon (Washington, D.C.: Georgetown University Press, 1995) 166.

74. Daniel Westberg, "Aquinas and the Process of Human Action," in *Moral and Political Philosophy in the Middle Ages*, ed. B. Carlos Bazán et al, 816–25, at 818.

machine whose inner workings are quite beside the point, came to be evaluated in terms of what was produced, and this production was understood as good or evil in terms of its conformity or lack of conformity to law. Intentions ought not to be pitted against causes, insofar as intentions cause actions; yet intentions cannot be reductively understood simply in terms of external effects. Hence, it is unsurprising that Gury, although he still speaks of human action, does not offer any analysis of the phenomena, but concentrates almost exclusively on differentiations of "voluntariness" in order to facilitate judgments about culpability before the law. Human action, in this late scholastic mode, is understood in terms of its effects, and these effects are imputed or not imputed to the agent depending upon whether or not the effects were voluntarily brought about. The entire "treatise" on human action found in Thomas is missing from the manuals. It became thought of as superfluous.

Advocates of proportionalism retain this manualist analysis of human action leading them to reject the I/F distinction. Proportionalism does not recognize the true basis of the I/F distinction in the nature of the acting human person in judgment, deliberation, and execution of acts, supposing rather that it arose from intrinsically evil acts. Proportionalism also suggests what would be an impossibility in the Thomistic account of human action, namely that one could desire evil for itself *(per se)* when it parses conflict situations not in terms of the I/F distinction but rather in terms of a distinction between disapproval of evil, i.e., only using evil as a means *(in se sed non propter se)* and approval of evil, i.e., desiring evil on its own account *(in se et propter se)*. Many proportionalists seem not to treat human action as an intransitive process beginning in the intellect and proceeding through many stages to execution but rather as the mere production of external effects.

In fact, human action comes to be understood as unintelligible aside from production of effects. In the words of McCormick, "'To act' means intentionally to bring into being certain effects, or to refrain from doing so. If we prescind from effects, we can no longer speak of action. In this sense, everyone judges actions by their consequences."[75] Or as Knauer puts it,

Moral evil, I contend, consists in the last analysis in the permission or causing of a physical evil which is not justified by a commensurate reason. Not every permission or causing of a physical evil is a moral evil, but every moral evil depends on the permission or causing of physical evil.[76]

In the first instance, we simply do not have human action unless we have effects; in the second, moral evil is defined in terms of bringing about physical evil, by definition excluding sinful thoughts and desires, a move difficult to reconcile with the "interiorization" of the moral life as presented both by Thomas and earlier and more authoritatively in the Sermon on the Mount. The remarks of both authors suggest a lack of appreciation for the depth of human action in all of its elements that precede the production of an exterior effect.

Presumably, judgments about good or evil follow from judgments about what a thing is or could be. Only by having some sense of what a human action is can we tell whether a human action is good or evil. Hence in Thomas's account, the questions describing human action, I-II, 6–17, precede the question treating goodness or badness of action, I-II, 18–22. But having addressed the nature of human action and important related issues (namely, the goodness/rightness and foresight/intention distinctions), we now turn to the topic of the formal evaluation of human action. Thomas organized this formal evaluation around a discussion of the object, end, and circumstances of human action.

---

75. McCormick, *Notes on Moral Theology, 1981 through 1984,* 119.

76. Knauer, "Hermeneutic Function," 1. Knauer says: "There is no constituting intention without performing an action. This is just what distinguishes a real intention from a merely imagined one. . . . There is no intention without an action" ("Concept of Intention," 8 and 13). Here "real intention" is understood as not existing without "performance," and the interior acts preceding execution or performance are seemingly forgotten.

Good and Evil in Human Actions

Thomas's account of good and evil human action presupposes, as one would expect, his account of human action. "[A] man is deemed good on account of his possession of a good will, through which he may put into act whatever good there is in him. Now, the will is good because it wills a good object."[77] The will bears on the proximate end (the 'object') through choice of means *(electio)* and more remote ends through intention *(intentio)*. Since the will bears on object and ends, and circumstances, at times, can alter the moral character of the object and ends, these three characteristics—object, ends, and circumstances, the fonts of morality *(fontes moralitatis)* as they are later called in the nineteenth century—become essential to moral analysis.

Thomas places his understanding of moral goodness within the context of his metaphysical understanding of goodness in general. Moral goodness is a specific kind of goodness: goodness pertaining to the will. Goodness in general, for Thomas, is a fullness of being and due perfection, and evil a defect of due perfection. Thomas applies this general understanding of good and evil to human action in the first article of *Summa theologiae* I-II, question 18: "Each action, insofar as it has something of being, to that extent has something of the good. But insofar as something is lacking to it of the fullness of being, which is due to a human action, to that extent it falls short of the good, and thus is called evil."[78] An action may have some particular good but be missing others, as when an action good in object and circumstances, nevertheless is spoiled on account of a bad intention, or vice versa. "An action is not good simply unless all goods concur, since a single defect causes evil and good comes from an integral cause."[79] Just as beauty comes from all the aspects of one's appearance being beautiful and properly ordered to one another, and just as sickness results from any one system of the body not functioning

---

77. *ScG* III, 116, 3.
78. *ST* I-II, 18, 1, r.
79. *ST* I-II, 18, 4, ad 3. See also *De malo* q.2, a.4, ad 2; *De malo* q.2, a.5.

properly,[80] so also for a human act to be good each of its aspects must not be lacking any due perfection.[81] Since object, remote ends, and circumstances make up a human action, the goodness of a human action depends on all three of these aspects.[82]

Thomas reiterates this teaching explicitly in a number of places. In order for a human action to be good, the object or proximate end of the act cannot be evil,[83] the remote end or intention must not be evil,[84] and the circumstances must be appropriate.[85] The teaching would seem clear and easily applied. One cannot steal in order to give alms, since stealing (bad object) is not altered in its description, despite the good end the thief has in mind. In the same way, to give alms for vainglory is wrong, not, of course, because giving alms is bad, but because the remote end, vainglory, is bad. Finally, even if one gives alms (good object) in order to help a neighbor (good end), the act might still be bad if the money given should have been spent elsewhere, as for example, parents who donate so much money to charity that they cannot reasonably maintain their responsibilities to clothe and feed their own children.[86] In this case then, both object and remote intention are good, but the circumstances are not fitting.

In similar manner, William H. Marshner suggests that Thom-

80. *Sententia libri ethicorum*, II, 7, [320]; *De malo* q.2, a.1, ad 3; *De malo* q.2, a.4, ad 2.

81. See *ST* I, 5, 4, ad 1; *ST* I-II, 27, 1, ad 3; *ST* I-II, 71, 5, ad 1; *In De div. nom.* 4. 5, no. 349; *In De div. nom.* 4. 6, no. 367; for background, see Jan A. Aertsen, "Beauty in the Middle Ages: A Forgotten Transcendental?" *Medieval Philosophy and Theology* 1 (1991) 68–97, especially 78–86.

82. Circumstances are sometimes said to affect only the degree of the rightness or wrongness of an activity, but other circumstances, sometimes called specifying circumstances, enter into the very object of the human act.

83. *ST* I-II, 18, 2; I-II, 18, 5; *ST* I-II, 19, 1 & 2; *De malo* q.2, a.2; *De malo* q.2, a.3.

84. *ST* I-II, 18, 4, response and ad 3; and *ST* I-II, 19, 7; *De malo* q.2, a.2 ad 7; *De malo* q.2, a.4 ad 2.

85. *ST* I-II, 18, 3; *ST* I-II, 18, 6.

86. Here, one can speak of the "indirect voluntary." The sense of the term here is the one used by Thomas in *ST* I-II, 6, 3, when he writes that one acts from the will in two ways, directly when one acts and indirectly when one does not act. In *ST* I-II, 74, 6, ad 5, he adds: "for the indirect voluntary to be imputed as a sin, it is necessary that the will was able to and should have but did not act." In the example above, the parents could have and should have spent more money for the care of their children.

as's account of good and bad human acts is but another application of his account of good and bad generally.[87] In order to make
his point, he makes an analogy to grading in which the term
"good" can appear in two different places in the analysis. On the
one hand, such terms (excellent, good, fair, or poor) can mark
each exercise in the course of the semester, and such terms also
can appear in the final grade. Now, in determining the final
grade, evaluators have at least two options. Marshner writes:

> One kind of evaluation will sum and average the marks to reach the
> grade, and so it requires a commensuration of the features, and one will
> have had to import enough arithmetic to allow for computation. Anoth-
> er kind of procedure introduces an order of rank among the criteria, so
> that if a thing is good in one feature and bad in another, its grade will
> depend upon whether it is good in any feature that outranks the ones in
> which it is bad.[88]

On this account, elements of evil in the action do not necessarily
make the action bad. One cannot decide whether or not an action is bad without taking into account all the elements of action,
or all the features that could be good or bad. The final grade cannot be made without taking into account all features of the action.

Some proportionalists adopt this method of analysis. They
agree that evaluation of human acts cannot be done without an
analysis of object, end, and circumstances taken together. Joseph
Fuchs states the claim as follows:

> Because of the coexistence of premoral goods and premoral evils in
> every human act, we must determine moral rightness or wrongness of
> an act by considering all the goods and evils in an act and evaluating
> whether the evil or the good for human beings is prevalent in the act,
> considering in this evaluation the hierarchy of values involved and the
> pressing character of certain values in the concrete. Therefore, the real-
> ization of premoral values could be justified only because of the preva-
> lence of premoral goods as opposed to premoral evils.[89]

87. William H. Marshner, "Aquinas on the Evaluation of Human Actions,"
The Thomist 59 (July 1995) 347–70. Earlier, Jean Porter made a similar point in
the opening chapters of her book *The Recovery of Virtue: The Relevance of Aquinas for
Christian Ethics* (Louisville: John Knox Press, 1990).
88. Marshner, "Aquinas on the Evaluation of Human Actions," 353.
89. Fuchs, *Christian Ethics*, 82.

Fuchs, like many others, suggests that if one element of evil is in the act, if one aspect of the act is not as it should be, i.e. premoral evil is present, then the act on the whole may still be justified by commensurate or proportionate reason. On this account, one or more aspects of the act being evil does not mean the act as a whole is evil, for other good aspects of the act may be more prevalent.

On the other hand, Marshner notes, one could evaluate every aspect of the act as good or evil, with the total grade being good if and only if every aspect of the act is good. Marshner describes this position as follows:

> No matter how many features need to be checked, the marks applicable to each feature are just two ("good"/"bad"), and the overall grades are just two ("good"/"bad"), and the rule for getting from the former to the latter is this: the overall grade is "good" if and only if the mark on every required feature is good; otherwise, the overall grade is "bad."[90]

In this method of analysis, a single bad aspect of the act renders the entire act, even if good in all other respects, bad.

In at least some cases of judgment, we do clearly insist on this standard. Consider the case of the evaluation of an airline pilot. A good pilot has at least the following characteristics: (1) experience flying, (2) sobriety, and (3) alertness. If the pilot lacks any of these, if he or she lacks experience flying, is drunk, or daydreaming, then he or she is a bad pilot at least for the moment, even if the pilot has the other good characteristics to a high degree. In other words, if a pilot is drunk, even given extensive experience flying, even given efforts to be alert, he or she is not, at that time, a good pilot. The question for us is: which model should we adopt for analysis of human action?

First, advocates of proportionalism, when defending the GRD, argue that we *can* judge means independently of ends as, for example, in the case of someone who gives alms for vainglory.[91] The agent is morally bad because motivated by a bad end, but the act of giving alms is nevertheless right. Hence, we can

90. Marshner, "Aquinas on the Evaluation of Human Actions," 353.

91. Hoose, *Proportionalism*, 48, also 62–63; Ugorji, *The Principle of Double Effect*, 175; Salzman, *Deontology and Teleology*, 240.

judge a means, in this case alms-giving, independently from its end, in this case vainglory. Thus, on the one hand, it is claimed that one cannot judge means save in relation to their ends taking everything into account. But on the other hand, in arguing for the goodness/rightness distinction it is presupposed that means can indeed be evaluated independently of their ends.

Secondly, most human acts can be placed in a long chain of means-end relationships and in detailed and complex social contexts. If means cannot be evaluated as bad, save in relation to ends, and these ends turn out themselves to be means to further ends, then we have to take each and every one of these means into account, no matter how remote. The problem is not one of infinite regression, since there is a final end: happiness. Rather the problem is one of plausibility.[92] It seems clear that we can judge the act of assault wrong without taking into account everything, however remotely connected with the assault.

From a slightly different point of view, Bartholomew M. Kiely has suggested the impracticality of the proportionalist demand to take "everything" into account based upon the difference between systematic and non-systematic processes. He draws the distinction from both Bernard Lonergan and Alasdair MacIntyre. Systematic processes repeat themselves in a predictable way, just as the movements of the stars or the interaction of certain chemicals in set conditions. By contrast, non-systematic processes, such as every human interaction insofar as human beings have free will, simply cannot be reliably predicted. Hence, it is not that it is quite difficult to take everything into account, but that it is literally impossible to so do whenever other human free choices are involved.

One reason that proportionalism is intuitively plausible is that its advocates often rely on examples taken from systematic processes; for example, cases of ectopic pregnancy or cephalopelvic disproportion. In these cases, no other human agent is in-

---

92. See also Brian Thomas Mullady, *The Meaning of the Term "Moral"* and William May, "Aquinas and Janssens on the Moral Meaning of Human Acts," *The Thomist* 48 (1984) 566–606.

volved. One can reasonably predict the outcome of cases. However, it does not follow that since we can reasonably predict the outcome of systematic processes we can also reasonably predict the outcome of non-systematic processes. Since it is these non-systematic processes which make up the vast majority of moral decisions facing agents, proportionalism simply cannot offer a rational solution for the vast majority of moral decisions people face. At best, it can proceed on the basis of reasonable guesses about how other agents will react.

Thus, in the case in which a sheriff considers framing and executing an innocent black man for a rape he did not commit in order to avoid a deadly riot, advocates of proportionalism have considerable difficulty explaining what should be done. Presumably, the sheriff should not frame the innocent person, but why?

This question still awaits a satisfactory answer. In *Doing Evil to Achieve Good,* McCormick suggested that framing the man is wrong because of its long-term consequences. Critics argued that this was straightforward consequentialism. Conceding the point, McCormick withdrew this argument and came to agree with Bruno Schüller, who said that this action was wrong because it undermined the criminal justice system. Of course, the framing would undermine the system only *if* the judge's action were discovered. Thus, if a sheriff believed he could get away with framing the innocent undetected, he would have no reason not to frame the innocent. On the other hand, he would have a reason for not carrying out just sentences that *seem* to the public at large as unjust, for indeed this would undermine public confidence in the judicial system. Joseph Selling suggests that the sheriff should not frame the innocent because it undermines his role as sheriff. Once again, the distinction between the appearance of injustice and actual injustice comes to the fore. It is only the *appearance* of injustice that would undermine the sheriff's role in the community; actual but undetected injustice would not. Peter Knauer suggests that in the long run the sheriff's act would open the door to more and more acts of a similar type. A similar situation was the ultimatum of 1961 in which the communists hinted at the possibility of a third world war unless they were given full control of Berlin. Appeasing the tyrant in this instance would only have led to the handing over of one city after another. A difficulty for Knauer's response is that the two cases are in certain important ways disanalogous. The crowd is not a plotting tyrant with long-range plans for world domination. Believing that the rapist has been found and properly punished, the crowd has no incentive to demand the capture of more persons for the crime. The crowd lacks the organization to make such repeated demands.

The sheriff case is fictional, but there are real cases that bring out the same difficulty. Though "terror bombing" is decried as immoral, advocates of proportionalism have as yet not offered an adequate justification for a prohibition against intentionally bombing innocent civilians in war. If, at least at times, the intentional killing of civilians leads to less loss of life on the whole, then how could these bombings be wrong on proportionalist grounds? Often it is said that these bombings actually lead to more loss of life in the long run. This may be true in many cases, but is it true for *all* cases? Certainly, it is not true by definition, nor is it a matter of empirical fact, and concrete demonstration seems lacking. At best then, the norm against killing civilians in war would be *prima facie* wrong.

McCormick has offered an argument why killing innocent civilians in war is always wrong based on the association of goods.

[E]xtortion by definition accepts the necessity of doing nonmoral evil to get others to cease their wrongdoing. The acceptance of such a necessity is an implied denial of human freedom. But since human freedom is a basic value associated with other basic values (in this case, life) undermining it *also thereby undermines life*.[93]

"Necessity" here means that there is no other way imaginable to prevent greater loss of life, save the taking of life. If there is another way available, for example, the cessation of wrongdoing by others, then there is no necessary connection. If there is no nec-

---

93. Richard McCormick, *Doing Evil to Achieve Good*, 260.

essary connection, other goods are brought into play, and the original good comes to be undermined in the act. There is in such cases no truly proportionate reason.

Because there is not a necessary connection between avoiding the evil or achieving the good and intending the harm as a means, other basic goods (for example, liberty) are brought into play in using the harmful means. Because of the association of goods, undermining one undermines others, and thus the very value at stake, for example, life, will suffer more if the killing is done.[94]

Insofar as this requirement obtains, people may not threaten other people with non-moral evils nor may they inflict non-moral evils to prevent the possible wrongdoing of others.

However, McCormick's analysis ends up excluding much more than intentionally killing the innocent in war. Also excluded would be intentionally speaking a falsehood in order to save someone's life. No necessary, intrinsic, and deterministic connection exists between speaking falsehood and protecting threatened human life. The one threatening could simply abandon the intention to injure the innocent. Furthermore, the evil of speaking falsely now is done that the good of avoiding attack may come later. Hence, according to these secondary conditions of proportionate reason, proportionate reason does not justify saying a falsehood to save another's life. Speaking falsely to save another, by definition, accepts the necessity of doing nonmoral evil to get others to cease their wrongdoing. The acceptance of such a necessity implies denial of human freedom. But since human freedom is a basic value associated with the basic value of life, undermining it thereby also undermines life. Hence, speaking falsely to save the life of another, as well as killing in self-defense, would be excluded by the criteria adduced to exclude terror bombing.

The repeated emphasis in various forms of proportionalism on the importance of remote ends is not, however, misplaced. That a proximate end can be morally evaluated as good or evil without reference to remote ends does not mean that proximate ends are more formative of the agent than remote ends. In fact,

94. Ibid., 262.

remote ends, insofar as these architectonic ends govern and determine what proximate ends are sought, are of greater importance than proximate ends. They determine the person more significantly than proximate ends as they proceed further down the chain of human action. Thomas writes: "Hence, the philosopher says in the *Ethics* that he who steals so that he may commit adultery is properly speaking more an adulterer than a thief."[95] The remote end determines the agent more, although the proximate end determines in part. As Janet Smith notes: "One who steals to commit adultery is *more* of an adulterer (for this was the end of his act) than a thief (the object was to steal), but it is extremely important to note that he is *both* a thief and an adulterer for he intended both to steal and to commit adultery."[96] Given that we can judge means and not only insofar as these means are related to ends, we can call into question the often-repeated thesis that we cannot judge an act without taking "everything into account," while nevertheless retaining the insight as to the greater importance of remote ends over proximate ends.

More plausible accounts of proportionalism are available. McCormick, for instance, elsewhere argues that we do not need to take everything into account to make a judgment about a given means. The remote ends of an act (not paying for tuition/ adultery) can be separated from the act itself (procuring an abortion/taking a vacation).[97] The problem then, at least for some forms of proportionalism, does not have to do with an inability to judge means save in relationship to ends, but rather deciding

95. *ST* I-II, 18, 6. See too, *ST* I-II, 75, 4.

96. Janet Smith, *Humanae Vitae: A Generation Later* (Washington, D.C.: The Catholic University of America Press, 1991) 217.

97. See Richard McCormick, "Reactions to *Veritatis splendor.*" See too Knauer, "Fundamentalethik." For Knauer, a means is included in and cannot be evaluated independently from the end that it seeks to realize. If one does an act only for the sake of some end and not in any way for its own sake, then this means and end combination is one act to be evaluated by proportionate reason. See "The Concept of Intention in Theology and Ethics," 9–10. Thus, if Thomas is right, since all activity is ordered to the end of happiness, and no human action takes place save in seeking this end, we would on Knauer's account adequately and accurately describe all human action as "seeking happiness." This, of course, is in one sense true, but clearly there are more precise descriptions available, descriptions that afford a judgment of the means undertaken to achieve happiness.

what in fact is a means or an object of the human act and what is a further intention or motive.

Such an analysis of human action as good or evil in terms of object, end(s), and circumstances occasions many questions of both an interpretive and philosophical nature. These questions are central to an evaluation of the proportionalism. How can one distinguish "object" and "end"? What is the object of the human act? Which circumstances enter into the definition of the object and which do not?

Intentions, Acts, and Consequences

The interpretive difficulties of reading Thomas arise in part from the authentic philosophical difficulties of distinguishing an act from its consequences. Consider a man firing a gun (eventually killing the victim) in order to rob her. This event has indefinitely many descriptions. The agent first flexes muscles in his hand, pulls the trigger, there is a flash, the bullet and other debris leave the chamber, a loud noise is made, the projectile goes through the person's clothes, the projectile strikes her body, the victim bleeds (a few days later dying from complications), and finally the money is taken. Each aspect is a "consequence" in some sense, but they have different moral significance. How do we differentiate consequences of great importance from those of lesser importance? Which aspects of this full, but by no means exhaustive, description should count as the morally relevant object? When does the "act" end? Where do the "consequences" begin?[98]

Thomas's answer relies on his account of choice and intention. We differentiate the significance of these various consequences according to the intention of the agent. That which differentiates "act" from a merely foreseen "effect" is determined by

---

98. Of interest in this respect is Jonathan Bennett's *The Act Itself* (Oxford: Oxford University Press, 1995). As Bennett argues, if one cannot make a distinction between act and consequences, then consequentialist theory is inevitable. Those who wish to avoid consequentialism must retain the distinction between act and consequence.

the plan of means-ends relationships envisioned by the agent. For example, he may have planned to shoot the gun, to injure the victim, to take her money. Each means taken to each end can be considered an act, various aspects of one human action. The bullet's passing through her clothing, though physically necessary and chronologically prior to the bullet's entering the body, does not figure into his plan, and hence "ruining her shirt" does not define one of his moral acts. Similarly, though firing the gun may be quite loud, "making noise" does not properly describe his action. For agents in other circumstances, firing a gun may indeed be a means to the end of "making a noise"; for instance, at the beginning of the 100-meter dash or in order to startle horses. If killing her was part of his plan, then the object was a murder. If injuring her alone was part of his plan, the act was assault and battery with a weapon, but not murder. He is indeed causally and undoubtedly morally responsible for her death. He did not avoid an evil consequence that he could and should have avoided. Hence, the attacker is guilty of both stealing and reckless homicide, but not of what we would call first-degree murder.

IV. DEFINING THE OBJECT

OF THE HUMAN ACT

❦

In Thomas's moral thought, perhaps no single word causes more difficulty to exegetes and raises more questions for readers than *obiectum*.[1] The single most frequently recurring question of these debates may well be: what is the object of the human act? It is not difficult to understand why this question interests exegetes, since Thomas, as so many after him, places such emphasis on the object: "An act does not take its species from the circumstances as such as was said earlier; but good and evil are specific differences of the act of the will, as was said. Therefore the goodness or malice of the will does not depend on the circumstances but only on the object."[2] For Thomas, central to moral judgment is the determination of what constitutes the object of the action.

Recent disputes over the object of the human act come in at least two general categories. First, it is often said that the object of the action was previously understood in a physical sense, that is, as merely the externally visible state of affairs able to be captured by a third-person observer. This characterization of the object as an external, physical state of affairs is symptomatic of the

1. The best account of the introduction and use of this word in the Latin Middle Ages is found in Lawrence Dewan, "'*Objectum*': Notes on the Invention of a Word," *Archives D'Histoire Doctrinale et Littéraire du Moyen Age* (1982) 37–96.

2. *ST* I-II, 19, 2.

neoscholastic and manual traditions.³ Secondly, it was noted that there was a tendency to "preprogram" or "gerrymander" the object of the action to fit preconceived notions about what was fitting in a given situation. The object was expanded or narrowed arbitrarily. What should be said about these concerns?

Part of the confusion generated in this controversy has to do with the shifting meanings of a word that retained the same orthography. "*Obiectum*" generally in Thomas's thought does not correspond well to the "object" for modern English speakers and certainly not merely to a physical state of affairs. W. V. O. Quine summarizes the modern usage of the word:

> [W]e are prone to talk and think of objects. Physical objects are the obvious illustration when the illustrative mood is on us, but there are also all the abstract objects, or so there purport to be: the states and qualities, numbers, attributes, classes. We persist in breaking reality down somehow into a multiplicity of identifiable and discriminate objects, to be referred to by singular and general terms.⁴

In many contemporary discussions, "object" seems to be coupled with "subject," the object being that which exists independently of a mind or experiencing subject. An object in the modern sense of the word is not related to human agency because it is understood as explicitly distinguished from the subject.

For Thomas, no mere physical state of affairs, considered only as such, is subject to moral analysis. John F. Dedek is correct when he says, "St. Thomas knew nothing of intrinsically evil acts, that is, physical acts which are so morally disordered in themselves that they can never be good or licit in any circumstances or for any purpose."⁵ Thomas knew of no physical acts, considered merely under the formality of the physical, that are intrinsically evil, for no physical act considered exclusively under the formality of the physical is a human act. Only human acts

3. John F. Dedek, "Intrinsically Evil Acts: The Emergence of a Doctrine;" Hoose, *Proportionalism*, 107; Mary Jo Iozzio, *Self-Determination and the Moral Act: A Study of the Contributions of Odon Lottin, O.S.B.* (Leuven: Peeters, 1995) 67.

4. W. V. O. Quine, *Ontological Relativity and Other Essays* (New York: Columbia University Press, 1969) 1.

5. See John F. Dedek, "Intrinsically Evil Acts: The Emergence of a Doctrine."

can be morally right or wrong. The abstraction of a physical act is what Thomas calls an "act of nature" and as such is simply not subject to moral analysis, either as right or as wrong. There is then, in his thought, a distinction between acts *in genere naturae* and *in genere moris.*[6] Thomas, it could be said, was not a "physicalist."

In fact, some have suggested that the accusation of "physicalism" does not fit even the later scholastics. As Richard McCormick notes, "Authors have always admitted that the total object (or significance) of an action cannot be identified merely with the physical object."[7] We are concerned with the object of the *human* action. The fundamental distinction in Thomistic ethics between acts of a human being and human acts must not be overlooked. But the physicalist objection having been put aside, at least in relation to Thomas, many questions remain about the role of the exterior, sometimes physical act, in moral judgment.

If the object of the human act is not merely the external event, what part do external events play? Are not intentions themselves often intentions to do a certain external act? The answer to these questions hinges on the way in which external acts are considered. The ends sought in human action can be considered either as conceived, an element of a plan, or as carried out, the execution of a plan. Such a distinction is sometimes missing in analyses of the debate. Salzman writes:

Traditionalists maintain that [the object] can designate an external act such that, independently of the agent, the act can be considered evil *ex objecto.* Whereas revisionists assert that the moral nature of the external act cannot be determined detached from the human subject, i.e., the concrete situation of an acting, willing, human being.[8]

6. See Martin Rhonheimer, *Natural Law and Practical Reason: A Thomist View of Moral Autonomy,* trans. Gerald Malsbary (New York: Fordham University Press, 1999).

7. Richard McCormick, *Notes on Moral Theology, 1965 through 1980,* 218. A detailed study of Jean Pierre Gury's account of the object of the human act suggests that he, for instance, did not have a physicalist notion. Salzman, *Deontology and Teleology,* 426. See too Gerhard Stanke, *Die Lehre von den "Quellen der Moralität" Darstellung und Diskussion der neuscholastichen Aussagen und der neuerer Ansätze* (Regensburg: Freidrich Pustet, 1984) 30.

8. Salzman, *Deontology and Teleology,* 327.

These assertions are not so much correct or incorrect as undifferentiated. The relevant distinctions still need to be drawn. If one considers external acts solely *as performed* (i.e., from the point of view of a second- or third-person observer) proportionalists rightly assert that no moral judgment about the act can be made. The act may be accessed in terms of *technē* or artifice in the ancient sense but not as moral. On the other hand, if one considers the external act *as planned* in the mind of an agent, one can make judgments about it, as does the conscience of the agent him or herself. As Thomas writes:

> There are some sins in which the exterior acts are evil in themselves, as is clear in theft, adultery, murder, and similar matters. . . . [E]xterior acts are able to be considered in two ways: in one way, insofar as they are in the apprehension according to reason, the other way in respect to the execution of the act. Therefore, if we consider an act that is in itself evil, for example theft or murder, as it is in the apprehension according to its form, in this case the notion of evil is found first in it. . . . For considered in itself [the exterior act] is compared to the will as its object, as that which is willed. . . . Hence, the notion of evil and sin is thus found first in the exterior act considered, then in the act of the will. But the notion of guilt and moral evil is completed to the extent that the will follows. And thus is the evil of guilt brought to completion in the will, and in this way the evil of guilt is completely in the act of the will. Therefore, we say that first is the evil in the exterior act considered in the apprehension, the contrary however if it is considered in the execution of the work; since the exterior act is compared to the act of the will as an object which has the notion of an end. The end is later in being but earlier in intention.[9]

Human action begins in the understanding of the exterior act as conceived by the agent. The exterior act as conceived in the mind of the agent determines the character of the will as good or evil; the will determines the exterior act as performed as good or evil. The exterior effects of a human action are relevant to morality insofar as they are willed either directly or indirectly. Hence, proportionalists are right to insist that

> [T]he physical reality of killing (death = consequence) can be, as intersubjective reality, murder, waging war, self-defense, the death penalty,

9. *De malo* q.2, a.3.

or resisting insurrection, depending on the circumstances, especially depending on the reason *(ratio)* for which the act is done.[10]

No one, it would seem, would disagree with these suggestions. We begin, in Thomas's account, not with effects of human action (either immediate or more remote consequences) but with the intentions or plans of the acting person. These plans or intentions are often to do a certain external action as conceived in the intellect. This emphasis on intention is not mere subjectivism, for the intention is governed by the intellect's understanding or foresight, which in turn is governed by reality, which limits the possible objects of an agent.

If it is safe to say that the "physicalism" concern is misplaced, what of the seeming inconsistency in defining the object? Proportionalism, in almost all its manifestations, holds that we must take circumstances into account in order to make a fully objective judgment of the act. This statement is true in a number of senses. If one is to make a complete description of an act, so as to determine whether or not the act is good, one must take into account all the circumstances. This follows from the nature of goodness as the fullness of due perfection and evil as a defect of due perfection. Likewise, prudential judgment and providing counsel for action requires knowledge of all relevant circumstances. In addition, comprehensive judgment about the species of a morally bad act cannot take place without knowledge of relevant circumstances.

Thus, proportionalism is entirely correct in insisting both on the importance of circumstances and that circumstances alter cases. The next question to ask is how circumstances alter cases. It was suggested earlier that some circumstances, for example, motivation or remote intentions, do not alter an act's moral nature from evil to good, but can vitiate an action that has a good object. A question that demands an answer is: Which circumstances enter into the very object of the act? Which do not?

Consequences that follow acts, consequences that are therefore circumstances of an act, become themselves defined as acts

10. McCormick, *Notes on Moral Theology, 1981 through 1984,* 118.

relative to the agent's intention. As was suggested in the example of a person firing a gun, those consequences that are elements of the agent's plan and are chosen as such are intended and constitute "species" of action. Yet the original act as formed by proximate intention and the consequences as formed by remote intention or motive, and the end, remain distinct. The object of the human act is determined by the proximate intention. McCormick and many other proportionalists are exactly right in saying "Photographing a happening will not tell us the object of the act" and that actions are "distinguishable" by their object. How can one draw a distinction between remote and proximate intention?

One could distinguish proximate ends intended from remote ends[11] intended by considering what will or will not count as successfully achieving a given end. Consider the examples diagrammed in Figure 4.1. Two characteristics of objects become apparent when one considers these examples. The first is that the intention is accomplished *without remainder* in the handing over of the money. When one hands over the money, one *has* bribed or loaned or given a gift. The motives or remote intentions are *not* accomplished without remainder by the intended object. In other words, one can successfully bribe someone and *not succeed* in having accomplished that which motivated the bribe. One could bribe the guard to save Jay's life, but the guard could still not let Jay free from prison. Even though the motive remains unrealized, the intention of the agent allows the act to be properly characterized as bribing. Hence, that which could remain unrealized after realizing the intention is properly characterized as a motive or remote intention. We have then some means of distinguishing proximate from remote intentions in defining the object with respect to determining what should be considered a means.

Proportionalism, at times, wants certain motives or remote intentions to be included in the object of the act as if they were proximate intentions. "Thus, we refer to an *act of self defense*, not

---

11. One could also speak in this context of "motive(s)."

Figure 4.1

physical act	proximate intention	remote intention
handing $$ to another	bribing	to save Jay's life
handing $$ to another	loaning	to manipulate Jay
handing $$ to another	giving a gift	to show Jay love

to an act of killing for the added purpose of defending my life. We refer to an act of transplantation of organs, not to an act of mutilation done for the good purpose of saving another's life."[12] In these and other cases, proportionalists want a notion of the object that is expanded. "Organ donation from a living donor is not two acts, one a means to the other. It is a single act whose very object is saving the life of the recipient."[13]

These actions do not all have the same structure as those to which we referred to above. An attacker strikes, and a man seeks to defend himself. By what means? Fleeing, injuring, and killing the aggressor are all normally possible means of self-defense. If fleeing and injuring, in a given case, are not sufficient for self-defense, and killing is the only means available, this does not making killing any less a means. Clearly one could kill the attacker (object) and yet fail to defend oneself (remote intention). On the other hand, when one hands over the money, depending on one's intention, one has succeeded in bribing, loaning, or giving a gift whether or not the remote intention comes to be realized. In the self-defense case, to elide the proximate intention to kill into the remote intention or motive of saving one's life is to exclude *a priori* the position of Thomas, but more importantly to exclude means from their proper consideration.

Likewise, the example of transplantation of organs does not seem to prove the point at hand. Removing a healthy organ from someone is an object as specified by intention. Another object is to ship it across town. Still another is to implant it in a needy patient. Excising an organ, transporting it across town, and trans-

---

12. McCormick, "Reactions to *Veritatis Splendor,*" 495.
13. Ibid., 499.

planting it into another are clearly three different acts. Removing an organ is not without remainder "organ transplantation" in the same way that handing money to another is without remainder "bribing."[14] Just as someone could bribe another and fail with respect to a remote intention or motive, so one could successfully remove an organ and not successfully transplant it into another person. Further, these three different acts could be done by three different people, ignorant of what the others were doing.[15]

Organ transplantation can be considered one object, as winning a just war, running for re-election, or seeking happiness can be considered one object. But each means that contributes to these large architectonic goals or objects has a status of its own. One cannot simply subsume everything that is done in order to achieve some end under the aegis of that end as one object. Oth-

14. To say that this is simply and only but one action obscures the reality that, in fact, (1) a surgeon removed an organ, (2) a nurse packed it in ice, (3) a delivery man brought the package of ice and organ to the airport, (4) a pilot flew the organ across state, (5) an orderly unpacked the organ at the hospital, (6) a nurse reheated it, and (7) another surgeon reimplanted the organ in a needy patient. On at least one reasonable account of this, the intention is of (1) removing the organ, the motivation for removing the organ is (2) so that it can be packed in ice. The motivation for this is (3) so that the package can be brought to the airport, and so on until (7). Given that people could participate in (3) and (4), *without any knowledge whatsoever of* (7), indicates that grouping (1)–(7) is not simply the intentional object "saving a life," since one could participate in some of the steps leading to the end without knowing what one was doing. As Thomas and Anscombe have suggested, one cannot intend what one does not know.

However, the one organizing the whole affair knows. Could not his involvement be characterized as single object (1–7) "organ transplantation"? This objection would seem to fail, as we could replace the original agent acting at stage (7) with another surgeon implanting the organ in a needy patient with some other end making the separate objects more clearly individuated. Perhaps, a wicked person might use the threat of damaging the living organ to blackmail someone or to perform a medical experiment. Since this form of proportionalism absorbs all discrete actions (1–7) into the last (7), on his analysis all that we could say of (1–7), given the new final end, is that the act was "blackmail" or "experimentation." Although this may indeed be the case, it would seem that much more is going on here than this single object characterization would lead us to believe.

15. Is this "mutilation done for the good purpose of saving another's life" (McCormick, *"Reactions to Veritatis Splendor,"* 495)? This depends upon what one means by mutilation. What will count as mutilation is not clear. Not *all* alterations of the body are mutilations—blood transfusions, breast reduction, and such. The distinction between alterations of the body that are mutilations and those that are not depends upon the function of the organ in the donor. If the substantial function of the body is not impaired by the removal of the body part, then removal of such a body part is not mutilation.

erwise, all sorts of behavior would be simply subsumed under such architectonic expanded objects as "winning a just war," "running for re-election," and "seeking happiness." Such architectonic ends are indeed objects so to speak in their own right, but the means taken to achieve these ends are *also* objects of human acts. It makes a difference what means one takes to achieve one's architectonic ends, whether one wins the just war by means of killing civilians, whether one wins re-election by means of deceiving voters, or whether one seeks happiness by means of misrepresenting one's achievements. That the means taken to achieve these ends are chosen only for the sake of the end, or with regret, or as a last resort, does not alter the fact that they are in fact chosen as means and shape the moral character of the one choosing them. The notion of the "expanded object" has always remained ambiguous as to what will be included and what will not be included in the object, in part because of a lack of appreciation of the place that the choice of means has in self-determining human activity.

On the other hand, at times proportionalism suggests a restricted notion of the object. For instance, giving alms is considered an object definable without recourse to any further intention, as is intercourse against another's will. Problems arise however in reconciling these narrow accounts of the object vis-à-vis the rest of proportionalism. Almsgiving has already been treated in this regard. Questions arise in the second case as to whether proportionalism has the resources to define the act of "intercourse against another's will" in a "narrow" way as a single object and further whether this single object could be said to be intrinsically evil.

Richard McCormick has answered these questions: "Of course, no one says that [having sexual intercourse with someone against that person's will is considered only a premoral disvalue]. As soon as one adds 'against that person's will,' a qualifier has been added that makes the described action morally wrong, much as does 'against the reasonable will of the owner' in the definition of theft."[16] When the circumstance, "against a person's

16. Ibid., 486.

will" is added to the genus of sexual intercourse, the object is defined as intrinsically evil.

The cases of theft and rape, however, are not perfectly analogous. Acting against someone's reasonable will suggests moral qualification (with the word "reasonable"). This is lacking when one speaks merely of acting against someone's will. This circumstance (against a person's will) can be overridden by other considerations in favor of an "expanded" object in a good many cases. Often pedagogical discipline, punishment in the criminal justice system, and the thwarting of various crimes take place against someone's will. Most killing takes place against the victim's will. Nor will a definition of rape in terms of use of force provide the needed "narrow" object that is nevertheless always evil. If "by force" is connected with appropriation of goods or killing, we still need to know, according to advocates of proportionalism, more about the situation.

Noticing this problem, Janssens holds that the reason such a circumstance renders the sexual act wrong, and not other acts, is that intercourse by force or against someone's will contradicts the very nature of the sexual act, as "free reciprocal self-giving."[17] Intercourse against someone's will always and by definition contradicts the sexual act which is understood as a mutual self-giving. Hence, this act is always evil as self-contradictory and therefore contrary to reason.

This justification does not accord well with other aspects of proportionalism in terms of both theoretical suppositions and practical conclusions. Theoretically, proportionalism distinguishes "is" from "ought" and seeks to avoid the naturalistic fallacy, par-

---

17. "As a descriptive term the noun rape means 'the use of physical or psychic violence in order to compel somebody to sexual intercourse against his or her will.' Violence is a premoral disvalue and its use can be justified by a proportionate reason. But truly human sexual intercourse is an expression of mutual love and thus a free, mutual self-giving which is radically opposed to the use of violence." Louis Janssens, "Norms and Priorities in a Love Ethics," 207–38, esp. 217–18. "In the action [of rape] itself there is an inner contradiction: on the human level sexual intercourse is an expression of mutual love and of free reciprocal self-giving and the use of violence contradicts these requirements." Louis Janssens, "Saint Thomas Aquinas and the Question of Proportionality," *Louvain Studies* 6.3 (1982) 41.

ticularly with regard to questions of sexual practice. On this view, appealing to what can accurately be described as the nature of the sexual act as "mutual self-giving" in order to determine the morality of a given sexual act cannot be a sound basis for ethical judgment. Practically speaking, it is not clear why acting "contrary to nature" should be absolutely illicit in this one case but licit, according to proportionalism, in many others. Speaking a falsehood likewise contradicts a speech act's order to communicating the speaker's mind. In terms of sexual acts, both self-stimulation and contraception contradict "the mutual self-giving" necessary, according to Janssens, for a truly human sexual act. However, these acts are said to involve only "premoral evils," and thus can be on occasion justified. Of course, advocates of proportionalism, as all people of good will, hold that intercourse against a person's will is always morally illicit. Proportionalist theory, however, does not offer us resources to justify this conclusion.[18]

Thus, it would seem that proportionalism has not found a solution to a problem which gave rise to it, namely the ambiguously defined object. In another example of such ambiguity, Lisa Cahill writes:

When some of these circumstances are specified, we arrive at another sort of absolute norm: one which in addition to the physical *act*, includes specific *circumstances* in which it is wrong to perform it. Examples of norms *regarding acts plus specific immoral circumstances* are: "Do not kill to gain an inheritance (but do so in self-defense)," "Do not tell a falsehood to evade due punishment (but do so to save an innocent)," and "Do not mutilate a child for sadistic pleasure (but do so in a life-saving therapy)." Sometimes the "act plus circumstances" can be specified in a single word, such as "rape" or "adultery" or "mercy killing." Unlike an open ended word like "murder," these terms imply some specific sort of injustice, e.g., intercourse by force, intercourse with someone other than one's spouse, and killing the sick to avoid suffering.[19]

18. Knauer suggests that one must show only that the sought value, in the long run and on the whole, is undermined and that other values are not unnecessarily undermined. If the rapist seeks love and affection, then clearly the act would be counterproductive. On the other hand, if, as many feminist scholars have suggested, rape is an expression of violence and power, then it would seem that what is sought in the act of rape, namely, the domination of one over another, is not undermined in the long run and on the whole by the act.

19. Lisa Cahill, "Contemporary Challenge to Exceptionless Moral Norms," in

The first example given does not, in fact, indicate an act plus specific *immoral* circumstances. For example, "killing," as proportionalists point out, can be licit or illicit depending on other factors. The specific circumstances "to gain an inheritance" does not indicate an *immoral* circumstance, since when combined with "taking a walk in the park," we would say the action is *ceteris paribus* licit. As Janet Smith writes:

What is not clear from Cahill's account is why these particular circumstances make an action always wrong. Without an answer to this question, it seems right to speculate that some other circumstances might override the [*prima-facie*] immorality of the circumstances defining these norms. That is, could one kill to gain an inheritance if one had plans for the money that saved more lives than the life taken? Could one tell a falsehood to evade a due punishment, if one were on a mission to save many lives?[20]

We have not yet been given an account by proportionalists about the difference between the cases in terms of specifying circumstances and object. A common charge brought against the characterization of the object by proportionalists is that certain circumstances were brought into the object as specifying or left out of the object inconsistently. Proportionalists then face the same sorts of difficulties characterizing the object as those whom they criticize.

The explanation comes, in part, from the fact that the scholastic tradition did not differentiate between the "broad" and "narrow" concepts of intention as described earlier. If one adopts a broad conception in one case and a narrow conception in another, the object similarly will be broadened or narrowed. The other explanation for the discrepancy in object description has to do with the way in which circumstances are taken into account. Hence, there were in the earlier tradition, and continue to be in

---

Moral Theology Today (St. Louis: The Pope John XXIII Center, 1984) 123–24, emphasis in the original.

20. Smith, *Humanae Vitae*, 208. The other two examples given by Cahill indicate circumstances in which, whatever the agent does, he or she acts immorally, these being "for sadistic pleasure" and "to evade due punishment." Not just speaking falsehoods and inflicting pain are immoral under these circumstances, but also eating an ice cream cone and taking a subway ride or any other action.

proportionalism, inconsistency and gerrymandering of the object to fit preconceived notions of what is to be approved (e.g., organ transplantation) and disapproved (e.g., intercourse by force, killing to gain an inheritance).

Another cause of the ambiguity in the discussion comes from the perspectival use of object and circumstance.[21] The seemingly arbitrary inclusion or exclusion of circumstances grows in part from this perspectivity. John takes something from another person. At this general level of description, there is, of course, nothing wrong with the act as described. But let us come to a more specific level of judgment. Jean takes something that belongs to another person, another person's property. Here, the circumstance, "belonging to another," introduces something relevant to moral description, relevant to reason. This act of taking what belongs to another falls in the genus of what Thomas calls theft.[22] Leaving aside for a moment the question whether theft is always morally bad, at least according to Thomas, theft is a more or less serious sin depending on the circumstances. Stealing from a poor widow is worse than stealing from a millionaire, stealing a great deal of money is worse than stealing just a little,[23] but stealing remains stealing.

If this property is taken from a holy place, we can add further that the act in addition to being theft is also a sacrilege.[24] Nothing prevents one act from having a number of deformities.[25] If, to

21. *De malo* q.2, a.6. Certain authors, noting that circumstances stand as accidents to an action, suppose that the categories of Aristotle apply in a straightforward way to human acts as to objects in the natural world. The substance of a cat remains whether or not the cat has a thick or a thin coat of hair. The length of hair is accidental. Unlike the use of substance and accidents in relation to objects of natural philosophy, substance and accidents apply in an analogous sense to human acts, due to the perspectival nature of judgments about circumstance. One should avoid then reifying the "substance" of a human act, usually as its bare physical description. See, for example, Werner Wolbert, "Die 'in sich schlechten' Handlungen und der Konssequentialismus," and Bruno Schüller, "Die Quellen der Moralität."

22. *ST* I-II, 18, 10.

23. *ST* I-II, 73, 7

24. *ST* I-II, 18, 10. Sacrilege is the *"principalis conditio objecti."* It is the principle condition of the object because of its more direct injury of the agent's relationship with God. Nevertheless, the secondary evil of the object as theft remains.

25. *De malo* q.2, a.6, ad 11.

cite another example, the agent makes use of that which is not his or hers to make use of (theft), and that which is made use of is another person for sexual purposes (additional circumstances), Thomas speaks of fornication.[26] This example can further be specified by still additional circumstances as adultery, if one of the persons is married.[27] Thus, a circumstance, e.g., "belonging to another," sometimes reduces an act that is not a sin, "taking something," into a species of sin, "theft."[28] Other times, circumstances further specify a sin from a broad genus of wrongdoing (theft) to a more specified form (fornication).[29] In another example, if one lies in the circumstance of being under oath in a courtroom, one has not merely lied, but also perjured oneself.

Can further circumstances change this act from an ignoble to a noble one?[30] Yes, if the circumstances that rendered the act wrong themselves change, then the act can change from evil to good. So, for example, persons in dire need can take food in the possession of others in order to fend off starvation, for the circumstance "belonging to another" itself changes according to circumstance. In light of the universal destination of worldly goods, for example, the preservation of human life, property in such dire circumstances properly belongs to those who urgently need it for the sustaining of life.[31] Taking what belongs to another is theft, but "what belongs to another" varies according to circumstances. Belonging to another can change when something is sold, given away, or on Thomas's account, in dire shortages in which private property becomes common property. Hence, the manualist definition of theft as "taking the property of another against his reasonable will" was pleonastic, unless we assume a modern "legal" notion of property. Consistent with this analysis,

26. *ST* II-II, 154, 1.
27. *ST* I-II, 73, 7. See too, *ST* I-II, 88, 5.
28. *De malo* q.7, a.4.
29. See, for example, *ST* II-II, 154, 1; *De malo* q.7, a.4.
30. In *ST* I-II, 88, 6, Thomas argues that mortal sin cannot become venial sin through additional circumstances. Proportionalism suggests what would be a mortal sin can become not only not a sin but also a meritorious, obligatory act.
31. *ST* II-II, 66, 7; see also *ST* II-II, 66, 7 ad 2. See too Finnis, *Aquinas: Moral, Political, and Legal Theory,* 188–92.

Cardinal Frings delivered a famous sermon on theft to the faithful in the Diocese of Cologne during Advent after the Second World War. As trains brought coal out of Germany as war reparation, the people were suffering in the cold of winter. Cardinal Frings said that they could take coal from the trains, if this was the only way to avoid freezing. Germans coined a word to capture the concept. *Fringsen* refers to these reallocations of property during dire circumstances in light of the common good.[32]

Similar treatment of circumstances is seen in matters of sexual congress. Considering the sexual act specifically under a natural description *(ex specie naturae)*, it is a circumstance of the sexual act whether or not the partners are married to one another. Considered in a moral sense, this circumstance becomes a defining one. Once partners are married to one another, they "belong" in a sense to one another. There is no "use" of that which is another's.

Likewise, issues of killing depend on the same perspectival consideration of circumstances, circumstances which themselves can change. When one does not distinguish a specific level of description from a more general level, it will appear that an evil act is justified in certain circumstances. Consider the following example from Jean Porter:[33]

One person kills another. . . . It is surely circumstantial that the killer is a woman and the victim is a man, that the killer is young and the victim old, and so forth. But it is not a mere circumstance that the killer is an authorized executioner and the victim is a duly convicted criminal. Those details change the description of the act, *from murder to legal execution;* or to be more exact, they do if we accept the traditional Catholic account of murder and justifiable homicide (cf. II-II, 64.2).[34]

In this example, circumstances do change the act, but not from "murder to legal execution." Rather, the change is from an act

---

32. Wolbert, "Die 'in sich schlechten' Handlungen und der Konssequentialismus," 96.

33. See too, Wolbert, "Die 'in sich schlechten' Handlungen und der Konssequentialismus," 95.

34. Jean Porter, "The Moral Act in *Veritatis splendor* and in Aquinas's *Summa theologiae*," in *Veritatis Splendor: American Responses,* ed. Allsopp and O'Keefe, 283, emphasis added.

considered in a very general sense "killing a person" to an act more concretely considered "legal execution." One could begin with a very general description of the act as killing, more specifically described as killing a human, still more specifically described as killing an innocent person. This act may become worse still (killing your sister who is a consecrated religious because you want to terrorize her fellow sisters) but cannot become good.

A key difference in the way circumstances are treated arises from the difference between the institution of property and the institution of marriage. The universal destination of property differs from the ends sought in marriage and sexual intercourse. Hence, one cause for the felt inconsistency in treatments of object and circumstance arises from the assumption that the ends of various forms of human institutions and activities are the same. In both theft and bestiality, evil arises from relevant circumstances, namely, "belonging to another" and "with a beast." The circumstance "belonging to another" can disappear at the signing of a contract, the giving of a gift, or the rising specter of poverty, and only in fairy-tales does the beast not remain a beast. Hence, felt inconsistencies in describing the object derive from the various ways in which an object is bad (contrary to nature, contrary to justice), the way in which some circumstances change more easily than others, and the level of generality in which one considers the object.

Determining what is "intention" as opposed to "motive" is one difficulty in defining the object of the act. Another difficulty is determining what is included as a means to an end. What falls within intention and what lies outside intention? What is included in a means to an end? Thomas has no explicit answer to these questions, questions which have stimulated ongoing discussion.

Suggested Criteria for Determining
What Is Included in the Means to an End

Thomas Aquinas' account of human action constitutes one of his important contributions to philosophy. Although there is some dispute about the exegesis of *Summa theologiae* I-II, 6–17, one might summarize that Thomas describes the procession of human action from thought *(intellectus)*, wish for the end *(velle* or *velleitas)*, intention of the end *(intentio)*, deliberation about the means *(consilium)*, consent to possible means *(consensus)*, choice of means *(electio)*, command *(imperium)* and carrying out the deed *(usus)*, and enjoyment of the completed act *(frui)*. This account in fact helps provide an answer to the question of how one can non-arbitrarily distinguish intention from foresight in determining what is included in the means to an end.[35]

In the order of human action, intention, and not foresight, characteristically gives rise to deliberation about means to be taken in order to achieve the end. For the Terror Bomber (TB), as Michael Bratman has noted, how to effect the deaths of the civilians presents a problem of achievement for which a solution must be sought. The Terror Bomber may select the bombs that are most efficient for killing people, for instance chemical weapons. If the TB is seeking to especially terrorize the population, the TB may seek to bomb a school filled with children. A further problem may now arise as to when the children will be in the school and how the bombing can best take them by surprise. In contrast, for the Strategic Bomber (SB), how to effect the death of the children is not a problem the achievement of which occasions deliberation. The problem is simply how to blow up the munitions factory. Hence deliberation for the SB will be about what sort of bombs will best disable heavy machinery. Thus, if achievement of the evil effect presents a problem for the agent that results in deliberation about how to achieve the evil effect, the evil effect falls within intention.

Secondly, again as Bratman has noted, an evil effect is intended if bringing about the evil effect constrains one's other intentions, limiting those options for which the agent can give consent. Let us suppose that both bombers are also commanders

---

35. I am indebted here to both Thomas Cavanaugh and, perhaps more directly, Michael Bratman for drawing these characteristics to my attention. Readers familiar with their work will recognize their explicit influence throughout this section.

formulating further plans for defeating the enemy. The Terror Bomber-commander must be careful that other plans do not encroach on the plan to bomb the school. Hence, TB will not move troops into the area, an action that would cause the evacuation of the school, unless he or she aims to give up the intention of terror bombing. By contrast, the Strategic Bomber-commander is not constrained by the intention to blow up the school. SB can move troops into positions that will occasion the evacuation of the school without in the least affecting his or her intention to destroy the munition factory. He or she can give consent to other options without being constrained by the aforementioned prior intention. This is the "constraining" condition.

Thirdly, the Terror Bomber *endeavors* to kill civilians while the Strategic Bomber does not.[36] The Terror Bomber will keep track of the movements of civilians, adjust his plans to account for their movements and their defenses, while the Strategic Bomber need not. If the children have found secure defenses, the Terror Bomber will need to deliberate about the possible means to breaking down these defenses or about the possibility that the mission can in no way be successfully accomplished. In contrast, the civilians simply do not enter into the Strategic Bomber's calculations in the same way. He endeavors to destroy the factory, and his planning will be focused on achieving this end. This could be called the *endeavoring* condition.

Finally, the intended from the foreseen can be distinguished according to the criteria by which success is reckoned. If the Strategic Bomber were to learn, contrary to his expectations, that no children were killed, this news would not indicate any failure whatsoever in his planned attack. On the other hand, the Terror Bomber, having heard the news, would have failed his mission (even if he was partially glad to have failed). Hence, this criterion should not be construed as "approval" or "disapproval" as registered by one's emotions or feelings but rather with what one reckons as success or failure in a given endeavor. Failure to realize what one intends differs from failure to realize what one foresees.

36. For more, see Bratman, *Intentions, Plans, and Practical Reason.*

What is included in a means to an end? What falls within intention and what lies outside intention? The following characteristics help determine what lies within intention and is included in the means: (1) the achievement of the effect presents a problem for the agent that occasions deliberation; (2) the achievement of the effect constrains other intentions of the agent; (3) the agent endeavors to achieve the effect, perhaps being forced to return to deliberation if circumstances change; and (4) the failure of the agent to realize the effect is a failure in the agent's plan.

These four criteria are linked with Thomas's account of human action. For Thomas, deliberation *(consilium)* about how to achieve some effect arises only if that effect is intended. Insofar as actions with a single means require no deliberation, this condition would be sufficient but not necessary for establishing intention. The achievement of the effect constraining other intentions of the agent belongs to *consensus* that again follows intention but not mere foresight and addresses which means are appropriate to realize the end. The agent endeavoring to achieve the effect, perhaps being forced to return to deliberation if circumstances change, captures the idea of *electio* or choice for Thomas, a striving to realize the intention by some means. Finally, (4) Thomas expresses the idea that a failure of the agent to realize the effect is a failure in the agent's plan by means of *fruitio* or enjoyment of the act, a rational evaluation of whether one's plan has been realized. Each of these criteria is a sufficient condition for distinguishing intention from foresight, though not all criteria may be met in every case.

Thomas's account of human action also helps avoid problems of circularity. The notions of (1) deliberation, (2) constraint, (3) endeavor, and (4) plan as explained seem to be notions that Thomas defines without reference to intention. Indeed, he even defines them as elements of the human act separate from intention, even though they always follow intention in the order of execution.

These criteria distinguish the cases of terminal sedation (TS) from physician-assisted suicide (PAS). First, the achievement of the evil effect presents a problem in PAS, and not TS, that occasions deliberation about what sort of dosage to give and perhaps even the choice to use not morphine but a drug that brings about death more efficiently. Secondly, the achievement of the effect constrains the other intentions of the agent. If, for instance, euthanasia is illegal or frowned upon in certain contexts, the physician may choose to kill the patient in a way or time that will be conducive to the act being seen as accidental, to mask the killing. TS requires no such further planning.

A difficulty arises with this analysis. The difficulty with (2) is that foreseen but unintended consequences can *also* constrain an agent's plans, so (2) cannot be sufficient to pick out intended consequences. Suppose I give Sam frequent doses of morphine to alleviate his pain. I know that the cumulative effect of the morphine will be to kill Sam within a month, but killing him is not my intention. The effect constrains my plans because I will no longer enjoy Sam's company. This is obviously a case of terminal sedation rather than PAS, but according to the criterion as stated the death of the patient seems to be intended.[37]

Although it is true that one's intentions are constrained not only by intended consequences but also by foreseen consequences, the constraint in question here involves the *ante rem* achievement of the effect in question, not the question of *post rem* constraint. Achieving the effect of relieving Sam's pain may constrain my intention to prescribe other drugs, such as Serevent, that would relieve Sam's asthma, but would partially inhibit pain relief. On the other hand, the *achievement* of his death does not constrain my other intentions, e.g, as it might if I were intending his death. Thus, one who intends to kill must be careful not to do anything that would interrupt the achievement of *this* effect. The objection then does not distinguish between constraints arising from efforts to achieve an effect before that effect is realized and constraints arising from the simple fact of some foreseen effect having been realized. In the first case, if one desires to achieve an effect, say pain relief, one must not realize another possible intention that might interfere with the original intention, e.g. the

37. I thank Paul Weithman for this objection.

intention to relieve asthma. In the second case, the factual existence of some effect constrains one's intention. Thirdly, the physician assisting the suicide of another endeavors to achieve the effect of death, perhaps being forced to return to deliberation if circumstances change, or the first attempt fails. Endeavoring to achieve death does not interest the doctor whatsoever in TS. Finally, a failure of death to be realized is to be accounted as a failure of the first physician but not the second (who does not intend to kill), though both may share the same remote end of relieving pain.

How do these criteria apply to the Hysterectomy Case (HC) and the Craniotomy Case (CC)? Although such cases are from a medical standpoint practically, if not entirely, non-existent,[38] they help illustrate the analysis at issue. Grisez, Finnis, Boyle, and others have noted that in neither the hysterectomy case nor the craniotomy case is it the *death* of the child that secures the life of the mother. Indeed, applying the suggested criteria above to CC, the death of the child is not intended. The physician does not deliberate about how to achieve the death of the child, nor does seeking the death of the child constrain the doctor's other intentions. Unlike the situation with a partial-birth abortion, the doctor does not endeavor to achieve the death of the child. If the child did not die, its survival would not constitute a failure of either the proximate or the remote ends planned by the doctor. Thus, the death of the child in the CC is not intended.

On this view of intention, one could still believe that craniotomy is prohibited by maintaining that it is the crushing of the skull that is wrong and not the death of the child. Donald Marquis notes a weakness in the strategy, a weakness that threatens to undermine the distinction on which double-effect reasoning relies.

The difficulty with this strategy is that if we ask *why* crushing the child's skull is morally wrong, the answer surely is that it causes the death of the child. If the child's skull could be crushed without irreparable harm

---

38. At least in the view of T. P. Cunningham, "The Contumacy Required to Incur Censures," *Irish Theological Quarterly* 4 (1954) 332–56, and Thomas J. O'Donnell, *Medicine and Christian Morality* (New York: Alba House, 1976) 154–55.

or death to the child and the child could be removed from the mother's
birth canal thereby saving the mother's life, it is hard to believe anyone
would want to condemn the action. Hence, strictly speaking, crushing
the child's skull is in itself wrong only because the action can, as a matter of fact, be redescribed as killing the child. But, of course, we can describe the hysterectomy . . . in the same way.[39]

There may, however, be an option that both preserves the account of intention described here and also excludes the craniotomy case. Even if crushing the head of a child is not killing as a
means to saving the mother, it may involve another evil means,
namely the mutilation of the child. Were this to be true, we
could distinguish CC and HC and yet retain the insight that CC is
not killing as a means to saving the mother. But is it mutilation?
And is this mutilation nothing other than killing, as Marquis assumes?

Mutilation is the destruction or removal of an organ (or other
body part) that inhibits the function that the organ (or body
part) had in maintaining the health of the one possessing the organ. Hence, removal of a diseased or threatening organ is not
mutilation, because the organ either no longer contributes to the
good of the body or threatens no longer to contribute to the
good of the body. Nor is removal of superfluous or duplicated organs mutilation, because this removal does not inhibit the function that such organs may have had in maintaining health. Thus,
kidney donation is licit because removal of a single kidney does
not inhibit the function that the kidney once had in the body of
purifying the blood supply.

Now, in CC, the crushing of the skull, along with the removal
of the brain, destroys the functioning of the skull as protecting
the brain and destroys the most important organ of the human
person. This mutilation does indeed lead to death, as does the removal of other organs without due replacement such as the liver
or heart, but mutilation in itself is not defined in terms of this
consequence. Thus, removal of two healthy eyes is mutilation,
even though it does not lead to death. Is this mutilation, the

39. Donald Marquis, "Four Versions of Double Effect," *Journal of Medicine and
Philosophy* 16 (1991) 523.

crushing of the skull and removing of the brain, intended? First, the achievement of the crushing of the skull presents a problem for the doctor that occasions deliberation about what clamps, forceps, and other tools are best for crushing. Secondly, the achievement of the effect constrains the other intentions of the agent. All intentions that are contradictory to the intention to crush the skull must be set aside. Thirdly, the agent endeavors to achieve the effect, perhaps being forced to return to deliberation if circumstances change and earlier attempts at crushing the head are unsuccessful. Finally, a failure to crush the child's head will be accounted as a failure by the agent.

What can be said about the ectopic pregnancy case? In cases of ectopic pregnancy, the embryo implants in the fallopian tube (or even more rarely, elsewhere), eventually leading to profuse bleeding and loss of both maternal and embryonic human life. The four options of treatment most often discussed in the literature are: non-intervention, salpingectomy (removal of tube with embryo), salpingostomy (removal of embryo alone), and use of methotrexate.[40] In approximately 40 percent of the cases, non-intervention leads to the embryo naturally being expelled from the fallopian tube. This option preserves the fallopian tube, has no bad side effects for the mother, and does not even logically exclude the possibility of implantation of the embryo in the uterus. Unfortunately, non-intervention does not always result in the embryo naturally leaving the tube. The grave situation ensues in which both the embryo and the mother may die.

Another option in treatment is salpingectomy, the removal of the entire fallopian tube with the embryo in it. The tube is pathological and thus can be removed by the conditions of DER. The embryonic child is within the tube, but the surgeon does not intend embryo's death but only foresees it as a side effect of removing the tube that threatens the woman's life. The result is

---

40. See, Jean DeBlois, "Ectopic Pregnancy," in *A Primer for Health Care Ethics: Essays for a Pluralistic Society,* ed. Jean DeBlois, (Washington, D.C.: Georgetown University Press, 1996) 209; Charles Curran, "The Manual and Casuistry of Aloysius Sabetti," 180–83; James Keenan, "The Function of the Principle of Double Effect," 303–15.

that both the child and the tube are lost, the loss of tube diminishing the woman's fertility. On the other hand, salpingostomy, the removal of only the human embryo, leaving the tube intact, preserves the tube for further use in reproduction.

A number of authors have pointed out the counter-intuitiveness of the judgment that salpingectomy alone is licit. If one removes the tube with the baby in it, both the baby's life and one-half of the potential fertility of the woman are lost. Why not just remove the child (salpingostomy), saving the only thing that can be saved, the fertility of the woman?[41] This case is, in a way, even more intuitively powerful than the craniotomy case. The newly conceived is surely doomed, so why not preserve the only value that one can in this situation preserve, the fertility of the tube? Use of methotrexate, which inhibits cellular reproduction in rapidly dividing cells, has the same advantages and one advantage further of being non-surgical intervention.

When one applies the suggested criteria for distinguishing the intended from the foreseen to these cases, the embryo's death is the means to the end in neither the salpingectomy nor the salpingostomy. In neither case does the death of the embryo present a problem that occasions deliberation, nor does an intention to bring about death constrain the other intentions of the agent. The agent does not endeavor to achieve death in either case, nor is a failure to bring about death reckoned as a failure of the agent's proximate or remote aims. As surgeons intend to facilitate the implantation of the child in its proper place, it seems probable that the chances of implantation and flourishing would rise. It is possible that techniques and methods might be perfected to make this transfer a relatively common and practical occurrence. There is one documented case of a salpingostomy resulting in the live birth of a healthy baby boy, and there are other cases reported.[42] Advances in microsurgery could make salpingostomy an even

---

41. This consequentialist analysis usually leaves out one important consideration. In cases of salpingostomy, the chances of future ectopic pregnancies increases by 26 percent, while on the other hand, removal of the pathological tube reduces the chance of ectopic pregnancy.
42. C. J. Wallace, "Transplantation of Ectopic Pregnancy from Fallopian Tube

more attractive option for preserving the newly conceived life while also retaining the fertility capacity of the fallopian tube.

The negative effects involved in the use of methotrexate, a drug which inhibits cellular reproduction in the embryo, to treat ectopic pregnancy cannot be in the same way considered foreseen. The effects following upon use of methotrexate are both the death of the embryo and the end of the threat to the mother. However, like the CC, the means taken cannot be otherwise construed than as mutilation, mutilation of the tissues of the embryo responsible for cellular reproduction. How to inhibit cellular reproduction presents a problem for the agent that occasions deliberation about how powerful a dose and at what frequency doses should be given. The achievement of the effect constrains the other intentions of the doctor, who must be careful not to prescribe any medications that will interfere with methotrexate's ability to inhibit cellular reproduction. The doctor endeavors to achieve the effect, perhaps being forced to adjust dosages if the desired effect does not occur. Finally, it will be accounted a failure for the doctor prescribing methotrexate if the cellular inhibition does not take place. The use of methotrexate to treat ectopic pregnancy may not be intentional killing, but it is intentional mutilation.[43] Fortunately, there are other less risky ways of treating the problem of ectopic pregnancy that are less morally problematic as well as arguably more healthy for women.[44]

---

to Cavity of Uterus," *Surgery, Gynecology, and Obstetrics* 24 (1917) 578–79. In an article still in preparation, Dr. John O'Neill reports four other cases more recently.

43. There is, however, a case of ectopic "pregnancy" in which the use of methotrexate *per se* is not morally objectionable. These are cases of what is called "persistent ectopic pregnancy." See, for instance, Hans-Göran Hagström et al., "Prediction of Persistent Ectopic Pregnancy after Salpingostomy," *Obstetrics and Gynecology* 84 (1994) 798–802. Sometimes, although the human conceptus is no longer present, the trophoblast (the layer of tissue which normally nourishes the newly conceived) continues to develop. This continued growth can lead to hemorrhaging equally as dangerous as the growth of the human embryo in the tube. Use of methotrexate in cases of "persistent ectopic pregnancy" would be neither intentional killing nor intentional mutilation, and hence would not be, other things being equal, illicit.

44. The most promising way of treating this vexing problem seems to be neither removal of the tube, removal of the embryo alone, nor use of methotrexate, but what is called the "milking" or "squeezing" technique. Physicians E. Diamond

One final case to consider is the set of conjoined twins Mary and Jodie born in Manchester, England on August 8, 2000. Although the twins were joined at the lower abdomen and shared a spine, Jodie's heart and lungs maintained both of their lives. Doctors predicted that Jodie's circulatory system would give out in a matter of weeks under the strain of supporting both girls. A decision to rival Solomon's: Should one twin be killed in order to save the other or ought both be allowed to perish? In light of this medical testimony, a British high court judge ordered that the twins be separated against the wishes of their Catholic parents, as well as the local Catholic bishop, who objected to the procedure as killing one person to save another. On November 7, 2000, surgeons in St. Mary's Hospital following a judge's ruling separated the twins and Mary died.

If one were to distinguish intention from foresight in the way proposed, to formulate the question in terms of killing one or letting both die is to misframe the issue. In separating Jodie and

---

and A. DeCherney describe this technique as follows: "In this procedure, the tube is grasped just proximal to the site of dilation and then compressed, advancing toward the infundibular aspect of the tube. In this manner, the products of conception are excluded from the fimbria." E. Diamond and A. DeCherney, "Surgical Management of Ectopic Pregnancy," *Clinical Obstetrics and Gynecology* 30 (1987) 205. Like the salpingectomy, the "milking" technique avoids the intentional bringing about of the evil effect on either a broad or a narrow account of intention. This "squeezing" technique leaves open the possibility of the pregnancy proceeding in a normal way. Most often the newly conceived dies; but implantation in the uterus is not excluded and presumably could be facilitated by microsurgery. This "milking" technique, when compared with the use of methotrexate, is better not only for the newly conceived but also for the mother. The milking technique avoids the side effects associated with the use of methotrexate while also being effective in preserving both maternal health and respect for the newly conceived. A study in *Clinical Obstetrics and Gynecology* concludes: "[T]he postoperative results [of the milking technique] are remarkably good, even when compared with the more popular salpingostomy. When tissue is handled gently and vigorous 'milking' efforts are avoided, this procedure is not only harmless but may technically prove to be the simplest and the most beneficial in terms of subsequent fertility." E. Caspi and D. Sherman, "Tubal Abortion and Infundibular Ectopic Pregnancy," *Clinical Obstetrics and Gynecology* 30 (1987) 162. Some studies report an increase in the rate of future extrauterine pregnancies, e.g., G. Oelsner, "Ectopic Pregnancy in the Remaining Tube and the Management of the Patient with Multiple Ectopic Pregnancies," *Clinical Obstetrics and Gynecology* 30 (1987) 226; other studies note no such increase, e.g., Caspi and Sherman, 162. Although other studies suggest an increase in the rate of future ectopic pregnancies as a result of this technique, this option at present seems like the most promising way of treating ectopic pregnancy detected at an early stage.

Mary, the achievement of Mary's death does not present a problem for the doctors that prompts deliberation. If Mary's death were the goal, there would be more efficient ways of achieving the lethal effect that would also be less dangerous to Jodie. Secondly, achievement of the effect of Mary's death does not constrain the other intentions of the doctors. They would not hesitate to follow a given means of separating the children because it risked the possibility of Mary's living. Thirdly, the doctors do not endeavor to achieve the death of Mary, nor would they "finish the job" if by some miracle Mary survived. Finally, were Mary *per impossible* to survive, the original plan of the doctors would have been in no way thwarted. Thus, in separating Mary and Jodie, the death of the weaker twin is an unfortunate side-effect, but not an intended means, of saving the stronger twin.

The four criteria suggested can help us define the object of the human act. They can help us determine what is properly murder, mutilation, theft, or adultery. It is another question, of course, whether or not these acts, understood in a properly non-tautological way, are always bad. For instance, one could hold that to appropriate the goods of or to kill another, though a disvalue or premoral evil, could be justified by a proportionate reason. An action considered at a high level of abstraction may be wrong, but considered more particularly could be right. Further circumstance may make evil still remaining within the act tolerable.[45] Similar analysis could be provided for the actions whose

45. The single quodlibetal question referred to by McCormick above was originally offered as evidence for Aquinas holding this view by Janssens in articles in 1977, 1982, and 1987. Mark Johnson has argued that Janssens has misunderstood a fourfold division of human action referred to by Aquinas in *Quodlibetum* IX, q.7, a.2. "[O]ne cannot say, I honestly think, that the young Aquinas holds here the distinction between premoral and moral evil upon which moderate teleology depends." Mark Johnson, "Proportionalism and a Text of the Young Aquinas: *Quodlibetum* IX, Q. 7, A. 2," *Theological Studies* 53 (1992) 699. A student of Janssens, Joseph Selling, suggests that Janssens has indeed gone beyond Thomas and thus should not be faulted for certain incongruities between him and the letter of Thomas's text. According to Selling, Janssens sought "to demonstrate how Thomas himself *might have* incorporated such a concept [i.e. premoral evil] into his work." Joseph Selling, "Louis Janssens' Interpretation of Aquinas: A Response to Recent Criticism," *Louvain Studies* 19 (1994) 66. The use of the subjunctive contrary to fact seems to be a tacit admission that in fact the central premoral/moral evil distinction was not actually in *Quodlibetum* IX, q.7, a.2.

names are used here in a merely descriptive and not morally pejorative sense: fornication (sexual intercourse of an unmarried couple), adultery (sexual intercourse in which at least one party is married to another), bestiality (sexual intercourse with a beast), lying (speaking what one believes to be an untruth with the intention of deception), perjury (speaking what one believes to be false under oath in a court of law), murder (intentionally killing an innocent person), and legal execution (capital punishment). Hence, the analysis given here of circumstances does not exclude proportionalism *a priori* or implicitly smuggle in the notion of intrinsically evil acts, but is rather presupposed by proportionalism insofar as "premoral evil" often derives from such circumstances. Are adultery, theft, murder, and capital punishment defined in the non-pejorative way above always wrong? Can one intend a disvalue or premoral evil in order to bring about a greater good? The answers to these questions depend in part on the account of practical reasoning one adopts.

Human actions are good insofar as they are ordered by reason: on this Thomism and proportionalism agree. This reason is practical reason, and in light of practical reason the object, circumstances, and ends of human action are judged.

Hence good and evil in acts as far as we are concerned now is understood concerning that which is proper to man insofar as he is man: this however is reason. Hence, good and evil in human acts is considered according to whether the act accords to reason informed by divine law, either naturally or through instruction or through infusion: Hence, Dionysius says that it is evil for the soul to be contrary to reason and the body contrary to nature. Therefore, in this way, if being according to reason or opposed to reason pertains to the species of human act, it should be said that some human acts are in themselves good and others in themselves evil.[46]

Reason judges human action and its elements as good or evil. Practical reasoning, then, is an important hinge of the entire debate, and it is to rival forms of practical reasoning to which we turn in the next two chapters.

46. *De malo* q.2, a.4.

V. PROPORTIONATE REASON

AS THE FIRST PRINCIPLE OF

PRACTICAL REASONING

Proportionate reason is the form of practical reasoning that is at the very heart of the teleological as opposed to the deontological approach to morality. What exactly is proportionate reason? Misunderstandings of proportionate reason have appeared among those critiquing proportionalism, for instance in the work of John Connery. In response to these misunderstandings, McCormick writes as follows:

> Proportionate reason is not in addition to an act already defined; it constitutes its very object, but in the full sense of that term. Take amputation of a cancerous limb to save a patient's life as an example. Connery would see amputation as the object and "to save a patient's life" as a motive. But the literature he is critiquing sees "to save a patient's life" (the proportionate reason) as the object in the full sense of that term. In other words, proportionate reason enters into the very definition of *what* one is doing. If one conceives proportionate reason as *in addition to an act already definable by its object*, then one does indeed get into some mischievous results.[1]

Proportionate reason however is not defined merely in these negative terms, i.e., as not intention and not some addition to the object. It has a positive definition which will be explored later. But these denials themselves are very instructive for evaluat-

1. McCormick, *Notes on Moral Theology, 1981 through 1984*, 64.

ing whether or not proportionate reason, as this term is used in the context of proportionalism, has a firm basis in the Thomistic tradition about which we have been speaking.

Chapter I suggested that the term "proportionate" meant something quite different for Thomas in *Summa theologiae* II-II, 64, 7, than for Gury in his *Compendium*. For Thomas, who does not speak of proportionate *reason* in the famous self-defense passage, proportion describes the relationship between means and end. The act is proportioned to its end if the defender uses the least violent means possible to achieve the end of self-defense. In speaking of this act/end proportion, Thomas says nothing here about taking "everything" into account, or about the necessity of weighing the goods and evils that follow from the act of self-defense. For Gury, on the other hand, proportionate reason is in part the justification for allowing the foreseen evil effect and obtains only when one is not obliged from justice or charity to avoid the evil effect. In the manuals following Gury, this connection to virtue was lost and replaced with a weighing or balancing of goods. Here, the act/end proportion of Thomas is replaced by effect/effect proportion.

Does then "proportionate reason" as the term is described by McCormick arise from this late neoscholastic context? Does not the fourth condition of double-effect reasoning, that there is a proportionate reason for allowing the evil effect, indicate that proportionate reason has long been accepted in the tradition?

If proportionate reason is not separate from the object already defined in a moral sense, then the answer must be negative. Proportionate reason, in this sense, is something quite different than proportionate reason as employed by Gury in the nineteenth century or as meant by late neoscholastics following him up to Knauer. For Gury and these neoscholastics, proportionate reason was not part of the object of the human act. In Gury's account of double-effect reasoning as recounted in Chapter I, as for other neoscholastics, one condition of double-effect reasoning is that the object is not bad and another that there is a proportionate reason for allowing the bad effect. Hence for these writers, the object can be defined independently as good, bad, or indifferent without reference to a possible proportionate reason.

Thus, the concept of proportionate reason as entering into the very object of the act cannot be said to be "utterly traditional"[2] but rather arises for the first time in 1965 with Knauer and those writers following him known as proportionalists. It is inconsistent both to claim that proportionate reason defines the very object of the act and simultaneously to claim that proportionate reason enjoys a centuries long undisputed status as exemplified in its use in DER. Underlying this claim is an equivocation.

Proportionate reason has many synonyms in the contemporary literature, among them *debita proportio,* commensurate reason, *recta ratio,* and the teleological norm. A common though perhaps not universally accepted definition of proportionate reason can be found in the work of James Walter:

First, the word "reason" means a premoral, i.e., a conditioned, and thus not absolute, value that an agent seeks to promote in the whole act. Second, the term "proportionate" refers to a proper relation that must exist between the premoral disvalue(s) contained in, or caused by, the means and the end or a proper relation between the end and the premoral disvalue(s) in the consequences of the act.[3]

This definition of proportionate reason reintroduces terms that have occurred a number of times in the discussion thus far. Often, we have encountered the very same idea in different terminology. The "reason" is a reason for action, that is, a premoral (McCormick), ontic (Janssens), or non-moral (Knauer) good or value sought in the act. The counterparts and opposites of premoral goods are premoral evils or disvalues. Since premoral good and (by implication) premoral evil enter into the very definition

2. McCormick, "Notes on Moral Theology: 1985," 69–88, at 87; Fuchs, *Christian Ethics,* 83.

3. Walter, "Proportionalism," 1058. See also Walter's article that structures my own treatment here, "Proportionate Reason and Its Three Levels of Inquiry: Structuring the Ongoing Debate," *Louvain Studies* 10 (1984) 30–40, and Brian V. Johnstone, "The Meaning of Proportionate Reason in Contemporary Moral Theology," 223–47.

of proportionate reason, the meaning of these terms is germane to the discussion.

The distinction between moral and premoral evil (and good) is essential for proportionalism. McCormick writes about the pair as follows:

> Moral evil refers to those evils that render the person as a whole bad: e.g., the desire of and will to injustice or unchastity. But such evils do not tell us what concrete acts count as injustice or unchastity. That is, they do not tell us what concrete acts are morally right or wrong. Premoral evils do not touch directly the moral goodness of the person, but only on the person's well being. But they are relevant to moral goodness. How? The morally good person will avoid causing them unless there is a proportionately serious reason.[4]

Fuchs adds "Moral evils, contrary to 'morally good', are those which, if freely realized, make the human being (as a whole) morally bad."[5]

Arguably the most influential author in explaining the proportionalist use of ontic, premoral, or physical evil is Louis Janssens, who in a series of articles in the 1970s and 1980s developed and defended the relevance of the ontic evil/moral evil distinction for moral theory especially as related to St. Thomas. Although the distinction between premoral and moral does not seem to be influential among moral philosophers, with the possible exception of William K. Frankena,[6] this distinction is absolutely central to the proportionalist project. Death, illness, ignorance, violence, pain, etc. are examples of premoral evils; and for a proportionate reason, an agent may intend these premoral evils.

"We call ontic evil," Janssens writes, "any lack of a perfection at which we aim, any lack of fulfillment which frustrates our

---

4. McCormick, *Notes on Moral Theology, 1980 through 1984*, 110.

5. Fuchs, *Christian Ethics*, 80.

6. William K. Frankena, *Ethics*, 2d edition (Englewood Cliffs, N.J.: Prentice Hall, 1963) 62. Here, Frankena speaks of moral value and non-moral value and their relation. He does, it should be noted, later have some connection to revisionists writers with whom he takes issue. See Frankena's "McCormick and the Traditional Distinction," in *Doing Evil to Achieve Good*, ed. McCormick and Ramsey (Chicago: Loyola University Press, 1978) 145–64.

natural urges and makes us suffer."[7] This definition, in terms of its reference to privation, i.e. a "lacking," accords with Thomas's and Augustine's definitions of [physical] evil. Evil has no substance of its own, since all substances come from a good Creator whose creation expresses *(manifestat)* his goodness. Janssens refines his definition later: "Ontic evil" says Janssens, "is a lack of perfection, a deficiency which frustrates our inclinations."[8]

How, according to Janssens, is ontic evil causally related to moral evil? Before answering this question, we might first consider how ontic evil relates to human action in general. In light of the fact that every concrete choice excludes other goods which could have been the object of concrete choice, according to Janssens

ontic evil is *always* present in our concrete activity. If this approach is true, it cannot be concluded that it is inevitably morally evil to cause ontic evil or to allow it to remain in this world by our actions. If this were the case, there would not be any way to act morally.[9]

Though one finds many proportionalist writers holding this thesis,[10] the origin of the supposition among them perhaps may be traced to Knauer: "Every human act brings evil effects with it. The choice of a value always means concretely that there is denial of another value which must be given as a price in exchange."[11] Janssens offers basically the same argument: "[T]he fact that we have the ability to *decide* and to determine what to do is the positive aspect of our freedom. But there is also a negative side. When we choose a certain action, we must at the same time, at least for the time being, postpone all other possible acts."[12] The agent's inability to realize *all the values* that he or she

7. Janssens, "Ontic Evil and Moral Evil," 60.
8. Ibid., 69.
9. Ibid., 67.
10. Schüller for example writes: "It is universally agreed that a man is responsible for all the foreseen (negative) consequences of a free act." Schüller, "Direct Killing/Indirect Killing," in *Moral Norms and Catholic Tradition*, ed. Curran and McCormick, 140.
11. Knauer, "Double Effect," 16. Knauer, "Zu Grundbegriffen der Enzyklika 'Veritatis Splendor,'" *Stimmen der Zeit* 212 (1994) 22.
12. Janssens, "Ontic Evil and Moral Evil" 61; See also Janssens, "Norms and Priorities," 212.

could have potentially realized is ontic evil.[13] <u>Since every act involves premoral evil, then every act becomes justified through of the presence or absence of proportionate reason.</u>

Proportionalism then is not merely a solution for conflict situations and moral dilemmas but rather is the fundamental moral principle to be used in evaluating each and every human act.[14] In the words of Bruno Schüller:

> All ethical norms which govern our actions and omissions among our fellow men and the world surrounding us can only be particular applications of this general first principle. . . . From two concurrent and mutually exclusive values, one must determine which from the two deserves preference and act to realize it.[15]

We have in proportionate reason a rival first principle to Aquinas's that good is to be done and evil to be avoided.

The Secondary Conditions of Proportionate Reason

Though maximization of premoral goods and minimization of premoral evils *primarily* define proportionate reason, there are other *secondary* conditions that establish it as well.[16] The relationship between the conditions does not seem to be clearly established. However, it would seem that these secondary conditions are necessary conditions for a truly proportionate reason.

First, proportionate reason is present only when one takes the *long-term view*. The means cannot undermine the end in the long run, as, for example, excessive studying undermines the pursuit of knowledge in the long run and on the whole *(auf die Dauer und im ganzen).*[17]

13. Janssens, "Ontic Evil and Moral Evil," 62; For similar argument, see Fuchs, *Christian Ethics,* 82.

14. *Pace,* McCormick, "Notes on Moral Theology: 1985," 77.

15. Bruno Schüller, "Zur Problematik allgemein verbindlicher ethischer Grunsätze," *Theologie und Philosophie* 45 (1970) 1–23, at 4 and 3; and also 9.

16. I am indebted here to the summary of James Walter, "Proportionate Reason and Its Three Levels of Inquiry," 30–40, esp. 33–36. I have changed his order of presentation and slightly altered the list itself.

17. These words from Knauer are explored in McCormick, "A Commentary on the Commentaries," 193–265. As was suggested in the first chapter, these two conditions, in the work of Peter Knauer and a few others, are not secondary but primary. They constitute "counter-productivity."

Second, proportionate reason includes a _condition of intrinsic_ 2
connection.[18] The premorally evil means used by the agent must
stand in a necessary causal relationship to the premoral good
sought.[19] Hence, in the classic case of abortion to save the life of
the mother, one may legitimately intend the death of the child in
order to save the life of the mother. On the other hand, a sheriff
may not frame an innocent person for a murder he did not commit in order to prevent a riot that will kill others, even many
others. One may not intend premoral evil in order to prevent the
wrongdoing of others. For this reason, McCormick and Knauer
also argue that there is no proportionate reason present in the
Bergmeier case (in which a woman commits adultery to escape
from prison), for extra-marital sex and escaping from prison
have no intrinsic, necessary, or essential connection.[20]

Third, proportionate reason has a condition of _chronological si-_ 3
multaneity. Proportionate reason is present only in the preservation of a good here and now, not some future good. One cannot
have an abortion because one wants to avoid paying the unborn
child's college tuition; one cannot sleep with the prison guard to
be reunited with one's family. On the other hand, one can kill in
self-defense, since the killing preserves the good of life here and
now.[21]

Fourth, proportionate reason is not present if the evil used to
secure some sought good undermines other goods that are associated with this originally sought good. McCormick argues that if

18. McCormick, _Notes on Moral Theology, 1965 through 1980,_ 718–19;
McCormick, "A Commentary on the Commentaries," 238.

19. Richard McCormick, "A Commentary on the Commentaries," 209–12,
236–39.

20. Ibid., 238.

21. Of this condition, McCormick writes: "Here [in the work of a critic of pro-
portionalism] we have evil _now_—good _to come._ Thus it is sometimes said that adultery now justifies a future good. This misrepresents what Fuchs-Schüller-Böckle-
Janssens-Scholz-Weber-Curran and many others are saying. What they are saying
is that the good achieved _here and now_ (though it may perdure into the future) is
sometimes inseparable from premoral evil. Thus, an act of self-defense achieves
here and now the good of preservation of life. A falsehood achieves _here and now_
the protection of a professional secret. Taking property (food) of another saves the
life of the taker _here and now_" (McCormick, _Notes on Moral Theology, 1981 through
1984,_ 3, n.10).

the associated goods are undermined the original good is also thereby undermined.

5   Finally, proportionate reason excludes causing *more evil than necessary*. If one can defend oneself by injuring, rather than killing, then one should only injure. If one can defend oneself, without even injuring, then one is obliged to take this course of action. This final secondary condition excludes the causing of *superfluous evil*. These five secondary conditions of proportionate reason (namely, the long-term approach, the intrinsic connection of the good achieved with the evil used, chronological simultaneity, association of goods, and the curtailing of superfluous evil) are said to sharply delineate proportionalism from straightforward consequentialism, especially if each is construed as a necessary rather than as a sufficient condition.[22]

Let us examine these secondary conditions, beginning with the last. That one should not cause more evil than is necessary in pursuing one's end seems self-evidently true. In this sense, Thomas speaks about the act of self-defense being proportioned to its end as discussed earlier. In medical treatments, for example, a doctor should prescribe, other things being equal, drugs that cause the least harmful side effects. Bringing about superfluous evil, i.e., not taking due care to avoid causing evil that one can and should avoid, is, all in this discussion would agree, wrong. In fact, by definition, unjustified evildoing is wrong. Hence, this secondary condition does not really advance our understanding of what counts as a proportionate reason; rather it restates the obvious, that unnecessary or unjustified evil should not be brought about.

The other four secondary conditions of proportionate reason do advance our understanding of what courses of action are right or wrong. Knauer holds that lack of proportionate reason is present when the sought value, universally considered, is undermined in the long run and on the whole *(auf die Dauer und im*

---

22. Walter suggests that we know whether or not a proportionate reason is present through (1) human experience, (2) our sense of outrage, (3) trial and error, (4) analysis and argument, (5) long-term consequences, and (6) feelings of guilt or harmony following an action.

ganzen). This understanding of proportionate reason is not a secondary condition for Knauer, but the primary and solitary condition of proportionate reason. This condition, construed as primary or secondary, is made up of many elements. One of these elements answers the question: should one maximize value in the short run or in the long run? This criterion of proportionate reason entails that one should seek long-term benefit rather than short-term.

Although on first view this seems self-evident, in fact this answer is not uniquely or unquestionably rational. For example, undertaking some public work such as a subway system can fail a cost-benefit analysis based on a 75-year time-line but succeed on a cost-benefit analysis based on a 125-year time-line.[23] Is it irrational to conclude that even though in the long run the system pays for itself, the long run is in fact too long? Is it patently irrational in this case to prefer the short-term benefit accrued in 75 years to the long-term accrued in 125 years? Or again, given the financial history of the last fifty years, it makes no long-term sense to invest one's money in a mere savings account rather than in the stock market. Given that the rate of inflation is consistently greater than the rate of interest offered in a simple savings account, in the long run it makes no sense to keep one's money in a savings account. Long-term return is best realized through investment in stocks. However, it is not uniquely rational to plan for the long term. Although "financial well-being" remains in both cases the goal, sometimes one will have need of the financial security of a savings account over the long-term, but momentarily risky, fiscal growth of the stock market. Here again, what best realizes the value sought in the act in the long term contradicts what best realizes the value sought in the short term. Yet, we have no reason to say that putting one's money in savings is irrational or counter-productive. Given the "long-term" criteria, these acts are unacceptable, for the value gained in the short term undermines the same value in the long-term perspective. But clearly it is the assumption that long-term

23. The example comes from Alasdair MacIntyre.

thinking is uniquely rational which is unacceptable and not the case in the acts considered here.

Other elements of this condition of proportionate reason are also problematic. Who can reasonably say what the outcome on the whole and in the long run of any given act may be? As Richard McCormick in his original review of Knauer's first article on the topic suggested, who can tell whether an abortion here and now will undermine life on the whole and in the long run or not? The outcome of any new life, and its effect upon other lives, simply cannot be known or reasonably predicted.

The allure of this criterion is, in the end, its indeterminateness. The "value considered universally" is even more formal and abstract than the Kantian categorical imperative of universalizability. It is made even more indeterminate by the qualification that this value should not be "undermined on the whole and in the long run." This indeterminateness allows one to invoke the seemingly objective "proportionate reason" as a validation of one's prior convictions on any given matter. Proportionate reason understood in this way becomes a Rorschach Blot upon which one projects one's own intuitions, feelings, or desires.

The final three secondary conditions of proportionate reason allow advocates of proportionalism to avoid contradicting some of their own moral assumptions about behavior in conflict situations, especially wartime. Supposing that intentionally killing of the innocent is not always wrong in principle, can one threaten to or actually kill innocent civilians in order to end a war more quickly? No, the advocates of proportionalism answer. First, there is no intrinsic connection between killing civilians and the end of a war. Secondly, the evil of killing the civilians is done now so that the good of an end to war may come in the future. Killing civilians in terror bombing violates two secondary conditions of proportionate reason, namely the conditions of necessity and simultaneity.

Terror bombing also violates the final condition of the "association of goods." "[E]xtortion by definition accepts the necessity of doing nonmoral evil to get others to cease their wrongdoing. The acceptance of such a necessity is an implied denial of human freedom. But since human freedom is a basic value associated with other basic values (in this case, life) undermining it *also thereby undermines life.*"[24] "Necessity" here means that there is no other way imaginable to prevent greater loss of life, save the taking of life. If there is another way available, for example the cessation of wrongdoing by others, then there is no necessary connection. If there is no necessary connection, other goods are brought into play and the original good comes to be undermined in the act.

Because there is not a necessary connection between avoiding the evil or achieving the good and intending the harm as a means, other basic goods (for example, liberty) are brought into play in using the harmful means. Because of the association of goods, undermining one undermines others, and thus the very value at stake, for example, life, will suffer more if the killing is done.[25]

Insofar as this requirement obtains, people may not threaten other people with non-moral evils nor may they inflict non-moral evils to prevent the possible wrongdoing of others.

However, these secondary conditions of proportionate reason—intrinsic necessity, simultaneity, and association of goods—applied consistently exclude much more than intentionally killing the innocent in war. Also excluded would be intentionally speaking a falsehood in order to save someone's life. No necessary, intrinsic, and deterministic connection exists between speaking falsehood and protecting threatened human life. The one threatening could simply abandon the intention to injure the innocent. Furthermore, the evil of speaking falsely is done now that the good of avoiding attack may come later. Hence, according to these secondary conditions of proportionate reason, proportionate reason does not justify saying a falsehood to save another's life. Speaking falsely to save another by definition accepts the necessity of doing nonmoral evil to get others to cease their wrongdoing. The acceptance of such a necessity implies denial of human freedom. But since human freedom is a basic val-

24. Richard McCormick, "A Commentary on the Commentaries," 260, emphasis in the original.
25. Ibid., 262.

ue associated with the basic value of life, undermining it also thereby undermines life. Hence, speaking falsely to save the life of another does not meet the criteria that exclude terror bombing.

Likewise in corrective punishment, according to proportionalism, one inflicts a premoral evil, and threatens to inflict more later, in the hopes that the criminal and others noting the punishment will not commit crimes in the future. As McCormick notes, "Do we not spank children [now] so that in the future their conduct may be less self-threatening?"[26] Elsewhere he writes: "If I apprehend one of two thugs on the way to execute my brother or sister (at the time, I am not sure which one), I would apply a very effective and increasingly painful arm lock to find out which, so I could warn him/her."[27] In these examples, we find the chronological condition, the necessity condition, and the condition of long-term association of goods all violated. The premoral evils (punishment/pain) are caused in the hope of achieving some future good (deterring wrongdoing/safety of siblings). These acts violate the chronology condition. There is furthermore no *necessary* connection between punishing and inflicting pain on another and his or her avoiding future wrongdoing or giving in to a request.[28] The one undergoing suffering can relapse into wrongdoing or, in the other example, refuse to answer. Since there is no necessary connection, the one threatening to inflict harm undermines the goods associated with liberty such as life. Thus, to deter someone with threat of punishment

---

26. Richard McCormick, *Notes on Moral Theology, 1965 through 1980,* 765, n.50.
27. McCormick, *Notes on Moral Theology, 1965 through 1980,* 766.
28. The necessity condition of proportionate reason proves more than that an agent may not intend premoral evil in the Sheriff and Bergemier cases. Also, killing in self-defense, just war, and punishment undertaken to deter others would also be excluded. In these cases too, there is no necessary deterministic connection between the evils inflicted and the goods brought about. The attacker *could* stop his attack, leaving the victim unharmed; the unjust military force could withdraw, ending the aggression; those contemplating breaking the law could cease their wicked musings. Lying for the sake of protecting a professional secret or even someone's life would not be justified by a proportionate reason. *Ex hypothesi,* the one asking does not have a right to the truth, and the defender of the secret could avoid speaking an untruth if the one unjustly seeking the information would merely withdraw the question.

so that they do not undermine the life of the community is itself to undermine this life.[29]

Of course, advocates of proportionalism do not reject punishment as a deterrent or as an aspect of rehabilitation. Nor does proportionalism exclude telling falsehoods to those seeking to harm innocent third parties. In fact, these acts are brought forward as paradigm cases of right acts involving evil. Hence, it is more likely that the secondary conditions spoken of here are not in fact always the necessary or sufficient criteria for determining whether or not one has a proportionate reason for intending some non-moral evil. Rather, these secondary conditions are invoked (or not invoked) to include and exclude that which is antecedently judged as right or wrong on other grounds. _Subjective & ad hoc_

In addition to reasons of consistency, there are also external reasons for rejecting these secondary conditions of proportionate reason. All the non-tautological secondary conditions of proportionate reason, construed either as sufficient or as necessary, rest as deontological norms in the midst of a teleological theory. What teleological grounds do we have for accepting them? What may be operative here is some form of rule teleology or more accurately consequentialism. Can we know however that following these conditions or rules will always and in every case lead to better outcomes? If these rules must be obeyed even in cases where the outcomes are worse, even much worse, then there is no reason to exclude that there might be still other rules that must be obeyed in every case regardless of outcome, e.g., no intentional killing of innocent human persons. If, however, these secondary conditions of proportionate reason are _prima facie_ guidelines, then in fact we should just maximize goods or minimize evils in each and every case, taking the value of following the rules into account, but only as one of many elements and not as a definitive deontological command. Hence, these secondary conditions or rules would be no different than other general moral rules, e.g., "do not kill." This rule applies, except when one

29. See Sanford S. Levy, "Richard McCormick and Proportionate Reason," _Journal of Religious Ethics_ 13 (1985) 258–78.

has a proportionate reason. Construed as strict requirements, the secondary conditions make room for the exceptionless norms that proportionalism seeks to undermine. Construed as only *prima facie* rules, the secondary conditions do not define proportionate reason, which remains in every case, a straightforward principle of maximizing and minimizing, a form of consequentialism.

The Primary Criteria of Proportionate Reason: Maximizing Non-Moral Goods; Minimizing Non-Moral Evils

Proportionalism proposes judgment of an act and its relationship to the agent as follows. Good agents, agents who act from a good disposition and according to virtue, seek to do right actions. Right actions are those actions that maximize premoral goods and/or minimize premoral evils.[30] Premoral evils include death, pain, hunger, sterility, ignorance, etc., while premoral goods are their contraries. The fundamental categories for analysis of acts as right or wrong are premoral goods and premoral evils. Rightness and wrongness of acts are defined in terms of these values, and goodness and badness of persons are defined in terms of the seeking of right and avoiding of wrong acts. Fuchs illustrates this

---

30. Peter Knauer and Garth Hallet are two who reject this thesis. For Knauer, wrong action is action that contradicts the sought value universally considered in the long run and on the whole. For Hallet, an act is right insofar as it maximizes both non-moral *and* moral values. See his *Greater Good*, 109–12. As John Finnis, *Moral Absolutes: Tradition, Revision, and Truth* (Washington D.C: The Catholic University of America Press, 1991) 15–16, has pointed out, a Thomistic account of providence excludes a maximizing principle of non-moral and moral goods. Thomas writes, "God always draws a greater good [than that good which was deprived through the evil], not necessarily for that in which he permitted the evil to be, but in reference to the entire universe, whose beauty depends on that existing evils be allowed." *In Sent.* II, d.29, q.1, a.3, ad 4. See also, *ST* I, 22, 2, ad 2. Finnis writes: "[I]f you accomplish what you attempt, you can be certain that what you chose tended toward overall long-run net good (since God's providence permitted it), whereas if you fail to accomplish what you attempt, you can be certain your failure tended toward overall long-run good since God's providence excluded the success of your effort. So, try anything!" (*Moral Absolutes*, 15–16). Finnis is mistaken that this excludes all forms of proportionalism, for God's providence might maximizes both moral and non-moral goods; whereas standard forms of proportionalism (with the exception of Hallet's) seek to maximize only premoral goods. Thomas's account of providence does, however, bring difficulties for the proportionalism of Hallet in so far as both non-moral and moral goods are admitted.

view: "[A] morally good person [i.e. one who strives to do what is right] has to avoid, as much as possible, premoral evils; his purpose is rather to create premoral goods and values for the well-being of human beings."[31]

The moral life on this view is defined in terms of one's effect on the world. In the words of one author:

[O]ur activity is ordered to the realization of the objective culture for the promotion of the subjective culture for each and everyone. In this respect, ontic evil is anything which impedes the progress of objective culture and the increase of the share of each and everyone in the resources of the objective culture.[32]

"Objective culture" transforms the world. It is contrasted with "subjective culture" about which he later speaks, meaning that in culture which cannot be separated from the agent. "Objective culture," Janssens writes,

is realized by our human activity which transforms the world from a natural reality into a cultural environment, inhabitable for human beings. . . . If man is to develop, he must transform the world into a universe of objective culture, which, in its turn, shapes man and helps him attain a higher level of subjective culture. As Jean Mouroux wrote, "*man perfects himself by perfecting the world.*"[33]

The moral task is a certain production of that which realizes objective culture.

Edward Vacek makes the same point in another way. Here, the author rightly points out the difference between utilitarianism and proportionalism:

The usual value-theory of utilitarianism is reductionistic. There is more to being human than "maximizing pleasure," "preference-satisfaction,"

31. Fuchs, *Christian Ethics*, 81.
32. Janssens, "Ontic Evil and Moral Evil" 81; See also, Fuchs, *Christian Ethics*, 81.
33. Janssens, "Norms and Priorities," 222–23, emphasis added. Josef Fuchs writes: "The distinction between moral and premoral evil, on the one hand, and the demand of moral goodness, on the other hand, that we avoid premoral evil *as far as possible* and act morally rightly, introduces a question: Under what conditions is the realization of premoral evils morally wrong, and is it possible to determine 'intrinsic wrongness' in this way? The morally right act in our human world is clearly understood as *the realization of premoral goods or values.*" Fuchs, *Christian Ethics,* 81, emphasis added.

or "happiness for the greatest number." These common utilitarian criteria acknowledge only certain subjective values and are incomplete with
respect to the full range of values. P[roportionalism] aims at the en-
hancement of all values.[34]

Utilitarianism is faulted for being concerned only with production of some individual valuable result. Proportionalism demon-
strates its superiority as being inclusive of all valuable results.
However for both utilitarianism and proportionalism, human action is judged as right or wrong in terms of its production: "In
the best of all possible worlds," he writes, "that aim [of enhanc-
ing all values] would lead to human happiness, but even in such
a world happiness would be the result, not the criterion, for
moral living."[35]

As was suggested previously, Thomas's Aristotelian conception of the moral life is quite different. Aristotle, as mentioned in
the second chapter, speaks of the distinction between human action and the products of human action. One evaluates the first in
terms of virtue *(arētē)* and the latter in terms of the standard of
craft *(technē)*. If, however, it turns out that we can evaluate an
act as right or wrong insofar as an act creates or destroys premoral values, then it turns out that right and wrong action can
be assessed in terms of the practices of crafts. In the words of
McCormick, "[A critic of proportionalism, Servais] Pinckaers
contrasts the 'technical finality' asserted by 'proportionalists'
with the true moral finality, which involves a conscious and voluntary tending toward God as one's final end—as if these were
somehow competitive and mutually exclusive."[36] Technical finality or craftsmanship is indeed neither competitive with nor mutually exclusive of the tending of a person toward God, but on
the other hand, neither should one be confused with the other.
It is surely unsound to believe that the better the craftsman the
better the person morally. The good craftsman may be a good

34. Vacek, "Proportionalism: One View of the Debate," 298.
35. Ibid. One can see here quite clearly the difference between Thomas and
proportionalism. For Thomas on the other hand, happiness precisely *is* the criterion for moral living. *ST* I-II, 1–5.
36. McCormick, *Notes on Moral Theology, 1981 through 1984,* 112.

person, but the good craftsman may also be an evil person. Craftsmanship and virtue are not co-extensive, which leads Thomas in *ST* I-II, 57, 4 to distinguish art from prudence.[37] Proportionalism confuses the third order of reason and order with the fourth, *actio* and *factio,* and therefore cannot properly distinguish *aretē* from *technē.*[38]

According to some writers, Knauer for instance, moral evil cannot be defined other than in relationship to some non-moral evil. Moral evil consists in trying to realize an ontic or premoral good in a counter-productive way.

This thesis that "sin consists in doing harm to God's creation,"[39] as well as the emphasis in some forms of proportionalism on defining wrongdoing solely in terms of the causation of various premoral disvalues,[40] does not accord well with the example of Christ in the Sermon on the Mount as understood by Thomas. Here wrongdoing is understood not merely as the exterior act of murder or adultery, but even those interior acts of *wanting* to commit murder or adultery "in one's heart." In the *Confiteor* of the Catholic liturgy, one says, "I confess to Almighty God, and to you my brothers and sisters, because *(quia)* I have sinned through my own fault. In my *thoughts* and in my words . . . " Sins of presumption, despair, and even the sin of pride have no *necessary* connection with the production of premoral evils whatsoever. Likewise, sins of blasphemy and sacrilege as well as good acts of prayer, forgiveness, contemplation, worship, and contrition cannot be properly understood in terms of causing of certain premoral evils or goods. Rather, by such acts, one retreats from or approaches God without, at least at times, any "exterior act" or "effect" visible from a third-person perspective.

Not only is there more to the moral life than merely how one

37. See too, *ST* I-II, 57, 5, ad 1.

38. Other scholars have noticed this, including John Finnis, *Moral Absolutes,* 13–14; Dewan, "St. Thomas, James Keenan and the Will," 153; Romanus Cessario, "Virtue Theory and Human Life Issues," *The Thomist* 53 (April 1989) 173–96, at 174–82, 192–96.

39. Knauer, "The Concept of Intention," Lecture in Honor of Louis Janssens, delivered at K.U. Leuven (October 7, 1988) 15.

40. See especially in this connection, Peter Knauer, "Good End," 71–85.

affects the world, for Thomas there is no obligation to do the "best possible" (however defined) under penalty of sin. Thomas retains the distinction between precept and counsel that he finds in the Scriptures.[41] The pastoral reasons for adopting such teachings are obvious. For some people, the adoption of a maximization (or minimizing) requirement would lead to an unrelenting scrupulosity; for others, an indifference born of unrealistic expectations; and for most, an unhealthy combination of the two. Though in Thomas's view all are invited to perfection, one is not invited under penalty of sin. Unlike proportionalism, the perfection with which St. Thomas is concerned is of the person, not the material world.

What Is Premoral Evil?

Finally, although we have examined the maximization/minimization requirement of proportionate reason, what can be said of the premoral goods and evils that are to be maximized?[42] An examination of proportionate reason as the maximizing of premoral goods and the minimizing of premoral evils would be incomplete without a more thorough treatment of the chief terms.

Premoral evil is, in the words of Janssens, "any lack of a perfection *at which we aim,* any lack of fulfillment which frustrates our natural urges and *makes us suffer.*"[43] Perhaps not all unrealized potentialities count as premoral evils, but only those experienced by the agent as bringing about suffering. Janssens, for instance, in "Ontic Good and Evil-Premoral Values and Disvalues" distinguishes between states of feeling *(stationäre Gestimmtheiten)* and feelings which are directed and intentional *(gerichtete oder intentionale Gefühle).* The latter is important for his moral analysis: "Contact with certain realities evokes a *positive feeling* in us. . . .

41. Matt. 19:21; Matt. 13:45–46; 1 Cor. 7:35; 1 Cor. 7:38; Phil. 3:7–8; See, *ScG* III, 130 and 149.

42. For the most lengthy, sympathetic treatment of the distinction between moral and premoral, as well as its advocates and critics, see A. M. Weiß, *Sittlicher Wert und nichtsittliche Werte. Zur Relevanz der Unterscheidung in der moraltheologischen Diskussion um deontologische Normen* (Freiburg: Universitätsverlag, 1996).

43. Janssens, "Ontic Evil and Moral Evil," 60, emphasis added.

[O]ur intentional feelings aim at qualities in these realities that bring us joy. We call these qualities values."[44] He goes on to note: "[W]e refer to a concrete reality as a good or an evil because according to its characteristics it embodies a value or a disvalue; we could practically speak about goods or evils as well as about values and disvalues."[45] Understanding premoral evils in this way would make it that *not all privations of possible goods* would be premorally evil, but only those *experienced by the agent* as evil.[46]

Other authors deny that there is anything subjective about premoral goods and evils whatsoever. As Richard McCormick writes:

We understand by "value" an intrinsic good to man, not something that is good simply because it is evaluated as such by human beings. And it is only if premoral good and evil are understood as value and disvalue *in Quay's sense* ["value implies value to man in terms of his needs and desires"] that the multiple aberrations he details would follow.[47]

It seems important to most proportionalists to avoid a kind of subjectivism that defines value/disvalue or good/evil in terms of whatever the agent desires.

Although this explanation excludes a possible misunderstanding of premoral evil and good as based ultimately in the desires of any particular person, it does not tell us what premoral evil or good is. One author writes:

Moral evil refers to those evils that render the person as a whole bad: e.g., the desire of and will to injustice or unchastity. But such evils do not tell us what concrete acts count as unjust or unchastity. That is, they do not tell us what concrete acts are right or wrong. Premoral evils do not touch directly on the moral goodness of the person, but only the person's well-being.[48]

Here, "well-being" is understood in independence of moral goodness such that one could have well-being and not have moral

44. Janssens, "Ontic Good and Evil—Premoral Values and Disvalues," *Louvain Studies* 12.1 (1987) 71.
45. Ibid., 80.
46. I thank Richard McCormick for this rejoinder.
47. McCormick, *Notes on Moral Theology, 1965 through 1980*, 646.
48. McCormick, *Notes on Moral Theology, 1981 through 1984*, 110.

goodness or vice versa. Of course, one may have both. But one could also be a flourishing villain or a floundering saint.

Or again, another writes: "Premoral evil does not refer immediately to the moral goodness of a person, but rather to the well-being of human beings in the different areas of human reality."[49] However, for Thomas, following Aristotle, the moral goodness of the person is part of the well-being or flourishing of an agent. Only the morally good person can be said to be truly flourishing.

One non-circular definition of premoral evil is the following: "The non-realization of human goods and values is a premoral evil for human beings."[50] These lacks arise from the very nature of the human person as material, spatial, corporeal, and temporal. Since premoral evil is always involved in our action, the only way to justify our action is in terms of the proportion between the good and evil brought about. The conclusion that premoral evil is always present rests on the assumption that one's not doing something, that is, the non-realization of something of which we are capable, is in some sense an evil, though a premoral one.

Insofar as one believes in the moral significance of the distinction between intended and foreseen consequences, one has reason to question that every evil brought about by human activity has the same moral status.

But should we even say that every non-realized possible good is an evil? Thomas's definition of evil is "a lack of that which is due a being."[51] Hence, not to have wings is an evil for a bird, but not for a man. Lacking eyesight is an evil for a woman, but not for a rock. In other words, there is a distinction to be made between privations, which are evils, and negations, which are not evils but rather simple absences. If human beings cause premoral evil by not realizing every good that could possibly be realized, then one has to assume that a human being is able to realize every good that could be realized. But even an all-powerful, eternal, and omnipresent being cannot bring about all possible goods, for some goods exclude one another by definition.[52] It

49. Fuchs, *Christian Ethics*, 81.   50. Ibid., 82.
51. *De malo* q.1, a.1, ad 1.   52. *ScG* I, 84.

would seem that there is ontic evil caused by God. But God is perfectly good, so this limitation must be compatible with perfect goodness (which excludes all evil)[53] and hence this limitation is not really an evil of any kind. If there is no evil for God in not realizing every good, why should there be evil associated with human beings for the very same limitation?

Finally, proportionalism proposes that in the right act there is a proportion between a finite good brought about and the infinite amount of premoral evil simultaneously brought about by omission. I choose to do X, which means *ipso facto* I do not choose X_1, X_2, X_3, X_4, X_5 ... X_n. What sort of proportion could obtain between the finite good of the act and the potentially infinite premoral evil also caused? ⌒⌣

Questions sometimes arise about the "absolutizing" of certain relative human goods. Normally, death is surely a worse evil than speaking an untruth. Why then may an agent sometimes permit or even intend death, but an agent may never intend to speak a falsehood.[54] How can there be a just-war theory and not a just-falsehood theory? These objections are cogent, if one presupposes that the purpose of the moral life is to create values and minimize disvalues. Why seemingly absolutize some relative values, seemingly lesser values, to the disadvantage of higher values in a particular situation? Proportionalism begins with the effects of action (death, deception) and works backwards toward the agent. But these assumptions, at least on Thomas's account, misrepresent not only the nature of human action, but also the way in which one comes to judgment about human action. Killing is indeed defined by its end-state of death, but killing is not its end-state, nor is killing as a human act non-moral. Killing is either a bad act or, if Thomas is correct, in very special circumstances such as just war, a good one.

The plausibility of proportionate reason as a form of practical reasoning governing both cases of killing and other cases cannot

53. *ScG* I, 39.
54. See, for instance, McCormick, *Notes on Moral Theology, 1981 through 1984,* 115.

be properly assessed apart from the alternatives available. Thomas and proportionalists differ in their assessments of particular cases in part because they have different accounts of practical reasoning and of the moral life as a whole. The relationship between practical reasoning and virtue in Thomas offers an alternative to the account of practical reasoning advocated in proportionalism. The next chapter treats this alternative account of practical reasoning.

VI. DOING EVIL TO
ACHIEVE GOOD?

𝕊𝕪

As an alternative to the account given of practical reasoning by various proportionalists, one could look to Thomas. For him, the various ways in which reason, including practical reason, relates to order leads to the establishment of various divisions of sciences. In the preface to the *Sententia libri ethicorum*, as noted earlier, Thomas finds that reason relates to order in a four-fold manner, leading to the differentiation of four sciences, in the medieval sense of four ordered spheres of inquiry. Sometimes reason does not create but contemplates the order of a thing *(res)*. On Thomas's account of understanding, although everything which is received is received according to the mode of the receiver *(quidquid recipitur recipitur secundum modum recipientis),*[1] nevertheless the astronomer or the geometrician does not create the order that his or her reason contemplates, but rather learns by receiving that order. In the *Ethics* commentary, Thomas calls his relationship between reason and order "natural philosophy." Secondly, reason establishes order among its own considerations of concepts and signs of concepts. Logic *(rationalis philosophia)* is the study that considers the order of parts of verbal expression to one another and the order of principles to their conclusions. A third relationship of reason to order is that proper to the moral science *(moralis philosophia)*, an order reason can establish or rec-

---

1. Thomas Aquinas, *De veritate*, q.12, a.12.

ognize in the will. Finally, reason can introduce order into external things *(artes mechanicae),* as when a carpenter makes the rough wood of a tree into a finely finished chest or cabinet. This is the transitive sphere of activity, the introduction of change into external states of affairs, *factio.*

The third and fourth spheres of activity, the sphere of moral virtue and the sphere of art or skill, have much in common, though they also differ in a number of ways. Given the many similarities between what the Greeks called *arēte* and *technē,* it is easy to see how it is that the two might be confused. But though they have similarities, it is a mistake to overlook the significant differences between virtues and skills, for these differences distinguish Aristotelian teleology from consequentialist teleology.

Why be concerned with the distinction between *arēte* and *technē?* Much more than a fine point of typology is at stake. We all want happiness, and to flourish. And if Aristotle and Aquinas are right, happiness has something to do with virtue, for happiness is an activity in accord with virtue. Hence, an understanding of what virtue is (or is not) can help us know how to achieve happiness. On the Aristotelian account there are numerous similarities as well as differences between skills and virtues. What, then, are the similarities?

Virtue and skills have to do with the mean *(NE* 1106b 15). The craft or skill of making a computer disk is destroyed if one makes the disk too large or too small for the computer. Similarly, the virtue of fortitude is not exercised if one is cowardly and bolts in fear at the first sign of danger, or if one is foolhardy and needlessly seeks danger. Since reaching the mean does not come easily, he suggests that "Craft and virtue are in every case about what is more difficult" *(NE* 1105a10; trans. Terence Irwin). Neither virtues nor skills, though in accord with nature, are in us by nature. We must acquire them by practice in matters of difficulty. Hence, there is no craft of breathing spring air, brushing one's teeth, or tying one's shoes. These activities are normally so easily done that they cannot be considered crafts. One can express skill or craft only in difficult matters such as making a violin in the manner of Stradivarius, playing a concerto by Paganini, or performing heart surgery.

Similarly, virtues are only about that which is difficult. There is no virtue of looking out for one's own good. People do so naturally. However there is a virtue of taking due care with others' goods, the virtue of justice. Skills and virtues are alike in that both concern doing these characteristically difficult activities well, and on account of this difficulty those who do them well are praised. Being described as "skilled" or "virtuous" is a compliment precisely because of the difficulty in achieving skills or virtuous habits.

Repeated activity brings about both skills and (natural) virtues (*NE* 1103b). Insofar as both are habits, skills and virtues are similar. Just as one becomes skilled by practicing a skill over and over again, so one becomes just or unjust by doing just or unjust actions repeatedly. The habits of virtue and craft both require knowledge (*NE* 1105b). One does not have craft or virtue if one "unknowingly" performs the act that a craft master or virtuous person would perform. People not trained in medical arts who just happened to pick the right medicine off the shelf would not possess the craft of medicine, even were they to do this, by chance or cue, on repeated occasions. Likewise, the virtue of generosity would not be expressed were someone to give while falsely believing that he or she was compelled to give.

Both skill and virtue concern habit, and not one-time action. These habits have both intellectual and affective aspects. The intellectual aspect helps a person with a given virtue to determine what should be done here and now. In soccer, there is no best kick, run, or pass. The most important part of the field is wherever the ball happens to be. No general rules enable a player to know what to do at each moment. Unlike, say American football, the very nature of the game as fast-moving, continuous, and ever-shifting excludes this possibility. A skilled player, however, knows how to respond to the shifting conditions of the game, not because he has read books on soccer or heard lectures from coaches (though these may sometimes help a bit), but because he has accumulated experience and is habituated to the shifting particulars of the game. So, too, the person of virtue, the person of practical wisdom, knows what to do in the shifting particularities of life, a knowledge of what to do informed by general principles, but not specifically determined by them. Lacking sufficient knowledge of the particulars, the unskilled or unvirtuous lacks the understanding necessary to lead to good production of artifacts or good human action.

5   The skilled and virtuous also have an affective ease in acting in accord with their habit. Playing a musical instrument is one thing when one begins instruction; it is quite another having acquired the skill. A certain joy and ease in action characterizes the latter but not the former. Similarly, the virtuous person enjoys his or her virtuous action. With respect to, say, the virtue of temperance, the virtuous person actually enjoys eating in moderation and would not enjoy overeating. The pleasure the virtuous person characteristically, but not always, takes in virtuous activity allows that person to do what virtue demands without the same internal difficulty experienced by either a continent or an incontinent person.

The similarities between skill and virtue have led some to write as if there were no distinction between them, as if *arētē* simply were *technē*. Consider this passage from Josef Fuchs: "[A] morally good person [i.e. one who strives to do what is right] has to avoid, as much as possible, premoral evils; his purpose is rather to create premoral goods and values for the well-being of human beings."[2] The person of technical expertise invariably strives to create premoral values, through surgical procedures, artistic creation, or technological breakthrough. But is the person of technical expertise also the person of moral goodness and virtue?

Although Aristotle and Aquinas point out similarities between craft or skill and virtue, they also point out dissimilarities. Aristotle writes:

[T]he products of a craft determine by their own character whether they have been produced well; and so it suffices that they are in the right

2. Fuchs, *Christian Ethics*, 81.

state when they have been produced. But for actions expressing virtue to be done temperately or justly [and hence well] it does not suffice that they are themselves in the right state. Rather, the agent must also be in the right state when he does them. First, he must know [that he is doing virtuous actions]; second, he must decide on them for themselves; and third, he must also do them from a firm and unchanging state. (*NE* 1105b Irwin)

Aristotle suggests in this passage at least three important differences between virtue and skill. These differences are differences not merely with respect to the agent, but also with respect to evaluating the action. What are these differences?

First, although Aristotle mentions that knowing is shared with both the skilled and the virtuous, the kind of knowledge involved in each differs. Craft knowledge is more narrow than knowledge arising from virtues.

It seems proper then to an intelligent person to be able to deliberate finely about what is good and beneficial for himself, not about some restricted area—e.g. about what promotes health and strength [as this would belong to the medical art]. A sign of this is the fact that we call people intelligent whenever they calculate well to promote some excellent end, in an area where this is no craft. (*NE* 1140a25–30 Irwin)

Art concerns a more narrow area of expertise; virtue encompasses the action of a person in the whole of life. The craftsman's knowledge is limited to a constricted range of aptitude, i.e., bridle-making, computer technology, or archery. The person of virtue's knowledge ranges over the unpredictable diversity and particularity of life. In addition, for *activity* to count as virtuous activity, one must know what one is doing in a way not essential for skill. The *product* of skill may turn out to be good without such knowledge being possessed by the artisan, for instance when someone has success in a project by chance (though, as mentioned, the person cannot be considered an artisan, as one possessing the skill, if such knowledge is missing). In some skills, with habituation one can act mechanically; in contrast, virtue must engage the will and be the result, as well as exercise, of human action.

One might object that this is misleading, on two counts. Craft skills include knowledge, and thus no "product of skill" can be produced without knowledge. If the claim is somewhat different, if it is merely that those without knowledge can at times produce what craftsmen do, then nothing has been done to distinguish art and virtue. Even fools stumble unknowingly into a just act from time to time.[3]

Although for Aristotle having a skill or a virtue requires knowledge (*NE* 1105b), one can further distinguish between products of skill or products of virtue and having a skill or having a virtue. A product of skill may be produced without knowledge, as when someone accidentally makes the right move in a game. Novices lack the skill but can sometimes do the skillful action. By contrast, a fool cannot do a just act because for an act to be truly just it must arise from a stable character, which presumably the fool lacks.

These differences arise in part because a different relationship of order to reason is expressed in virtue than in skill. Virtue is the habit perfecting practical reasoning in the third way in which reason relates to order where reason introduces order into the will of a moral agent. Skill is a habit perfecting technical reason that introduces order into exterior matter-mechanical arts, as Thomas says. The former perfects an action *(actio)*, a self-constitutive choice. The latter facilitates a production or making *(factio)* whose perfection lies not in the maker but in the thing made (*NE* 10945a). Aristotle clearly distinguishes between them. "[T]he state involving reason and concerned with action is different from the state involving reason and concerned with production. Nor is one included in the other; for action is not production, and production is not action" (*NE* 1140a5 Irwin). Thomas in his commentary on the *Ethics* suggests that Aristotle here is distinguishing prudence from art.

[T]he difference between action and making has been explained. Action is an operation remaining in the agent, like seeing, understanding, and willing. But making is an operation passing into external matter to fash-

3. I thank John R. Bowlin for this objection as well as many helpful corrections and remarks on the manuscript as a whole.

ion something out of it, like constructing and sawing. Since habits are distinguished according to the object, it follows that the habit that is active by means of reason, i.e., prudence, is different from the habit that is productive through reason, i.e., art.[4]

Prudence is not art, nor art prudence. Neither is included under the genus of the other, but rather both are quite different, though of course not opposed, uses of reason.

For Aristotle and Aquinas, prudence has priority over art. We have the skill of house building for the sake of a product, viz., the house. In contrast, virtue is not merely for the sake of any end external to the agent, but rather activity in accord with virtue is partially constitutive of the end at which all human activity aims—happiness. Virtuous activity is both good in itself and good as a means toward some good outside the agent. Jonathan Lear puts the point as follows:

Aristotle distinguished between ends that are distinct from the actions which produce them and ends that are the activities themselves (*NE* 1.1). . . . House-building, for example, is directed toward the production of a house, which is distinct from the process of building. By contrast, one may jog in order to be healthy, but jogging is part of what it is to be healthy. Health is not some end-state that is produced after the jogging, swimming, eating well, and sleeping well. Being healthy is a state in which all those activities are carried out. This distinction is central to Aristotle's ethics, for acting virtuously is not a means to a distinct end of living a happy life. Acting virtuously *constitutes* a happy life.[5]

The distinction drawn here between an end state and a process is important not only for understanding Aristotle and Thomas correctly but also—something that will be addressed more fully later—for understanding the place of premoral evils in a moral account. But the point at issue, that virtuous actions are worthwhile in themselves, is addressed clearly by Alasdair MacIntyre in his book *Dependent Rational Animals: Why Human Beings Require the Virtues*. MacIntyre writes:

4. Thomas Aquinas, *Commentary on the Nicomachean Ethics*, translated by C. I. Litzinger (Notre Dame, Ind.: Dumb Ox Books, 1993) 1151.

5. Jonathan Lear, "Ethics and the Organization of Desire," in *Aristotle: The Desire to Understand* (Cambridge: Cambridge University Press, 1988) 152–208.

The acts required by the virtues are each of them worth performing for their own sake. They are indeed always also a means to something further, just because they are constitutive parts of human flourishing. But it is precisely as acts worth performing for their own sake that they are such parts. To assert of a given action that it was performed for its own sake is not at all incompatible with saying of that same action that it was performed for the sake of that individual or these individuals to whose good it was directed.[6]

For example, charity as an activity connected with God or neighbor both is directed to an outside end and is constitutive of the perfection of the agent, the agent's own happiness.

Secondly, virtues, but not craft, require decision, and decision for virtue's sake. One could be moved to produce some effect merely because motivated by fear or by an external, accidentally related good. A craftsman still is properly a craftsman if he makes his good, a car, while motivated by the fear of being fired or an external good such as financial reward. A surgeon is still a good surgeon when motivated by fear of liability or by desire for renown. On the other hand, a person does not yet exercise virtue if he or she does what a virtuous person would do but only for the sake of avoiding punishment or becoming famous. The craftsman but not the person of virtue is motivated primarily by what MacIntyre calls exterior goods rather than goods internal to practice.

Thus, virtues, unlike crafts, cannot be used for evil ends, for the corrupt motivation corrupts the very exercise of virtue but not of craft. In the exercise of skills, but not in the realm of vice and virtue, voluntary errors are more choiceworthy (*NE* 1140b25). Thus, skills but not virtues can be misused. One can practice a craft but not for the craft's sake. A doctor's knowledge can enable her to kill as well as to heal. So if the doctor practices the craft of medicine to injure patients (as, say, certain Nazi doctors did), this does not mean that the doctor lacks the craft or skill. On the other hand, an otherwise virtuous person doing nonvirtuous acts is to that very extent exhibiting a lack of virtue.

6. Alasdair MacIntyre, *Dependent Rational Animals: Why Human Beings Need the Virtues* (Chicago: Open Court, 1999) 111–12.

Finally, a virtuous action, but not the exercise of a skill, requires that it be done from a firm and unchanging state of character (*NE* 11055a33). What does Aristotle mean? One could understand him to mean that an artisan could bring about a good product despite his unstable character, and this product could be just as good in every respect as the product issuing from the person of stable character. Likewise, the actions of the stable and unstable could be alike in every externally visible way.

The action of the virtuous person contributes to the agent's happiness in a way that an action proceeding from a person of unstable character does not contribute to that person's happiness. Hence, for the person of unstable character, an action may be similar to the action performed by the virtuous person, but the action coming from the person lacking virtue does not contribute to his or her happiness. The merely continent person may perform what appears from the third-party perspective to be a virtuous action but derives no happiness from this operation. He or she can do activity that is exteriorly similar to the activity of the virtuous person, but insofar as the action does not flow from virtue, it does not partially constitute the agent's happiness. Lacking the proper pedagogy of the passions, even if the incontinent person knows more or less clearly the way to excellence, the incontinent person cannot bring himself to act in this way. The continent person, although she can mimic the exterior actions a virtuous person would do, lacks the stability of good character that leads one to delight in such execution.

There are other ways of understanding the importance of stable character in Aristotle's account. Stable character may refer to a unity of the life of virtue. One can be a great shoemaker and a lousy spouse, but one cannot on Aristotle's account be both a courageous and an imprudent person. There is a unity to the virtues such that one cannot really have one without having them all. For exercise of all the virtues requires prudence, and the person with prudence has all the other virtues.[7]

What importance should be given to the difference between

7. *ST* II-II, 47, 14.

skills and virtues? Given that technical reason and practical reason constitute, for Aristotle, two separate and independent realms, it is clear that on his account we are mistaken when we reduce moral questions to technical questions. What brings about the greatest premoral good is a technical question, not necessarily a moral one. Technical possibility does not determine the morality of the act in question, which can only be evaluated positively (but not negatively) by taking into account the character and motivation of the agent. Technical answers do not necessarily determine the answers to moral questions. The moral order is then of a higher order of priority: it is more "divine" than the technical order (NE 1178b20).

The difference between skill and virtue also leads the person of virtue to evaluate the "greater good" in a way that subordinates premoral goods to the moral good. The virtuous person chooses for himself the "greater good" precisely by giving his friends the "premoral goods" of wealth, honors, and offices, thereby himself suffering a deprivation of premoral goods (NE 1168a25). On a proportionalist account, it is the "gross" of premoral goods that matters and not the distribution of these goods to the benefit of others at a (premoral) cost to the agent. The focus on *impartial* maximization of premoral goods for all those involved seemingly excludes the self-sacrificial person who sacrifices his or her own physical (or non-moral) well-being for the sake of another's good. In the words of Schüller: "Acting from love *(agapē)* is morally good. Doing what on the whole is impartially beneficial to all persons concerned is morally right. Therefore, an action may be morally bad because performed from pure selfishness, but nonetheless be morally right on account of its beneficial consequences."[8] Hence the person who sacrifices for others at cost to himself or herself and thereby at cost of the greater premoral goods impartially considered would be acting wrongly for proportionalists but not for Aristotle.

When one compares Aristotelian virtue ethics to proportionalist ethics, the role of motivation also differs. For Aristotle, inso-

8. Schüller, "The Double Effect: A Reevaluation," 165–92, at 183.

far as bad motivation corrupts an action that in other respects seems virtuous, one cannot evaluate that action as a whole as good (but one could evaluate it as evil) without reference to motive. On a proportionalist analysis, the morally right is determined on the basis of beneficial consequences, what Thomas would describe as a "making." On a proportionalist account, the action of an ill-motivated surgeon is still good, though if badly motivated the character of such a surgeon could not be described as good.[9] For Aquinas, the surgeon's act, as a function of technical expertise evaluated in purely medical terms is good, but this technical sense of "good" Aquinas would distinguish from a moral sense of good. For although the act itself in the case of the surgeon may be morally good, the action as a whole is not. Schüller's and Fuchs's way of framing the issue confuses, then, the technical and moral senses of good by confusing or conflating the third and the fourth ways in which reason can relate to order.

In this context, a category confusion of proportionalism becomes clear. "Right" acts, for proportionalists, would fall under the category of "skill" rather than virtue in this Aristotelian schema. First, according to those versions of proportionalism which abstract from an agent's intention, one can properly describe an executed act as "right" and "wrong," independently of the agent's knowledge that the act is right or wrong. Women feeding babies with defective bottles can be said to be doing morally wrong acts, although they are morally good because they had no idea that this feeding would lead to the death of their children. Secondly, an action may be unqualifiedly described as right in proportionalism even though it is not chosen for its own sake. The doctor who cures many people, to use Fuchs's example cited earlier, does the right act even when motivated by greed. Finally, the agent's stable character or lack of stable character plays no role in determining the rightness of activity, for proportionalism draws a firm distinction between the goodness or badness of a person's character and the rightness or

[handwritten margin note: right acts are productive]

9. Fuchs, *Christian Ethics*, 81.

wrongness of a person's activity. The moral judgments drawn by proportionalism are, according to Aristotle's distinction between *arētē* and *technē,* more properly described as judgments about skill or technique than properly moral judgments.

Of course, one might respond by noting that this would be true of almost all theories of morality that are not strictly "virtue" theories, so the critique is not merely of proportionalism but of many other theories of morality as well. Why should virtue theory be *the* normative theory by which others are judged?

Although these remarks do not indicate that proportionalism or any other theory is false *per se,* they do indicate something about claims of appropriating Thomas. Insofar as proportionalism does not distinguish skill from virtue, the theory cannot be considered in any robust sense Thomistic or Aristotelian. The "teleology" of proportionate reason would thus be of a different kind than the "teleology" of Thomistic moral theory.

One can also illuminate the category confusion of proportionalism by MacIntyre's distinction between the goods external to practice and the goods internal to practice. To excel in skill or virtue is to have certain internal goods of that skill or virtue. MacIntyre takes the game of chess as an example. The internal goods of chess include "the achievement of a certain highly particular kind of analytic skill, strategic imagination and competitive intensity."[10] By contrast, "goods externally and contingently attached to chess-playing and to other practices by the accidents of social circumstances [include] in the case of the imaginary child candy, in the case of real adults such goods as prestige, status and money."[11] MacIntyre notes that if a child playing the game of chess is seeking the good internal—and not external—to the game of chess, then "if the child cheats, he or she will be defeating not me, but himself or herself."[12] Hence, to cheat is to act contrary to the good of chess.

For such skills, certain invariable laws apply such that to vio-

---

10. Alasdair MacIntyre, *After Virtue* (Notre Dame: University of Notre Dame Press, 1982) 188.
11. Ibid.
12. Ibid.

late them is not to excel at such skills. The rules of these activities vary from art to art, but for arts such as medicine or navigation, certain acts circumvent the achievement of the goods internal to that skill. If the end of medicine is restoring health to patients, then to kill the patient is to fail to achieve the goods internal to medicine (though it may bring about goods accidentally related to medicine). If the end of navigation is to move the boat into its destination, then to sink the boat is to exclude the good internal to the skill of navigation.

In Aristotle, skills themselves are ordered in an architectonic manner. Bridle-making is ordered to horsemanship, horsemanship is ordered among other ends to the military art, the military art to politics, a division of moral philosophy. Since lower-order skills are ordered to higher, it is irrational to excel at the skill of bridle making and its internal goods at the expense of horsemanship. It is likewise irrational to practice horsemanship at the expense of the military art. Proper pursuit of the military art retains its order to the goods internal to politics. Hence, to excel at the goods of craft at the expense of excelling in virtue is for Aristotle and Thomas irrationally to reverse the proper ordering of activities to one another. Correlatively, one mistake of moral reasoning would be to suppose that considering the internal goods of a lower form of activity could inform one about the goods of a higher form.

The virtues are habitual perfections of various aspects of the human person, aspects described by Thomas earlier in the *Prima pars*.[13] Prudence perfects the practical reasoning of the person, courage properly regulates the fears and aggressions of the person, temperance orders the tactile desires of the person, and the virtue of justice, the chief cardinal virtue, governs the interaction of the human person with others.[14] Mention must also be made of the infused theological virtues of faith, hope, and charity, which are necessary in order to have true and perfect natural virtues and thus are necessary in order to have genuine although

---

13. *ST* I, 78, 1–4; *ST* I-II, 85, 3.
14. *ST* I-II, 61, 2; *ST* II-II, 58, 12.

imperfect happiness in this life. Activity in accord with virtue is Thomas's definition of the happiness possible in this life. Just as skills or arts have internal good, one could speak of happiness as the internal good of activity in accord with virtue. Unlike the internal goods of skills, there can be no goods of a higher order than the internal goods of the exercise of virtue; hence the internal goods of this order cannot rationally be undermined for any further good.[15]

Leaving aside "unnatural acts," the modern discussion generated by proportionalism has focused almost exclusively on issues of justice.[16] Thomas holds that justice is the highest of the moral virtues (although he does rank it below the theological virtues, which are higher insofar as they have God Himself as their proper object)[17] because justice is the perfection of the rational appetite, which is more excellent than the sensitive appetites that the other cardinal virtues perfect.[18] Sins against justice, Thomas tells us, are mortal sins, since "each injury brought against another person is of itself repugnant to charity, which moves to wanting the good of another. And so since injustice always consists in an injury brought against another person, it is clear that to do an injustice from its genus is a mortal sin."[19]

Justice, Thomas tells us, is of two types. Following Aristotle, he distinguishes between distributive and commutative justice. He writes:

However a twofold order may be considered in relation to some part. One order is the order of a part to another part, to which there is a similar order of one private person to another, and commutative justice directs this order, which is concerned with the affairs between two persons. The other order being considered is of the whole to parts; the community in relation to individual persons is similar to this order. This order is directed by distributive justice, which is distributive of common

15. *Sententia libri ethicorum* I, paragraphs 250–60.
16. See, for example, D. Witschen, *Gerechtigkeit und teleologische Ethik* (Freiburg: Universitätsverlag, 1992). W. Wolbert, *Vom Nutzen der Gerechtigkeit. Zur Diskussion um Utilitarianismus und Teleologische Theorie* (Freiburg: Universitätsverlag, 1992).
17. See *ST* II-II, 161, 5.
18. See *ST* II-II, 58, 12.
19. *ST* II-II, 59, 4.

goods according to a proportion. Hence there are two species of justice, distributive and commutative.[20]

For Aristotle and Thomas, commutative justice governs relationships among individual private persons; distributive justice governs the relationship of individuals to their community. For instance, the community alone may justly prosecute and punish criminals. This duty does not pertain to the private citizen who, if he or she undertakes this task, is an unjust vigilante. Other tasks belong to this realm of justice, such as levying taxes. Those who have care for the whole can justly order the whole in its distribution of rewards and punishments. Hence, even if it would be just for those representing the polity to execute a certain act, the execution of that same act by those not representing the polity may be unjust.

These two forms of justice correspond to geometric and arithmetic proportionality.[21] Geometric proportionality gives each person that which he or she merits. If a speculator contributes 10 percent of an investment, *ceteris paribus* he or she should receive 10 percent of the return. "What the equality of justice consists in is like cases being treated alike and in proportional differences in merit being treated according to that proportion. So a distribution is just, if and only if, it preserves between two cases where the recipients are unequal in merit a proportionately unequal distribution (*NE* 1131a10–b24)."[22] The act of distributing due goods and punishments in the community, Thomas adds, belongs to those who exercise authority in the community.[23] Private execution of punishment (capital or otherwise) does not fulfill an essential aspect of just punishment. In addition to the private good, it is the common good that the criminal undermines by undermining the good of this or that individual; hence it is only those exercising jurisdiction over this good and only acting *qua* representative of this good (and not from private mo-

20. *ST* II-II, 61, 1. See also, *Sententia libri ethicorum*, prefatio.
21. *ST* II-II, 61, 2. See also, Ralph McInerny, *Aquinas and Analogy* (Washington, D.C.: The Catholic University of America Press, 1996) 143–46.
22. MacIntyre, *Whose Justice? Which Rationality?* 119.
23. See *ST* II-II, 61, 1 ad 3.

tives) that just punishment can be given out. These authorities, if they are just, act for the sake of the good of the community as a whole in this distribution of goods and punishments.

What may be just in one sphere of justice may not be just in another. Thomas's treatment of self-defense falls within commutative justice, the justice that pertains to the relationship of individuals. For Thomas, intentional killing in this sphere of justice is always evil, but intentional killing under the description of punishment in the sphere of distributive justice is not always an evil.[24]

Since the virtues, including justice, are necessary for happiness in this life, and any acts against virtue are necessarily irrational and counter-productive, there could never be a good reason for killing intentionally an innocent person. This can be clarified further by considering the importance of loving God and neighbor in achieving happiness.

According to Thomas, the ultimate end of human life is divine filiation, or the beatific vision to be possessed in the life to come. The way in which human beings attain this vision serves only to underscore the necessity of virtue. This goal is presupposed by the first principle of practical reasoning. The knowing of God, the perfection of the intellect, the highest faculty by the highest object, is the end of man. Virtue again enters the discussion. Although ultimate felicity lies in the *actio* of understanding God,[25] since there is a unity of the virtues (intellectual and moral),[26] acts not in accord with justice or temperance or courage can exclude one's felicity. In the *Summa contra Gentiles*, Thomas has this to say about the relationship of the will to the final end.

The union which is through the intellect receives completion by the union which pertains to the will. For through the will man in a certain way rests in that which the intellect apprehends. The will however adheres to a certain thing, either because of love or because of fear, but not in the same way. For indeed, the one who clings to something because

24. A defense of retributive punishment is offered in Plato's *Gorgias*, 476–81.
25. See *ScG* III, 31.
26. See *ST* I-II, 65.

of fear, clings because of something else, for instance, to avoid an evil which threatens unless he clings to that thing. But, if one who clings to a thing because of love, he does so for its own sake. Now what is for its own sake is more principal than that which is for the sake of something else. Therefore, the adherence to God in love is the most powerful way of clinging to Him.[27]

The union of the intellect with God, Thomas tells us, is completed by the will in this life.[28]

Hence, we could properly say that without love of God the union of the intellect is incomplete. If happiness is the complete possession of our good, then we need love for our happiness. Love of God is, then, essential for human persons to achieve their final end.

How then is love of neighbor essential for achieving the final end? Having established the necessity of the love of God, Thomas offers several arguments in *Summa contra Gentiles* chapter 117 for the love of one's neighbor.[29] Since man is a social animal, he needs to be helped toward his final end by others, and this cannot happen without mutual love. Another of his central arguments is as follows:

[W]hoever loves someone consequently loves those loved by him, and those related to him. However, men are loved by God, who disposes them to enjoyment of Himself. Therefore it is necessary that whoever loves God also love neighbor.[30]

Thomas adds that tranquillity and peace are needed to devote time to divine matters, and that the chief obstacles to this tranquillity and peace come from lack of mutual love. Hence, human beings must love others to achieve their final end.

What then does Thomas mean by love? If human action is to achieve the human end of knowing God, and knowing God requires loving God and loving neighbor, one cannot harm a neighbor, for "all harm brought against another in itself is repug-

---

27. *ScG* III, 116, 2.
28. I say "in this life" because the context indicates that Thomas is talking about the divine law which guides man to his end. In the next life, the *beati* have attained the end, hence the law is superfluous for them.
29. For other arguments, see *ScG* III, 128.
30. *ScG* III, 117, 3.

nant to charity, which moves to wishing the good of the other."[31] The one who intends to visit evil on another indicates that he does not love that neighbor; he does not wish and choose the good for him. "In common, man is obliged to this, that he bring harm to no one."[32] Such an agent has chosen some apparent good that excludes the good of the neighbor or, to speak more precisely, visits harm upon the neighbor. An agent could intend this harm as the proximate end of a human act, (e.g., murder), as a remote end (e.g., detraction), or from circumstances (e.g., studying for the sake of knowledge, but when one should be watching after the well-being of one's children). A good human act is good in all these respects, a bad human act lacks goodness in any one of these respects. Love of neighbor and commutative justice thus are closely linked. The love of a neighbor for another neighbor presupposes at the very least that the good of the neighbor not be harmed; this is, of course, the minimal requirement of commutative justice.

Thomas, then, has given us some reason to suppose that evil may not be done so that good may come. It follows from the first principle of practical reasoning, that good is to be done and evil avoided, that one may not make as one's end or means an evil for another person or oneself. Doing evil to achieve good is to contradict the virtue of justice on the one hand and the infused virtue of charity on the other. The effect of death, for instance, is indeed a non-moral evil *(factio)*, but the cause defined as "killing" is not non-moral but moral *(actio)*. It is an operation, a human act, and as such good or bad.

At once a flurry of objections may be raised, and rightly so. Is all harming of neighbor evil? Cannot one at times intend a non-absolute or premoral evil in order to achieve some good? These questions, along with a corresponding investigation into the tradition, have led some to the following conclusion. On this view,

---

31. *ST* II-II, 59, 4

32. *ST* II-II, 122, 6, ad 1. See also *ST* I-II, 100, 5; *ST* I-II, 95, 2; *ST* II-II, 10, 12; *ST* II-II 41, 1; *ST* II-II, 44, 7; *ST* II-II, 73, 3; *ST* II-II, 76, 3. Steve Jensen notes these citations and others, *Intrinsically Evil Actions According to St. Thomas Aquinas* (Dissertation. University of Notre Dame, 1993) 131.

the tradition, of which Thomas and later writers are a part, sanctioned intending harm to achieve good in at least the following instances:[33] (1) the deception of another when necessary to protect an important secret; (2) the amputation of a limb or organ in order to prevent the spread of disease; (3) the excising of an organ for transplantation; (4) the pain of a child whom we spank pedagogically; (5) the killing of another in self-defense; (6) killing in a just war; and (7) the death of the criminal in capital punishment.

Doing Evil to Achieve Good: A Reexamination

John Finnis in his book *Moral Absolutes* has treated these alleged instances of doing evil to achieve good at length. Here, I will summarize and expand upon his analysis. The first point brought forward, the deception of another when necessary to protect an important secret, does not seem to establish clearly the point in question. Rather, tradition following Augustine's and Thomas's account held that one can never lie, no matter what the consequences. Precisely because of this conclusion, the tradition has come under criticism by proportionalism.[34] One may, however, intend that a person in ignorance remain in ignorance. Here one is not intending an evil for the sake of a good, but merely not eliminating an evil that was in one's power to eliminate. In fact, one might argue that if the case in point involves intending that a person, who has no right to the truth in question, remain in ignorance, then there would be no evil involved but rather only an absence, for every evil entails a lack of "due" good, and in this case the good of knowledge is not due to the person in ignorance. The question whether or not this prohibition has reasonable justification will be postponed until the next chapter.

The amputation of a limb or organ in order to prevent the

33. Though altering the order of presentation, I rely heavily here on Richard McCormick, *Notes on Moral Theology, 1965 through 1980*, 657, and, in responding, often on Finnis, *Moral Absolutes*, 78–81.

34. Salzman, *Deontology and Teleology*, 164–65.

spread of disease is said to be another instance of doing evil so
that good may come. According to the analyses given by Janssens, Knauer, Fuchs, and McCormick,[35] the removal of a diseased
organ is a premoral evil, but that one is justified in causing this
evil because of the existence of a commensurate reason.[36]

On Aristotelian grounds one might say that it is no longer an
organ at all. Aristotle writes in *On the Parts of Animals:*

Again, what appears to be a hand is not a hand regardless of its disposition; e.g., a bronze or wooden hand is not a hand, unless the term
"hand" is equivocally used, just as a physician in drawing or a flute
made of marble is not a physician or a flute, respectively; for such a
hand cannot perform its function just as a flute or a physician cannot
perform the function proper to a real flute or physician respectively.
Similarly, no part of a dead man, such as we might call "an eye" or "a
hand" can perform the function of what is really an eye or a hand, respectively.[37]

In an Aristotelian analysis then, the amputation of a diseased organ is not properly speaking the removing an organ, since the
part removed cannot perform its proper function. Sometimes, although temporarily the organ does not function, nevertheless
given proper medication it can be returned to proper functioning. That which is only equivocally described as an organ is now
properly described as an evil to the body. Later in *Wholly Human,*
Bruno Schüller echoes this understanding: "If 'eye' equals organ
of sight, then a blind eye would be an organ of sight that was no
good for seeing. But an organ of sight that's useless for seeing
seems to be no organ of sight at all, and so a blind eye is apparently not any eye."[38] He notes also that surgeons themselves do

35. Louis Janssens, "Ontic Good and Evil—Premoral Values and Disvalues,"
73. Knauer, "Hermeneutic Function," 22; Knauer, "Zu Grundbegriffen der Enzyklika 'Veritatis Splendor,'" 25. Fuchs, *Christian Ethics,* 76. McCormick, "Notes on
Moral Theology: 1985," 60: "Nearly everyone would argue that direct mutilation
is justifiable to save a patient's life."

36. Knauer, "Hermeneutic Function," 21–22; Janssens, "Norms and Priorities
in a Love Ethics," 215.

37. Aristotle, *Aristotle: Selected Works,* trans. Hippocrates G. Apostle and Lloyd
P. Gerson (Grinnell, Iowa: The Peripatetic Press, 1986) 313.

38. Schüller, *Wholly Human,* 109. Despite these insights, Schüller speaks later
of surgery as "permissible bodily injury" (156), rather than considering the acts of
the surgeon not injury at all, but in many cases removal of what is injuring. Of

not believe that they "injure" or "harm" in order to heal. Harming patients is a violation of the Hippocratic Oath.

The removal of what is evil, other things being equal, is normally understood to be a good. If an organ itself is not healthy, indeed, is so diseased that it threatens the very life of the person whose organ it is, then to remove that organ is not an evil, but a good. Thomas writes: "Something is called evil due to the fact that it causes injury. But this is only so because it causes injury to the good, for to injure the evil is a good thing, since the corruption of evil is good."[39] Thus, the removal of a diseased organ is not really an evil needing to be justified by a commensurate reason. If one has a cancerous kidney, to remove *this* kind of kidney is not an evil; rather, in removing the kidney one is *removing an evil* that threatens the entire body. Thomas writes:

But if a limb on account of disease is corruptive of the whole body, then amputating the gangrenous limb for the sake of the whole body is licit as long as one has the permission of the person, for to each one is given the care of his own body. . . . Otherwise, however, damaging a limb is in all ways illicit.[40]

For Thomas then, removal of a diseased limb, so long as appropriate permission was granted by the person for operation on his or her body, is not in fact an evil.[41] The order of parts of a whole to one another is a subordinate good to the order of the whole to its proper end.[42] Hence, insofar as a part does not share the order to the whole, that part is evil. Unless the organs of the body are assumed to have a certain ontological status independent of the body, the removal of cancerous organs cannot be said to be an evil, but rather a good for the person.[43]

course, in some cases, the surgeon must cut open a person's body to remove the cause of injury. Is *this* not harming? Though the body is cut, this normally has no effect on the healthy functioning of the body. Thus, at least by this standard, it is not harming.

39. *ScG* III, 11, 4. He speaks similarly in *ST* II-II, 33, 1.

40. *ST* II-II, 65, 1.

41. See also *ST* II-II, 65, 1.

42. *Sententia libri ethicorum*, prefatio.

43. I thank Richard McCormick for the objection that indeed there is a "premoral evil" involved in the act, since the doctor wishes that she did not have to perform the surgery, since the patient must be put under general anesthesia and

These conclusions make it easier to see that an organ donation of a duplicated organ is not a case of intending evil for the
sake of good. The health of the body is the good of an organic
whole, not the sum of various parts. Insofar as removing an organ does in fact damage the goods of the person's body, it would
be bad. Brain donation or donation of the heart without replacement would be doing an evil to one so that good may come to
another. Thus, Finnis rightly points out that "the transplantation
of a duplicated organ such as the kidney, leaving the whole sub-
stantially unimpaired, need not be regarded as doing harm for
the sake of good."[44] Such donation is considered heroic however,
because in so donating an organ one does risk harm in undergoing surgery and in the possible future failure of the one remaining organ.

With respect to the fourth example, properly speaking, no
harm—no true harm—is done in spanking a child for pedagogical purposes. Spanking, as opposed to child abuse, merely causes
a child relatively superficial pain, not genuine harm. Is pain,
even superficial pain, always an evil? Is pain a lack of something—namely pleasure—due a being as its proper perfection?

In order to answer the question properly, one must first say
something about the nature of pain in general and also distinguish two very different kinds of pain. If a person felt no pain
when touching a red-hot stove-top, the *lack* of feeling pain
would be an evil, a lack of something that should be present. The
perpetual deadening of the nerves or the nervous system is itself
an evil. Hence, it would seem that pain in general cannot be described as an evil.[45] If pain itself is not an evil, it would seem that

---

be subject to the risks accompanying anesthesia. Certainly, the doctor regrets having to do the procedure, but what is regretted is not precisely having to remove
the cancerous kidney, but the fact the kidney is cancerous to begin with and that
all other options have been exhausted. Losing consciousness, an aspect of many
surgeries, is not an evil in every situation. Often it can be a good sought, as when
someone takes a sleeping pill and buries himself in a warm bed. That general
anesthesia may induce other problems, such as respiratory failure, certainly
would be an evil, *if* it were realized. Still, in the case in point, the anesthesiologist
does not intend this result; on the contrary, he precisely seeks to avoid this result.
    44. Finnis, *Moral Absolutes*, 79.
    45. Following Aristotle (*NE* 1153b), St. Thomas does describe pain as an evil

the description of "inflicting pain" would not itself be *per se* evil. Would this open the way for torture? I believe one must distinguish between superficial and torturous pain. Inflicting extremely high levels of pain, pain that causes or indicates damage to the physical or psychological good of the person, torturous pain, is an evil, as is all inflicting of harm. On the other hand, the inflicting of superficial pain, such as occurs in a spanking, does not indicate or cause damage to the physical or psychological good of the person. Thus, the inflicting of superficial pain is sometimes licit, but the inflicting of torturous pain would not be licit.

This leaves the final cases, cases in which harm is in fact inflicted on human persons: (5) the killing of another in self-defense, (6) killing in a just war and (7) the death of the criminal in capital punishment.

Thomas's treatment of these three cases cannot be understood aside from his understanding of the virtue of justice. We discussed in Chapter I Thomas's answer to the question of whether we can kill in self-defense. It is indeed the case that some in the tradition justified that, but insofar as one rejects a positivistic and legalistic framework for discussion, this precedent is only as important as the arguments that support it. Thomas's treatment of private self-defense falls within his treatment of commutative justice, the justice of individuals to one another, or of neighbor to neighbor. From what Thomas says above about charity and its relationship to justice, it follows that private individuals cannot intend to inflict harm upon one another.

It is significant to note the question with which Thomas begins his treatment of war: Whether warfare *always* is a sin?[46] Thomas offers arguments establishing that at times war can be just. He cites Scripture in the *sed contra*, noting that Christ gave soldiers advice about carrying out their profession, advice that

---

insofar as it is opposed to the good of "rest of the senses" (*ST* II-II, 65, 3). But considering the due order of goods, the substantial integrity of the body is characteristically preserved by means of pain in such a way that, sometimes, to lack pain would be to endanger this greater good which is a necessary condition for enjoying the rest of the senses.

46. *ST* II-II, 40, 1.

presupposes the legitimacy of the profession. Although waging war is not always a sin, the conditions in which it is justified are carefully circumscribed. Just war may be understood as the community's effort to defend itself against attack, both exterior and interior; and, like potentially deadly self-defense with weapons, clerics are not to engage in it.[47] Hence, insofar as it is not truly the community's defense, when private persons wage war *qua* private persons, the war will be unjust.[48]

Just war can be seen as governed by the same principles as self-defense, by commutative justice writ large. Thomas requires that the cause of undertaking war be just.[49] A community cannot use violence as a pretext for securing some other goal but solely in defending itself. In other words, not just the means but the remote end or intention must be good. Just as one person cannot intend to kill another in self-defense, so one community cannot intend to kill another community as such but only stop, by lethal means if needed, the aggressors; hence "total" war is excluded. Finally, one might add that it would be consistent with Thomas (and is found explicitly in later writers) that there must be a proportion between the means employed and the end such that the least amount of violence possible is used to secure defense of the community. If diplomatic negotiating can secure peace, war must not be sought. If one must wage war, the least violent and destructive ways of securing a just peace must be sought.

What Thomas explicitly says about the subject is rather sparse. In his 1978 article James F. Childress provides a wider and richer background to the question.[50] But Thomas's account differs in at least one very important way from Childress's. Childress speaks of killing (and hence waging war) as a *prima facie*

---

47. *ST* II-II, 40, 2, ad 4. Thomas's treatment of war (*ST* II-II, 40, 1–2) falls under his account of the virtue of charity, rather than justice. As one of the effects of charity is peace, Aquinas places his discussion of just war in this context. His discussion, however, could just as easily have been placed among other questions of justice.

48. *ST* II-II, 40, 1. "*Primo* quidem auctoritas Principis, cuius mandato bellum est gerendum."

49. *ST* II-II, 40, 1.

50. James F. Childress, "Just-War Theories: The Bases, Interrelations, Priorities, and Functions of Their Criteria," *Theological Studies* 39 (1978) 427–45.

evil. The phrase arises from W. D. Ross's *The Right and the Good*, and its meaning does not seem to apply to Thomas. For Childress, the phrase *prima facie* evil (or duty) may mean that the evil present in a given situation may be over-ridden or outweighed by other circumstances. For Childress, the *prima facie* evil of killing leaves the final judgment of the rightness or wrongness of an act, even containing an evil such as killing the innocent, as in principle undecided until the all circumstances are taken into account. The description of an act as killing counts toward evaluating the act as morally evil. To say an act is an act of killing is to begin with merely a presumption against it.

For Thomas, killing as such may be morally evil or morally praiseworthy depending on the circumstances. For him it would be an evil to intend to kill the innocent, that is, given the act as described, no further circumstances can over-ride or outweigh the evil present in the act. This evil would not be *prima facie*. Likewise, justice may sometimes *demand* killing in cases of war or capital punishment. Killing, like sexual intercourse, as an act of nature cannot be morally evaluated, even initially as good or evil, until it is described in more particularity. Surely in the vast majority of cases killing turns out to be wrong; as perhaps in the vast majority of cases sexual intercourse turns out to be morally right, but considered under these bare physical descriptions they are neither right nor wrong in themselves.

The death of the criminal in capital punishment falls under distributive and not commutative justice. Commutative justice, as mentioned earlier, governs the relationship of neighbor to neighbor; distributive justice on the other hand governs the relationships of parts to the whole. Hence, although it is unjust for a neighbor to punish a neighbor, the community as a whole, acting through those with care for the common good, can punish wrongdoers. What is the nature of this punishment? Thomas's account of punishment contains retributive, corrective, and preventative elements, but the retributive element predominates. Punishment as deterrent or preventative could only be just presupposing the punishment was already just retribution.

Natural equity seems to require that anyone be deprived of the good against which he acts, for by it he renders himself unworthy of such a good. And hence it is that, according to civil justice, he who offends against the common good is deprived completely of association with the common good, either by death or by perpetual exile.[51]

For some today, retributive punishment seems unchristian, if not inhumane.[52] Arguing against retributive punishment as a whole, though, seems ill-founded. When this justification for punishment has been excluded, only two common justifications are left, punishment as deterrent/preventative and punishment as reformative/corrective. In some cases, for instance with the very ill or elderly, we can have near certainty that a criminal will not commit the same or similar crimes again. Hence, punishment as reformative for the criminal in these cases cannot be justified. If it can be shown that punishment in general (or in these particular cases) also serves as no deterrent (as arguably has been shown, for instance, with capital punishment), then it would follow that we ought not to punish such criminals at all. If punishment offers no real deterrent and no possible future wrongdoing of like kind is remotely plausible, there should be, on this view, no justification for any punishment.

Such views would, for Thomas, unduly restrict the scope of punishment, which is at least partially to manifest divine justice and not merely for deterring or reforming criminals. Aged war criminals and sickly wrong-doers would, without retributive punishment, literally get away with murder. Take the case of Gregory Scarpa, Sr., "a mafioso with a penchant for brutality, extortion, and murder."[53] Scarpa suffered from a number of physical ailments the last time he stood for sentencing. He was missing his stomach and one of his eyes, but more significantly he suffered from AIDS with a zero-T cell count. Before Judge Jack B. Weinstein, Scarpa pleaded guilty to three murders and conspiracy to the murder of several others. Should Judge Weinstein send

51. See *ScG* III, 144, 4.
52. McCormick, "Notes on Moral Theology: 1984," 52 n.4.
53. Fredrick Dannen, "The G-Man and the Hit Man," *The New Yorker* (December 16, 1996) 68–81, at 68.

Scarpa home as he requested? Though Scarpa in all likelihood, given his health, would never have killed again and though punishment does not seem to deter Mafia gangsters, Judge Weinstein sent Scarpa to prison for the rest of his short life. In similar fashion, highly publicized trials have reminded us that the civil law often allows, over and above recompensatory damages, punitive compensation to be assessed. In fact, it would be treating wrongdoers in an inhumane way to respond to their crimes as if they were no more responsible for the evil they committed than a wild-fire or nefarious virus.

Plato's *Gorgias* famously suggests that it is worse for the wrongdoer himself (and Aquinas might add, for society) not to be punished. Retributive punishment recognizes and respects human responsibility, that which is distinctly human, and responds to this responsibility in an appropriate way.

If Thomas's argument for capital punishment does not fail simply for being retributive, does it fail for other reasons? And if so, where?[54] He bases his justification for capital punishment on the nature of the relation of a part to its whole. The ruler executes the criminal guilty of capital crime:

[J]ust as a physician looks to health as the end in his work, and health consists in the orderly concord of humors, so, too, the ruler of the state intends peace in his work, and peace consists in "the ordered concord of citizens." Now, the physician quite properly cuts off a diseased organ if the corruption of the body is threatened because of it. Therefore, the ruler of the state executes pestiferous men justly and sinlessly in order that the peace of the state not be disrupted.[55]

Acting from the point of view of the community, the executioner does not intend an evil, for the criminal's death is a good both as an instantiation of retributive justice and as the removal of a threat to the common good. Just as the removal of a diseased organ is not an evil but good, so Thomas says as much explicitly

54. Probably the two best discussions of the question are Steven Long, "*Evangelium Vitae*, St. Thomas Aquinas, and the Death Penalty," *The Thomist* 63 (1999) 511–52, and Germain G. Grisez, "Toward a Consistent Natural-Law Ethics of Killing," *American Journal of Jurisprudence* 15 (1970) 64–96.
55. ScG III, 146, 5.

about the value of the criminal's life: "To kill a man maintaining his dignity is evil in itself; nevertheless to kill a sinful man is able to be a good, just as killing an animal: for a bad man is worse than a beast, and more harmful."[56] Like a diseased organ threatening the body, the malicious criminal threatens the body politic, and thus the removal of both is justified in light of the common good.

This justification of capital punishment depends, of course, on a view of the relationship of individual to community that is, to speak understatedly, not widely accepted. It seems highly problematic to many to suppose that the good of individuals in a community must be subordinate to the good of that community. As such, the justification may not persuade many.[57] However, insofar as a defense of just war presupposes just such personification of the community vis-à-vis other threatening communities or individuals, rejecting Thomas's account on this ground also has its theoretical drawbacks. If the picture of the relationship of individual to community drawn by Thomas has its disadvantages, so too does the picture of an autonomous atomized self of modern individualism.[58] Thankfully, these are not the only options.

Some have misunderstood the traditional natural law account as merely the weighing of the good of the individuals versus the good of the community. In the words of O'Connell, the justification of capital punishment, if there is one, is that "the common good of society demands that his right to life be violated. That is, the justification for capital punishment is precisely that another value, the value of societal peace and order, must take precedence over the value of this individual life. It is, in other words, a thoroughly proportional justification."[59] This account of the natural law tradition's justification is incomplete insofar as it is not simply the balancing of an individual versus the

---

56. *ST* II-II, 64, 2, ad 3. *ST* I-II, 92, 1, ad 3.
57. For a critique of Thomas's position on capital punishment, see Germain G. Grisez, "Toward a Consistent Natural-Law Ethics of Killing."
58. On this point, see Alasdair MacIntyre, *After Virtue*, Notre Dame: University of Notre Dame Press, 1984, ch. 3.
59. O'Connell, *Principles for a Catholic Morality*, 168.

communal good that is at stake. If this were the basis of capital punishment, then the killing of the innocent as well as the guilty would be justified whenever the innocent threaten communal well-being. Rather, capital punishment is justified in the tradition *only* under the aegis of retributive justice. Although other conditions must also be met for capital punishment to be justified, it always remains one necessary condition that the one punished be justly *due* punishment. In the words of *Evangelium Vitae:* "The primary purpose of the punishment which society inflicts is 'to redress the disorder caused by the offense."[60]

However, even Thomas's account may not justify capital punishment as it is exercised in modern societies. The malicious criminal, whose threatening presence in the community can truly be described as an evil, should not be killed unless this truly manifests justice and defends the common good. As Steven Long points out, arguably in societies such as our own, prudential considerations mitigate against administering capital punishment.[61] The public misunderstandings of the nature of justice, bias in judicial systems, the possibility of reform, and the demands of mercy suggest that capital punishment should be a last resort. Just as potentially lethal self-defense and the removal of a diseased organ are licit only in those cases in which *no other course of action* can preserve the threatened good, so too capital punishment is justified only in cases where this is *the only way* to defend the common good. There is some discussion about how this good is to be defined. Should the common good be defined in a narrow sense that encompasses only the physical protection of society or is the common good "defined by its relation to a morally transcendent order" such that punishment must also be justified "for the manifestation and vindication of moral truth"?[62] Just as the evolving state of medical technology determines in which cases amputation is the last means available for protecting the life of the body, so too the changing capabilities of prisons

60. John Paul II, *Evangelium vitae,* 56.
61. Steve Long, "*Evangelium Vitae,* St. Thomas Aquinas, and the Death Penalty," 511–52.
62. Ibid., 541.

and other options available to society for punishing criminals determine whether or not capital punishment is the only way
available to defend the common good. On Thomas's account, it
would seem that in modern, Western societies, with sophisticated high-security prisons and problematic understandings of justice and state power, capital punishment might not be justified.
Capital punishment may not be necessary in these societies for
securing the community's well-being; hence, like unnecessary
amputation, capital punishment in such circumstances would
not be justified.

In each of these cases, (1) the deception of another when
necessary to protect an important secret, (2) the amputation of a
leg in order to prevent the spread of disease, (3) the excising of
an organ for transplantation, (4) the pain of a child whom we
spank pedagogically, (4) the killing of another in self-defense, (5)
killing in a just war, and (6) the death of the criminal in capital
punishment, Thomas never holds that we may intend an evil
that good may come.[63] What is taken to be a case of doing evil so
that good may come turns out on further analysis either not to
be morally licit (1, 4) or not to be evil (2, 3, 5, 6). Thomas's account of justice, distributive and commutative, is a key to understanding his teaching on these matters.

63. Thomas then does not justify doing evil so that good may come in any of
these cases, even on a broad account of intention. If one adopts a narrow concept
of intention, one can treat these last three cases of killing differently. Although
each involves "killing," it is not death as such that is sought in the unity of performance of the human acts of self-defense, just war, or capital punishment but
the cessation of aggression in the self-defense and just war or the good of restoring the order of justice in capital punishment. See, for instance, Germain Grisez,
"Toward a Consistent Natural-Law Ethics of Killing," 64–96.

VII. EXCEPTIONLESS NORMS IN THE CATHOLIC TRADITION

Moral norms often arise as various specifications of what is just or unjust. These norms are defined in terms of actions and not end-states. The purpose of such norms is not just to prevent the harm that comes to those who are subject to the actions of others (though they almost inevitably do this as well), but also to prevent harm that would come to the agent himself or herself in undertaking certain courses of action.

For Thomas moral norms that arise from the eternal law help human agents to achieve their happiness, a union with God: "The eternal law first and principally orders man to the end; consequently, however, it makes man related properly to those things which are for the end."[1] The eternal law that enters into the very definition of sin for Aquinas is connected to both the theological and the cardinal virtues.[2] These virtues, in turn, are various specifications of the first principle of practical reasoning in the aspects of the human person. Each of the cardinal virtues corresponds to a certain perfection of the human soul. The negative precepts begin the process of initiation to virtue by enjoining the agent to abstain from evil. The positive precepts bring virtue to greater perfection through the injunction to do good.[3]

1. *ST* I-II, 71, 6, ad 3.
2. *ST* I-II, 72, 4, r; *De malo* q.2, a.6; *ST* I-II, 92, 1.
3. *ST* I-II, 72, 6, ad 2; *ST* I-II, 94, 3, *ST* I-II, 100, 2.

At the structural center of the *Prima secundae,* one finds human action, not law. The internal principles of good human action are the virtues. The external principles of good human action are two-fold, corresponding to the two-fold nature of the human act itself as knowing and willing. These two external principles of human action are law and grace. Law and grace enlighten the intellect and strengthen the will. Just as the intellect and will are inextricably and reciprocally bound up in the human act, so too are law and grace influential on both of the highest human faculties. Law and grace liberate the human person from the four-fold shackle of original sin—ignorance, malice, weakness, and concupiscence—which oppose the virtues of prudence, justice, fortitude, and temperance, thereby freeing the human person to achieve happiness.[4] The importance of law and grace arises from fallen human nature with its darkened intellect and weakened will. God first, according to Thomas, reveals the law so that humanity might know right from wrong. Though the revelation of the Decalogue is a divine mercy, this revelation is a preamble of faith and not a mystery of faith. Human persons can, in principle, know without revelation that which is enjoined by the Decalogue.[5] Like the existence of God itself, moral truths can be gained through unaided reason, but these truths are revealed nevertheless as an aid to the weakness of the human intellect and a protection against an admixture of error. Thomas's understanding of law differs dramatically from characteristically modern conceptions in which law and freedom vie against one another. As noted, grace aids the will of human persons in doing good and avoiding evil. Law and grace are both, in Thomas's account, aids given to help the fallen nature of the human person in achieving his or her goal. Law and grace free the person for pursuit of happiness.

The differences in emphasis and conception of law between the *Summa theologiae* and the manuals that followed are striking. First, the importance of law becomes amplified later in the tradi-

4. *ST* I-II, 85, 3.
5. *ST* I-II, 100, 1.

tion, where the fundamental organizational principle of the moral life is law, knowledge of law (conscience), and ability to comply with law (voluntariness). This contrast is apparent, if one compares the *Summa* with Gury's *Compendium*. Herbert McCabe is not the first to notice that the emphasis in Thomas on law is not especially pronounced.

In my edition of the *Summa Theologiae*, of the 1,496 pages devoted to what we now call "moral theology," Thomas spends just 22 on law, of which seven are directly about natural law. All the rest is concerned in various ways with virtues and vices, though this includes 300 pages on the virtue of justice in which there are, from time to time, references to law.

Gury structures his work quite differently. The subject of law merits at least three separate treatments, *tractatus de legibus, tractatus de praeceptis decalogi,* and *tractatus de praeceptis ecclesiae,* or four if one were to count *tractatus de contractibus* as pertaining primarily to law. Gury, on the other hand, offers no thorough treatment of human action. With no independent treatment of the cardinal virtues of temperance, fortitude, prudence, or justice, only the theological virtues merit mention in Gury's *Compendium*. Gury orders his exposition around law; Thomas orders his around the human person and the human act.

Nor does law seem to have the same function for these later writers as it had for Thomas. In the *Summa*, the Decalogue is God's gift to wayward humankind. It indicates the right and the wrong. In the later tradition, law operates often as a suppression of human liberty,[6] or in a positivistic sense. An act came to be understood as wrong because prohibited by laws or norms, rather than laws and norms arising from the wickedness or the goodness of an act. In contrast to Thomas's conception, law and freedom are pitted against one another. Frequently in modern jurisprudence and philosophy of law, law is understood as constraint and freedom the absence of constraint. According to Isaiah Berlin,

I am normally said to be free to the degree to which no man or body of men interferes with my activity. Political liberty in this sense is simply

6. See Mahoney, *The Making of Moral Theology,* 225–31.

the area within which a man can act unobstructed by others. If I am prevented by others from doing what I could otherwise do, I am to that degree unfree.

He continues: "Law is always a 'fetter' even if it protects you from being bound in chains that are heavier than those of law."[7]

The debates among probabilists, equiprobabilists, and tutiorists in the seventeenth century were symptomatic of this conception of law.[8] As John Mahoney writes:

Given their view of morality as essentially compliance with laws of various kinds, and also given their view of law as primarily the expression of the will of the lawmaker to oblige his subjects to certain types of behavior, it was natural enough that they should view moral dilemmas as problems of doubt, either doubt about the law itself, as to its meaning or extent, or doubt of fact, as to whether this particular situation or case was one actually covered by a particular law.[9]

Seen through Thomas's eyes, inasmuch as law and grace are both gifts from God aiding human persons weakened through the fall, the debates about probabilism seem quite strange.[10] Theologians have never debated, so far as I know, whether or not grace was present in a given situation, so that, were grace not to be present, those acting would be free to do that which grace would have prevented them from doing were it present. How does this historical background relate to present concerns?

Proportionalism argues for different conclusions but presupposes the same questions as a manualistic account of the moral law. Like their predecessors three centuries earlier, proponents of proportionalism invoke even still "probable doubts" in efforts to show that this or that norm does not obtain in this or that case.[11]

---

7. Isaiah Berlin, *Four Essays on Liberty*, 118–72.

8. See Mahoney, *The Making of Moral Theology*, 226–27, 135; Edward Sunshine, "'The Splendor of Truth' and the Rhetoric of Morality," in *Veritatis Splendor: American Responses*, ed. Allsopp and O'Keefe, 157–76; Daniel C. Maguire, "Abortion: A Question of Catholic Honesty," *Christian Century* 100 (1983) 803–7.

9. Mahoney, *The Making of Moral Theology*, 227.

10. Yet, it seems to me that these debates are not altogether foreign from Thomas's thought. See, for example, his question on "Epikeia" (*ST* II-II, 120, 1–2) and other places (e.g. *ST* I-II, 96, 6) wherein the Angelic Doctor discusses when, exactly, one law ceases to bind in favor of a more ultimate law. Even here law is not considered opposed to freedom, but the higher law secures freedom.

11. Richard McCormick, *The Critical Calling: Reflections on Moral Dilemmas Since*

Law is voluntaristic, an expression of one will restricting the freedom of another.[12] The law for Thomas is given primarily to protect agents; the law of the manualists primarily to protect those receiving the action of agents.[13] With the majority of late manuals, proportionalism shares the emphasis on questions of law as central to the moral life and central to the task of the moral theorist. This can be seen both in what it takes to be the fundamental questions: "How do we make exceptions to norms?" and "How do we formulate moral norms?"[14] and in the answer to these questions through a fundamental distinction between two types of norms—the deontological and the teleological.

Although these terms originally come from C. D. Broad, Bruno Schüller first introduced the terms into this debate. We begin with ethical reasoning, according to Schüller, which determines whether deontology, mixed deontology, or teleology should formulate norms. These norms in turn are used to evaluate acts as right or wrong. A particular action is wrong (or right) because it violates (or complies with) a specific norm.

What, however, do these terms "deontology" and "teleology" actually mean? Salzman suggests:

Where concepts of obligation (such as right, duty, ought, and their opposites) take precedence and the concepts of value (good, merit, and their opposites) are identified in terms of them, the theory is deontological. When, however, the reverse is the case and the concepts of value take priority, then the theory is teleological.[15]

Vatican II (Washington, D.C.: Georgetown University Press, 1989) 26; McCormick, *Health and Medicine in the Catholic Tradition* (New York: The Crossroad Publishing Company, 1987) 73.

12. Carol Tauer writes: "Thus, in the *Declaration on Abortion*, the Sacred Congregation was actually considering the scope of the law 'Thou shall not kill'; and its argument, which rejects consideration of even the most probable opinion *favoring liberty*, is inconsistent with the Catholic moral tradition." Carol A. Tauer, "The Tradition of Probabilism and the Moral Status of the Early Embryo," *Theological Studies* 45 (1984) 3–33, at 33, emphasis added.

13. Representing another view, see Talvacchia and Walsh, "The Splendor of Truth: A Feminist Critique," 308.

14. Hence, the title of the book by R. M. Gula, *What Are They Saying about Moral Norms?* (New York: Paulist Press, 1982) 101–4, and the book edited by Charles E. Curran and Richard McCormick, *Moral Norms and Catholic Tradition*. See too, the discussion of proportionalism in McCormick's *Critical Calling*, 134–35.

15. Todd Salzman, *Deontology and Teleology*, 50.

This division is suggestive of, say, the differences between a Kantian-inspired theory and an Aristotelian-inspired one. But it would seem that all involved in the controversy would be on the latter half of that divide. No one in this debate presupposes that something is to be done or avoided simply because naked duty so demands. Rather, for those who hold that there are exceptionless moral norms, the "duty" of the moral law is an injunction to seek that which truly fulfills, truly satisfies, truly makes one happy. Insofar as this is the case, the nomenclature "deontological" is a bit misleading when applied to eudaemonistic accounts of the moral life. The concept of the moral life as a "duty" running contrary to all inclination or happiness arises later with Kant.[16] There are no deontological norms in this sense, at least for Thomas.

Although it is true that proportionalism shares a manualist conception of law, it also changes the scope and application of law in a number of ways, especially by introducing a distinction between formal and material norms. Proportionalism is compatible with exceptionless norms of a certain kind. Formal norms are indeed exceptionless: "Be just," "Be kind," "Do that which love demands." These norms, however, correspond to the goodness of the person and do not answer questions about moral rightness of action. These norms are analytically true.[17] When one understands the terms used in the proposition properly, immediately one recognizes that the predicate is implicit within the subject. It is suggested that "murder is wrong" or "adultery is wrong" is the same sort of sentence as "a bachelor is an unmarried male of marriageable age." Hence, no proportionalist justifies murder or adultery, because these terms by definition include a negative moral evaluation of the act.

In contrast, for proportionalism, rightness and wrongness of

16. Immanuel Kant, *Grundlegung zur Metaphysik der Sitten,* ed. Karl Vorländer (Hamburg: Meiner, 1994) 15.

17. Bruno Schüller writes: "Du sollst Gott aus ganzem Herzen lieben, Du sollst auf ihn Deine ganze Hoffnung setzen usw. Über die ausnahmslose Verbindlichkeit solcher Gebote ist man sich unter Christen einig. Alsdann zählt man dazu Normen wie: Du sollst gerecht handeln, Du sollst nie einen Menschen rechtswidrig töten usf. Diese Normen sind rein analytisch-explikativer Natur, sie sind tautologisch, insofern zweifellos evident, aber wenig hilfreich." "Zur Problematik allgemein verbindlicher ethischer Grundsätze," 3.

action is governed by *material* norms. These norms are not analytically true but synthetically true. The sentence "Jack is a bachelor" may be false or true depending on which Jack is in question and his marital status. Similarly, "one ought never to intentionally kill the innocent" or any other moral norms without value terms such as "unjust," "wrongfully," or terms that exclude any further considerations such as "only" are synthetic. The grounds for the synthetic exceptionless norms in the Catholic tradition, according to the proportionalists, are two-fold: contrariness to nature and lack of right. Both these grounds fail; hence, there are not synthetic material norms of an exceptionless nature.

For proportionalists, one must carefully distinguish the two ways of speaking corresponding to these realms of goodness and rightness. Parenetic discourse belongs to goodness, normative discourse to rightness. In the failure to distinguish parenetic discourse from normative discourse, Richard McCormick finds a fatal error.

We have here a failure to distinguish fact-description *(Tatsachenbegriff)* from value description *(Wertbegriff)*. Certain actions (killing) are present in terms of an already concluded value-description (murder) when the normative question is whether this or that killing is unjust killing, murder. Value-descriptions pertain to the area of parenetic discourse.[18]

Proportionalism fully accepts a number of exceptionless norms, provided these are understood in a formal and not material sense. Hence, proportionalism seeks to preserve our moral intuitions that certain norms are exceptionless, certain acts intrinsically evil. McCormick writes:

For instance, murder, adultery, stealing, genocide, torture, prostitution, slavery, etc., would have no defenders among Catholic theologians. These phrases, Cahill correctly notes, do not define acts in the abstract, "but acts (like intercourse or homicide) together with the conditions or circumstances in which they become immoral." The same is true of intentionally killing an innocent person. Cahill asserts that "about this there is little disagreement."[19]

18. McCormick, *Critical Calling*, 58.
19. McCormick, "Reactions to *Veritatis Splendor*," 492–93. See also McCormick, *Critical Calling*, 58–59; Wolbert, "Die 'in sich schlechten' Handlungen und der Konsequentialismus," 95; Werner Wolbert, "Konsistenzprobleme im Tötungsver-

Proportionalism unfailingly condemns murder, lying, and adultery. These terms are value terms whose condemnation lies in their very definition.[20]

When considered against the backdrop of contemporary philosophy a number of tensions arise for the proportionalist account. Insofar as the distinction between goodness and rightness is problematic, the distinction between formal norms and material norms would be likewise problematic. Likewise, the distinction between analytic statements and synthetic statements arising from Kant, on which the proportionalist account rests, has mostly fallen into disrepute among contemporary philosophers following the lead of Quine.[21] But let us assume these two suppositions for the sake of argument. Is it true, for example, that adultery and murder simply mean "unjust intercourse" and "unjust killing"?

The word "adultery" seems particularly difficult to understand in this tautologous manner. Thomas certainly did not understand "adultery" as meaning analytically "wrongful intercourse." Thomas comments that Aristotle "affirms that, on account of what has been said, people also are of the opinion that the just man can do injustice as readily as anyone else, because from the fact that he is just he knows not less but more and can do any one of the things called unjust, *like having sexual intercourse with another's wife.*"[22] None of the terms in the italicized proposition explicitly indicate moral evil, but it is connected synthetically with the "unjust." Likewise, Thomas defines the word elsewhere non-tautologically in the *Summa:* "Adultery is intercourse with another's wife."[23] Thomas's usage reflects common speech, in

---

bot," *Freiburger Zeitschrift für Philosophy und Theologie* 43 (1996) 203. Salzman, for instance, writes: "Adultery . . . is definitely an evaluative term which contains a negative moral judgment in its very definition." *Deontology and Teleology,* 463.

20. On this point, see, for example, Charles Curran, "*Veritatis Splendor:* A Revisionist Perspective," 236, 238; James Walter, "Joseph Fletcher and the Ends-Means Problematic," *Heythrop Journal* 17 (1976) 59.

21. W. V. O. Quine, "Two Dogmas of Empiricism," *Philosophical Review* 60 (1951) 20–43.

22. *Sententia libri ethicorum* b.5, lect. 15, para. 1076, emphasis added. Thomas does not always speak in this way, however: cf. *Sententia libri ethicorum* b.5, lect. 10, para. 1018.

23. *ST* I-II, 94, 5, ad 2. *De malo* q.2, a.6; Karl Rahner has suggested that an

which it is not senseless to ask, as surveys sometimes do, "Is adultery always wrong" in the way that is it senseless to ask, "Is wickedness, avarice, or pettiness always wrong?"

Certainly adultery has always been condemned in the tradition, but the condemnation is not simply a recognition of the meaning of words. It does not seem right to say that the phrase "another's wife" already implies a transgression of justice the way that "wickedness" or "avarice" does. Clearly, we can think of many circumstances in which "another's wife" has no such connotation.[24] For example, "He saved both his own wife and another's wife from the fire." As John Finnis has noted about the parallel passage in the *Eudemian Ethics*, it is even harder to understand as condemning "adultery" by reference merely to the meaning of the word.[25] The history of commentary on the famous passage in Book II, Chapter 6 of the *Nicomachean Ethics* about intrinsically evil acts accords with the interpretation that "adultery" does not simply mean unjust intercourse.[26] Such intercourse is, in the tradition, always wrong.

Does the word "murder" simply mean "unjust killing"?[27] It does seem true that the word "murder" differs from "adultery" in

---

underlying problem in this debate is the Kantian difficulty in accepting true, universal synthetic judgments. I believe that he is right, but a defense of these judgments takes me too far beyond the tasks at hand, and in any case, is not taken up by the authors discussed here.

24. One might object here by saying that if you examine "deeply" the meanings of the words "intercourse with another's wife" you will find that adultery is intrinsically wrong. In other words, if one sees that the nature of the term "wife" includes the notion of a woman who has morally and until death bound herself to exclusive conjugal union with her husband such that her body becomes his body to which he alone has the right of conjugal union (all of which is included in St. Thomas's notion of a wife), then it would seem that "intercourse with another's wife" (i.e., adultery) becomes in itself evil by definition, provided that one examines the meanings of the term "deeply." This seems not only to read too much into the word "wife" but is especially problematic to maintain in light of some cultures that retain the concept of "wife" without any such prohibition of adultery, e.g, Eskimo and 1970s "wife-swapping" culture.

25. John Finnis, *Moral Absolutes*, 31–37.

26. Ibid., and Christopher Kaczor, "Exceptionless Norms in Aristotle? Thomas Aquinas and Twentieth-Century Interpreters of the *Nicomachean Ethics*," *The Thomist* 61 (1997) 33–62, esp. 56–61.

27. Bernard Hoose, *Proportionalism*, 60; Werner Wolbert, "Konsistenzprobleme im Tötungsverbot," 203; As McCormick writes: "When one intermingles these two [fact and value words] indiscriminately as if there were no difference,

this regard. Common language use suggests that while one can sensibly ask, "Is adultery always wrong?" one cannot sensibly ask, "Is murder always wrong?"

However the common use of "murder" is not the same as its meaning. The word "murder" is most commonly used to express disapproval, e.g., "Fur is murder." The use of a word, however, is not the same as its meaning. As MacIntyre notes:

> The angry schoolmaster, to use one of Gilbert Ryle's examples, may vent his feeling or attitude by shouting at the small boy who has just made an arithmetical mistake, "Seven times seven equals forty-nine!" But the use of this sentence to express feelings has nothing whatever to do with its meaning.[28]

It does not follow then from the use of the word "murder" to express disapproval that "murder" *means* "unjust killing" the way "bachelor" *means* "eligible unmarried male."

This lack of equivalence in meaning can also be shown through substitution. Words or phrases with the same meaning can be substituted in most sentences *salva veritate* without altering the meaning of the sentence. For instance, the sentence "John is a bachelor" does not differ in meaning from "John is an unmarried eligible male." However, we cannot make the same substitutions with "murder" and "unjust killing." Drunk drivers sometimes commit "unjust killing" but they do not commit "murder." Even more clearly, if a person kills the dog of his neighbor because its bark is irritating, there has been an "unjust killing" but not a "murder." "Murder" then does not simply mean "unjust killing."

While the typical proportionalist account of the meaning of the word "murder" encounters these difficulties, there are more sophisticated accounts. Joseph Selling writes: "'Murder' is such a [value] word, for it implies not only what is done (killing) but also the perpetrator's freedom (voluntary) and understanding

---

then one whose analysis justifies a killing is seen as one who justifies *murder* (=unjust killing)" (*Critical Calling*, 136).

28. Alasdair MacIntyre, *After Virtue*, 13; see too, Christopher Kaczor, "MacIntyre and Emotivism: Gaps Between the Meaning and Use of Words," in *Resurrecting the Phoenix*, ed. David Durst (Sophia: EOS Publishing, 1998) 38–46.

(intentional) as well as all the relevant circumstances (this killing was unjustly perpetrated on an innocent person)."[29] This account of the word is in fact the same meaning as that used by the tradition, save for the addition of "unjustly." Is murder intentionally killing the innocent or intentionally killing the innocent unjustly?

The answer to the question depends of course on who is using the word. Let us then distinguish between murder with a synthetic definition, intentionally killing the innocent (murder-s, the traditional definition) and murder with a tautologous definition, intentionally killing the innocent unjustly (murder-t, the proportionalist definition). The debate is about murder-s. We cannot bring reasons for or against a norm forbidding murder-t, for by definition it is always wrong; nor could someone be confused about the fact that murder-t is wrong, once the meaning of the word was made clear. Is the "murder" forbidden by the fifth commandment murder-s or murder-t?

Thomas believes that the Ten Commandments, the primary precepts of the natural law, were revealed by God, even though they could be known by human understanding. They were revealed to clarify that about which human reason could be and had become confused. Now surely, this confusion was not about the meaning of words, but rather about what good was to be done or evil avoided. The primary precepts of the natural law, among them the law forbidding murder *(homicidium)*, were not then, on Thomas's account, merely tautologous statements about which no one could possibly be confused, having understood the meaning of the word. This brings us back to common use of the word.[30]

29. Joseph Selling, *"Evangelium Vitae* and the Question of Infallibility," *Doctrine and Life* 45.5 (May/June 1995) 330–39, at 331.

30. In his article "Problems on Norms Raised by Ethical Borderline Situations: Beginnings of a Solution in Thomas Aquinas and Bonaventure," in *Moral Norms and Catholic Tradition,* ed. Curran and McCormick, Frank Scholz writes: "In distinguishing objectively between 'to kill' and 'to murder' (letter and meaning) Thomas's distinction between factual concept (to kill) and anti-value laden concept (to murder) aids in clarification. The misunderstanding results from the equation of fact and anti-value-laden concepts (to kill = to murder). The solution

It can make sense in common speech to ask, "Is murder always wrong?" This question is often asked when considering scenarios such as the one proposed by Bernard Williams in which one is given the choice between killing a native or allowing someone else to kill ten natives. This seems to indicate that although common *use* of the word is pejorative, expressing in its very use moral condemnation, the common *meaning* of the word is not. For when someone asks, "Why is a bachelor always an unmarried eligible male?" we answer by explaining the meaning of the word "bachelor." However, if asked why murder is wrong or whether murder is always wrong, we would not respond "because of the meaning of the word 'murder'" but by saying that murder violates the requirements of justice, or perhaps God's dominion over human life, or human rights, or the charity due one's neighbor. We would give a reason for the judgment that murder is wrong, not a definition of the word murder.

Are there exceptionless, non-tautological moral precepts governing the moral life? The proportionalist answer is no,[31] and this for a number of reasons we have already seen. Moral norms cannot be exceptionless, it is said, because of the complex nature of the moral life, a response to the concrete particular that is unable to be captured by any rule, no matter how nuanced and complex. The objection from the totality of the concrete situation runs as follows. In the words of Josef Fuchs:

The *a priori,* hence universal, non-historical social ethics that stands opposed to this [taking into account the entire reality of the action], that provides norms in advance for every social reality, sacrifices the indis-

---

to the problem is therefore begun by distinguishing the two concepts" (168). I do not believe that this distinction is in Thomas. The distinction between "Facts" and "Values" (on which a distinction between "factual concepts" and "anti-value laden concepts" rests), usually is traced to Hume's *Treatise on Human Nature* III, 1, 1, written in the eighteenth century (1739), some five hundred years after Aquinas. Such a distinction could not have been maintained by Aquinas, for in Thomas since (if value = good) good, as he says so many times, is convertible with being. Being or Existence, I take to be synonymous with "that which is" or with facts. There could not be, on Thomistic grounds, a fact/value distinction of the kind Scholz reads into the text.

31. Excluding of course what are called "formal" norms or norms such as "counter-productive actions are forbidden without exception."

pensable objectivity and therefore validity of duly concrete solutions to an *a priori* universalism.[32]

Ethics cannot provide "rules" that cover every case, just as we cannot provide a rule-book to cover every eventuality in medicine or navigation. Just as we cannot navigate a ship to shore or cure a patient by means of *a priori* rules which cannot possibly take into account every specific detail crucial for right action, so too in the ethical sphere we cannot possibly have rules be our guide without sacrificing the particular. Certain rules may be "virtually exceptionless,"[33] but every (non-tautologous) rule is, in principle, open to exception.

It is not clear that various kinds of norms have been properly distinguished. There are four different possible types of norms: (1) positive norms admitting exception, (2) positive norms admitting no exception, (3) negative norms admitting exception, and (4) negative norms admitting no exception. Let us clarify what is meant by each category of norms in turn.

Most positive moral norms admit exception; for example, "Return borrowed objects," "Take care of your spouse and children," and "Pay back debts as promised." These norms do not need to be considered at all times, nor do they bind all agents at all times. If one has not borrowed objects, then one need not observe the norm: "Return borrowed objects." Even if one has borrowed an object, let us say a sword, and the owner intends to kill himself with it, again one is not bound to return the sword, because one judges that not returning the sword in this case is a rightful exception of the positive norm that applies *in pluribus*.[34]

However, other positive norms apply always and without ex-

---

32. Josef Fuchs, "The Absoluteness of Moral Terms," in *Moral Norms and Catholic Tradition*, ed. Curran and McCormick, 115.

33. See, for example, Louis Janssens, "Norms and Priorities in a Love Ethics," 207 and 217–18; and Richard McCormick, *Notes on Moral Theology, 1965 through 1980*, 710.

34. Thomas recognizes this: "Such is the nature of human actions that they are not done always in the same way but are done otherwise in certain infrequent instances. For example, the return of a deposit is in itself just and good, as it happens in most cases, but in a particular situation it can be bad, for instance, if a sword is returned to a madman" (*Sententia libri ethicorum* b.5, lect. 16, para. 1085). Advocates and opponents of proportionalism offer different accounts of

ception. We are always and without exception bound by the norm: We are to love God with all our heart and our neighbor as ourselves.[35] Norms such as these are true, but the norm is so general that it often lacks practical application, not in the sense that one cannot apply it, but that applying the rule constitutes one of the difficulties of the moral life.[36]

The third type of norm, negative but not exceptionless, likewise helps us to make prudential judgments but does not and cannot be our sole guide to action. W. D. Ross in *The Right and the Good* called these guidelines *prima facie* duties. Examples of these types of norms include "Do not break promises," "Do not inflict pain," and "Do not put your life in danger." A morally good agent keeps these in mind as important rules of thumb that help guide people to know what many situations, but not all, demand.

For Thomas and for the Catholic tradition as a whole, there are also norms that the one seeking to be morally good must not violate under any circumstances. Norms of this type include the Ten Commandments. For Thomas, these norms are exceptionless and non-tautological.

Let us return to Fuchs's objection, an objection that gains support, it would seem, from Aristotle:

Questions about actions and expediency, like questions about health, have no fixed answers. While this is the character of our general account, the account of particular cases is still more inexact. For these fall under no craft or profession; the agents themselves must consider in each case what the opportune action is, as doctors and navigators do.[37]

---

why this, justly refusing to return borrowed objects, is the case, but they agree that it is the case.

35. Louis Janssens concurs in identifying the existence of such norms: "The formal norms constitute the absolute element of morals. For instance, it will remain true, that always and in all circumstances, we must be just" ("Norms and Priorities in a Love Ethics," 208).

36. Ibid., 208–9. He writes: "Formal norms do not determine the concrete content of our actions. There is, for example, the norm requiring us to be chaste: we have to order our sexuality in such a way that we respect ourselves as human subjects, our relationship to others, and the demands of social life. The formal norm, though describing our inner attitude, does not tell us which concrete actions are able to embody a chaste disposition."

37. Aristotle, *Nicomachean Ethics*, 1104a3–10 (Irwin).

William Charlton glosses this statement by saying: "Aristotle would hold, then, that a general principle of conduct can establish at best a prima facie rightness *and wrongness* . . ."[38] The italicized portion of Charlton's gloss does not have support in the Aristotelian text cited. We cannot determine "what is advantageous," Aristotle says. He does *not* say that we cannot determine what is disadvantageous or what is wrong in the sense of exclusive of the end. In NE 1107a 1–22, Aristotle indicates some actions that he considers inherently disadvantageous. Thomas in the *Sententia libri ethicorum* concurs with Aristotle's judgment in commenting on this passage, and he confirms the point elsewhere.[39]

Aristotle and Thomas draw analogies between the practice of virtue and the arts of medicine and seamanship.[40] To be sure, these analogies indicate the way in which the moral life cannot be simply deduced from universal norms; yet these analogies tell us more than that alone. Is it not the case that in these activities there are certain individual acts such that to do them is not to do these activities well? In the art of medicine, the art of healing, it is without doubt true that the proper medicine to give to an ailing patient cannot be learned by deduction from an *a priori* universal norm, but it is also the case that certain treatments ought never to be given to the patient whom one is trying to heal. Before considering all the relevant and particular characteristics of a patient, a medical doctor cannot determine whether Theodur, Serevent, or Proventil will best alleviate the bronchitis of an asthmatic. But the doctor does know that forcing the patient to inhale car exhaust will not help his condition. The art of seamanship as analogous to the moral life suggests that rules have a part, but only a small part, to play in the moral life.[41] Although it is the case that we cannot sail a boat to shore by *a priori* positive

---

38. William Charlton, *Weakness of the Will* (New York: Blackwell, 1988) 117, emphasis added.

39. Cf. *Sententia libri ethicorum* b.2, lect. 7, para. 329. For a further exposition, see Christopher Kaczor, "Exceptionless Norms in Aristotle?"

40. See Martha Nussbaum, *The Fragility of Goodness* (New York: Cambridge University Press, 1987) 303.

41. Ibid.

dictates, this is not to say that we cannot thwart the effort to move a ship to shore by violating negative precepts. Given that winds and waters vary in channels and seas, the ship's captain must make prudential judgments in light of relevant and highly specific factors to chart a course for port. In sailing, without experience and knowledge of relevant particulars, one cannot say whether or not a port tack upwind is or is not more advantageous than running a spinnaker downwind. However, certain negative norms apply if we want to sail a ship at all. Thus, it is an exceptionless norm of this activity that we must not destroy the ability of the boat to float. To cause the boat to sink is to exclude naturally and necessarily the end of moving that boat in to shore. Similarly then, intentionally to kill an innocent person (to murder), to have sexual intercourse with the spouse of another (to commit adultery), to say what one believes is untrue under oath (to perjure oneself), or to take that which is not one's own (to steal) is to act against the virtue of justice. In terms of the ordering of activities to one another described in Chapter V, there can be no advantage to be gained from "premoral goods" that would justify exceptions to these norms. However, what we ought to do remains always within the realm of prudential judgment, as what we ought to do in sailing or the medical art cannot be determined by rule.

Is the Tradition Overwhelmingly Teleological?

Do non-tautological exceptionless norms contradict the entire tendency of the rest of the Catholic tradition of moral reasoning? Is McCormick right to suggest: "Anyone familiar with the centuries-old tradition of Catholic moral theology would have to agree with Schüller 'that the normative ethics of Catholic tradition . . . is overwhelmingly teleological.'"[42] The claim that the Catholic tradition is overwhelmingly teleological is clearly an historical one. And this claim is rather specific and far reaching. That is, save for three areas of human conduct, marriage, acts

42. McCormick, *Critical Calling*, 63.

contrary to nature, and the taking of innocent human life, the tradition made judgments about right or wrong by reference to the greater good or the lesser of two evils. Even the norms governed in these areas are parsed so as to include teleological considerations and narrow the inflexibility of exceptionless precepts.

The truth or falsity of this view can be assessed only on the basis of evidence brought forward from the testimony of Scripture, patristic teachers, doctors of the Church, councils, schoolmen, Pontiffs, saints and martyrs. Schüller's assertion is true insofar as one looks at how exceptions were made to both positive law and what were referred to above as positive exceptionless precepts. On a wide range of issues, this teleological orientation is quite pronounced. A preference for the greater good or lesser evil is prevalent in traditional reasons justifying disobedience of human law or authority such as dispensation from Sunday observance, the breaking of promises, secret keeping, the obligation to say the divine office, and the duty of fraternal correction.[43] These exceptions, however, are either for positive ecclesiastical laws or those positive norms talked about above which do not apply in every circumstance (e.g., return borrowed objects).

The historical record is, however, more rich and varied than Schüller's account suggests. Although it is true to say that the Catholic tradition of moral inquiry is, in certain instances and aspects, teleological, i.e., showing a preference for the greater good or lesser evil, there seems to be an equally strong rejection of such a tendency, especially insofar as this teleology is understood as a demand to be "impartially beneficial" to all persons.[44]

A rejection of this form of teleology is shown throughout the patristic, medieval, and modern tradition—for instance, in (1) the distinction between precept and counsel designating two courses of licit action, even though following counsel secures a greater good than merely following precept; (2) the division between heroic or supererogatory acts and ordinary acts, in which the heroic act achieves a greater good or avoids a greater evil,

---

43. Hallet, *Greater Good*, 42–43.
44. Schüller, "Double Effect: A Reevaluation," 183.

but the ordinary act is nevertheless licit; (3) the prerogative to protect one's own life in self-defense, even at the risk of a greater number of attackers's lives; (4) the division between active and contemplative lives, which assumed that the contemplative life was the "better part" but that the active life was nevertheless fully permitted; (5) the traditional understanding of the Pauline prohibition of doing evil so that good may come; (6) the prohibition against baptizing the infants of unbelievers, though the good of salvation is greater than the good of respecting the wishes of others;[45] (7) the denial that one ought to bring about the death of a pregnant woman in order to baptize an unborn child in danger of death, though the moral good of salvation is greater than the non-moral good of life;[46] (8) the prohibition against various forms of coercion in leading a non-Christian to religious belief, though suffering coercion is a lesser evil than lacking faith; (9) the legitimacy of the use of painkillers, though sacrificial suffering may be a greater good; (10) the assertion that the status of the person sinned against and the status of the person sinning make a difference in the gravity of sin;[47] (11) the view that those taking religious vows have chosen a better part than mere secular priests though both vocations are fully licit;[48] and finally, of course, (12) the numerous other norms, many of which are involved in this controversy, such as those governing lying, taking of innocent life, revealing the secrets of the confessional, renouncing faith, and engaging in unnatural sexual activity. Given these aspects of the tradition, it is overstating the case considerably to say that the tradition is "overwhelmingly" teleological in its preference for the greater good or lesser evil.

Similarly, the narrowing of the scope of moral norms in the tradition, though true enough when understood in a modest way, is exaggerated and put to use as an apologetic for "making the tradition consistent with itself" through adoption of proportionate reason applicable to all (conflict) situations. The argument begins with the observation that the tradition gave a more

45. *ST* II-II, 10, 12.
47. *ST* I-II, 78, 8; *ST* I-II, 78, 10.
46. *ST* III, 68, 11, ad 3.
48. *ST* I-II, 98, 5, ad 3.

and more restrictive interpretation of the norm forbidding lying.[49] Although Augustine forbade speech *contra mentem* even to
save innocent life, and following him Aquinas also condemned
all lies, later scholastics permitted narrow and sometimes wide
"mental reservations." One may utter a misleading statement,
but qualify it mentally in such a way that the statement is true.
Still later scholastics narrowed the norm even further by adding
to the definition of lying that the one deceived "must have a
right to the truth." Proportionalism is the final and logical step in
this development. In light of the fact that arguments from contrariness to nature fail, proportionalism simply recognizes and
develops a tradition of restrictive interpretation to its logical conclusion: one can speak a falsehood, but only for a proportionate
reason.[50]

Regarding the taking of human life, proportionalism offers a
similar history and a similar conclusion. "Thou shall not kill"
seems absolute and exceptionless, but in fact this norm governing the most important of values is parsed teleologically.[51] Tradition sanctioned exceptions to this norm, e.g., capital punishment, just warfare, and self-defense.[52] The norm forbidding
killing does not forbid all killing of human beings but only the *direct* killing of the *innocent*. These qualifiers are added to make
room for killings in war, in self-defense, and in cases of removal
of a gravid cancerous uterus. The norm forbidding killing has
been narrowed in light of teleological considerations. Like lying,
over time the norm forbidding murder has been narrowed, to
"one may not to kill the innocent." Even this norm, however, is
narrowed even more by the addition, one may not *directly* kill
the innocent. But even this rule is subject to exception. Abraham, after all, was ordered by God to kill his innocent son Isaac.
Killing the innocent intentionally was said to be wrong, *ex defectu*

49. For a short history supporting these theses, see Ugorji, *The Principle of Double Effect*, 124–33.
50. Cf. Bruno Schüller, "Zur Problematik allgemein verbindlicher ethischer Grunsätze," 7.
51. McCormick, *Notes on Moral Theology, 1981 through 1984*, 4; McCormick, *Critical Calling*, 64.
52. James Gaffney, "The Pope on Proportionalism," 63.

juris in agente, from a defect of right in the agent. We cannot kill in this way because God has not given permission for us to kill in this way. Insofar as we are to have a rational and not voluntaristic basis for norms, and insofar as we cannot say when God does or does not give permission to kill, the basis for any exceptionless norms in this area is lacking. "The rule is, in a sense, as acceptable as it is capable of being restricted to accommodate our sense of right and wrong, and our firm commitment to save more lives than we lose in situations of conflict."[53] We may kill, but only for a truly proportionate reason.

There are both historical and philosophical grounds for questioning these conclusions. The historical reality of the treatment of lying and of the taking of human life in the Catholic tradition is a good deal more complex, varied, and nuanced than the account suggested by proportionalism.[54] In the early patristic tradition, lying was not universally condemned in cases of "necessity," though in some quarters, particularly by Augustine, it was severely condemned.[55] With the rise of Augustine's prominence in general, and given that Augustine was the only patristic author who wrote extensively on the topic, the views expressed in *De mendacio* and *Contra mendacium* became widely accepted. Augustine defined a lie, or at least that which surely must be a lie, as "speaking falsely for the sake of deceiving."[56] Later scholastics of the high Middle Ages, such as Aquinas and Bonaventure, as a whole but not exclusively tended to accept a definition of lying that was broader. Any speech *contra mentem* was regarded as a lie regardless of intention to deceive. Some authors in the seventeenth through nineteenth centuries introduced an addition to the definition of the lie: that the one deceived must have a "right to the truth" in order for the falsehood to be truly a lie. We have then, in the broadest terms, not a norm that is steadily restricted

53. McCormick, *Critical Calling*, 64.
54. The best source on the topic is still Gregory Müller's *Die Wahrhaftig-keitspflicht und die Problematik der Lüge* (Freiburg: Verlag Herder, 1962). I rely on his treatment throughout the historical analysis of lying.
55. Hence, "lying" was not, by either party, considered merely wrong by definition.
56. *De mendacio* 5.

in light of teleological considerations but one that changes over time with various authors, characteristically being most rigorous during the high Middle Ages and less so in both the patristic and neoscholastic eras.

However, even in the relative laxity of the seventeenth century, the norm governing lying was not progressively narrowed. Consider the following example taken from the Dean of Durham writing to Lord Salisbury, State Papers of 5 February 1606, the interrogation of a suspected Catholic during religious persecutions.

First he swore he was no priest, that is, saith he (in subsequent explanation), not Apollo's priest at Delphi. Second, he swore he was never across the sea, it's true he saith, for he was never across the Indian Seas. Third, he was never at or of the Seminaries. *Duplex est Seminarium, materiale et spirituale*, he was never of the spiritual seminary. Fourthly, he never knew Mr. Hawksworth; it is true, saith he, *scientia scientifica*. Fifthly, he never saw Mr. Hawksworth, true, he saith, *visione beatifica*.[57]

The "broad reservations" employed by the Jesuit speaker in this example were never universally endorsed, though for a time they were widely endorsed. In fact, the trend of broadening exceptions is reversed later in the tradition. The common opinion on the matter changed in the seventeenth century, and finally the "broad reservation" was condemned both by casuists and then, in 1679, by Holy Office.[58]

Moral norms governing lying were not simply progressively narrowed on teleological grounds, but underwent shifts that reflected shifting definitions of the "lie"[59] and various shifts in the vocabulary and frameworks used by authors to conceptualize and speak about the moral life. Nor are proportionalists capturing the full diversity of the history when they assert that lying is

57. Jonsen and Toulmin, *The Abuse of Casuistry*, 205.
58. Ibid., 214. It is this historical account on which I have based my remarks here.
59. The three most popular are the asserting of something believed to be false, the asserting of something believed to be false with the intention of deception, and the asserting any proposition with the intention of deception. Note that none of these definitions defines a "lie" as morally wrong simply by definition. In fact, some early Fathers in fact spoke of a justified lie, which of course would be nonsense were "lie" simply to mean an unjustified speaking of a falsehood.

said to be wrong because *contra naturam* without mentioning other reasons given in the tradition.

Gregory Müller's magisterial survey of the tradition on lying *Die Wahrhaftigkeitspflicht und die Problematik der Lüge* suggests that the justification of the exceptionless prohibition on lying in the Catholic tradition, indeed in the broad tradition of Western philosophy, is more varied and complex than a mere appeal of contrariness to nature. Augustine and Thomas do indeed suggest that lying is wrong because it perverts the faculty of speech and as such is activity contrary to nature. However, they also both suggest that lying is wrong because contrary to the virtue of truthfulness and contrary to Scripture. As the development of moral thought in the Catholic tradition became systematically divorced both from a conception of virtues and from its relationship to Scripture, these arguments were left behind. When advocates of proportionalism examine the history of the prohibition against lies, it is this truncated tradition to which they usually turn, or when reading earlier authors, it is in light of this truncated tradition that the patristic and medieval sources are read. Hence, the proportionalist history would lead us to conclude that lying was held to be wrong solely because contrary to nature.

Augustine, as well as so many others in the tradition, adds other arguments against lying that have not yet undergone scrutiny and that seem to be entirely absent from the literature. For instance, Augustine suggests the liar in speaking untruth, introduces into himself or herself a division and discord inconsistent with proper love of self, and therefore love of neighbor. Lying with the mouth then introduces a lie in the soul. The soul of the liar is then divided, part holding fast to truth, but part embracing a lie.[60] This alienation from oneself constitutes sin.

Secondly, for Augustine, lying *ipso facto* separates one from God, insofar as one cannot separate oneself from the truth and not separate oneself from God who is the truth. Since God is our greatest good, it never makes sense to lie.[61] These reasons may be

60. Augustine, *Contra mendacium* 7, 17.
61. Augustine, *De moribus ecclesiae catholicae* 13 (CSEL 90). Boniface Ramsey,

more or less persuasive, but to this point in the discussion these arguments from very traditional sources have not been treated at all. For instance, Müller notes some 63 arguments given by Catholic authors and some 26 by non-Catholics against lying.[62] Likewise untreated are the arguments of contemporary philosophers including Jorge Garcia, Sissela Bok, and Alasdair MacIntyre for either exceptionless or nearly exceptionless prohibition of lying.

What may drive Augustine and Aquinas to this conclusion, the "hard saying" that one ought not lie even to preserve innocent human life, is the example so present and central in the tradition of the martyrs. Augustine notes that the opinion that lying is sometimes permissible for the sake of a greater good makes the martyrs of the Christian Church evil-doers or at the very least fools rather than models to be imitated.

This judgment dishonors the holy martyrs, in fact it abolishes martyrdom altogether. For they would have acted more justly and wisely, according to these people, if they had not professed themselves to be Christians to their persecutors and by their confession make them killers. Rather they should have, by lying and denying what they were, preserved the advantage of the flesh and the intention of the heart and not allowed their persecutors to carry out the wicked deed they had already conceived.[63]

If the rightness of an act is determined by the foreseen non-moral goods (life, health, culture), then the martyrs of the Christian tradition clearly did the wrong act. Foreseeing that they would die and that their families, friends, and fellows be bereft of their presence (a great premoral evil) and that their persecutors would be killers (possibly a great moral evil), they chose instead to speak the truth (a relatively small premoral good) and not to tell an untruth with the intention of deceiving (a relatively small premoral evil).

However, to deny Christ, one might respond, is to act against

---

"Two Traditions on Lying and Deception in the Ancient Church," *The Thomist* 49 (1985) 504–33, at 512.

62. Gregory Müller, *Die Wahrhaftigkeitspflicht und die Problematik der Lüge*, 321–25 and 327–30.

63. Augustine, *Contra mendacium* 3.

the good of salvation. One cannot, on proportionalist grounds, act against a moral good such as salvation. However, this response fails on two counts. It is true that, according to common Christian belief, for a Christian to reject Christ would be to act against a moral good, but why would it be against a moral good for the Christian merely to *say* that he or she rejected Christ, when in fact the Christian did not? In addition, a number of martyrs, for instance Thomas More, were required, not to deny Christ, but rather merely to give assent to some contingent fact that they knew was not in fact the case. Is the King's marriage legitimate or not? A simple lie, which hurts no one and helps many, the least sinful kind of lie for Augustine and Aquinas, would have saved More's life.

One response is that the martyrs, by not lying, set a good precedent that leads others in the future also to heroic goodness. One should not deny that one is a believer, because this denial could have a snowball effect on others. Saints Thomas More and John Fisher provide heroic models of personal integrity for others to follow. This consequence of the act must itself be included in whatever calculations are made. Given this very good effect that follows from not denying that one is a believer, then to deny that one is a believer (when in fact one really is) is to do the wrong act.

This "precedent effect" argument, that one ought not to lie in a particular situation because of the precedent such a lie would have on others, has certain weaknesses. In many cases, for instance the disappearance in 1996 of Bishop Su Chimin in China, the public at large has no idea whether or not the believer eventually lied, denied the faith, or not. If the believer could reasonably foresee that the lie would never come to light, then there would be in fact no need to factor in the effect of precedent.

Secondly, the precedent effect seems to be a consideration mostly for "high profile" persons such as Thomas More rather than for mere plain persons. Perhaps, the sin of the high profile person is accidentally worse than the sin of the normal person, insofar as it causes scandal. But are the standards judging the acts themselves different for the two classes of persons? In the end, according to Bernard Williams, the precedent effect rests on confusion. For whom would the lie be a precedent? If someone were in an identical situation—one must either lie or face terrible persecution—then once again one should lie. If one is in a significantly different situation—one must either lie or suffer embarrassment—then the original situation serves as no true precedent.[64]

For Augustine, the conclusion that the martyrs acted wickedly is unacceptable, and he assumes that his Christian audience, both Catholic and Priscillian, would find this unacceptable as well.[65] The martyrs died rather than tell what Thomas would have considered the most venial of lies, i.e., a lie about a contingent fact that hurts no one and helps others. If it is a repugnant conclusion that one cannot lie to save innocent life, including the life for which one has greatest responsibility, it may be an equally repugnant conclusion that the martyrs were in fact modeling not virtue but foolishness and material wrongdoing.

Let us return, however, to the other norm in question, forbidding the killing of the innocent. Once again the history offered by proportionalism is rather incomplete. Some aspects of what is taken to be a teleological approach to parsing norms stem from the manualist habit of considering norms the fundamental coin of moral discourse and understanding all other moral terms in their relationship to norms. Within the more modest and limited account of moral norms adopted by Thomas, the distinction "direct versus indirect"—or better, the intentional versus the unintentional or merely foreseen—is not simply a contrivance that is useful for limiting the scope of norms. The

64. Bernard Williams and J. J. C. Smart, *Utilitarianism: For and Against* (Cambridge: Cambridge University Press, 1973) 107.

65. John Finnis concurs: "The oppressors, the tempters, the crowd, all persuasively present the [proposed] act as an evil lesser than death, disgrace, ruin for the martyr's family; a Thomas More or a Maria Goretti judges the act to be wrong *per se* and *in se* and, precisely because immoral, to be an evil greater than any amount of evil set in train by refusing to choose such an act." Finnis, *Moral Absolutes*, 9.

concept of intention is not simply an instrument for gerrymandering norms to avoid bad consequences, but rather the distinction is that which defines a performed act as this or that kind of act. In the same way, for Thomas, the difference between a private person taking guilty human life and a person acting on behalf of the common good taking guilty human life arises from characteristics of the virtue of justice. That such considerations limit the number of cases in which norms forbidding killing would apply is true enough, but intention or the characteristics of a virtue are not invoked so that norms can be parsed. The specification that the innocent should not be killed arises not from a desire to narrow the application of a norm but rather from an account of the virtue of justice. For Thomas, rules are to be understood as related to the central concepts of intentions, virtues, and human actions and the human end. In the manualists and the proportionalists following them, intentions, virtues, and human actions are to be understood in relation to what is seen as central to the moral life—rules.

As in the case of lying, the history of norms forbidding killing in the Catholic tradition is a good deal more complex than the proportionalist account would suggest. Exceptions to norms forbidding killing were in fact broadened until sometime in the late manualistic period. It was suggested by some that, since one could intend to kill to protect one's property, and since honor is a good greater than property, one could licitly kill another for merely an injury to one's honor, e.g., an insult.[66] However, from this high-water mark of permission, the norm restricting killing has been steadily broadened, not narrowed, by both schoolmen and the magisterium so as to admit fewer and fewer exceptions. This is true especially in the recent history: Pius XII made the criteria for waging a just war more demanding, the Statement on Liberation Theology renounced the use of violence to overthrow injustice, and John Paul II suggested in *Evangelium vitae* that the just use of capital punishment was very rare, if not non-existent,

66. For a more detailed account, see Jonsen and Toulmin, *The Abuse of Casuistry.*

in modern societies. The "consistent life ethic" is an expression of this effort at broadening of the scope of the norm forbidding killing, rather than limiting it in favor of "teleological" considerations.

The basis for the absolute prohibition against intentionally killing the innocent is also rather misplaced in the proportionalist history. Thomas, in the *Summa theologiae*, suggests that killing the innocent is licit if God gives such a command.[67] Revisionists, perhaps following earlier manualists,[68] are led to the conclusion that killing the innocent is wrong *ex defectu juris* or from a lack of authorization. Killing the innocent is wrong, notes one author, *"precisely because of a lack of right* given to human beings by God to take life is this way."[69] Unlike those who follow him, Thomas, in his discussion of the liceity of killing the innocent, does not trace the wrongness of murder simply to lack of right.[70] As in the case of suicide, one aspect of the wrongness of murder is this lack of right, but there are other aspects as well, such as the lack of charity displayed by the act and injury to the community.

Divine Dispensations and Moral Perplexity

The denial of the norm excluding intentionally killing the innocent, at least insofar as this denial depends on an analysis of *"ex defectu juris,"* is based on invalid reasoning, which begins with the premise that God can authorize the killing of the innocent and argues to the conclusion that killing the innocent is wrong because of lack of authorization. But what may be said of this premise? Usually, it is presupposed that God may kill an innocent person because in the Old Testament it appears that God had indeed given authorization for such acts. Thomas based his judgment that one could licitly kill the innocent given God's authorization on his reading of the Old Testament, a reading that prominent modern Scripture scholars have rejected. Three fa-

---

67. *ST* II-II, 64, 6, ad 1.
68. Gury, *Compendium theologiae moralis*.
69. McCormick, "A Commentary on the Commentaries," 217.
70. He does, however, argue in this way against suicide: see *ST* II-II, 64, 5.

mous cases illustrate a similar problem: Abraham's choice to sacrifice Isaac (Gen. 22:1–19), Hosea's marriage to a prostitute (Hos.
1:2), and the Israelites's plundering of the Egyptians (Ex. 12:35).
Does Scripture suggest that God commanded murder, adultery,
and theft? According to proportionalist L. U. Ugorji:

> [Modern] exegetes do not take these texts literally. The first is seen as a
> test of Abraham's faith. The fathers saw it as prefiguring the passion of
> Jesus, the only begotten Son. The second is seen as symbolically repre-
> senting Yahweh's marriage with Israel. In spite of Israel's repeated acts of
> flirtation with alien gods, Yahweh still loves this faithless people and
> cherishes them when they repent. The third, the willingness of the
> Egyptians to provide gold, silver, and clothing, is explained to match the
> Egyptian mentality: God has proved his strength, to allow his people to
> leave empty-handed is an affront.[71]

Insofar as modern moral theology relies on modern commen-
taries on Scripture, it would seem that the problem faced by
Thomas, the problem of reconciling exceptionless norms with
God's commands to break exceptionless norms, no longer exists.

What if we took these *prima facie* exceptions as a given? "[I]f
God can command certain acts (such as killing, and I know of no
one who doubts He can), this shows that such acts are not intrinsically evil in May's sense, scil., that one necessarily takes on the
moral character of an evildoer in performing them."[72] The question is a deep one, and may be rephrased as follows: Does God
intend or choose *per se* non-moral evils?

The disagreements among the authors in question extend to
the very notion of God's power and will. Hallet, Schüller, Dedek,
Milhaven, Walter, and McCormick assert that God can will *per se*
non-moral evils, but not moral evils. Finnis asserts that willing
any sort of evil, moral or non-moral, is incompatible with the
goodness of God. On which side would Aquinas fall?

In the *Summa contra Gentiles*, Thomas argues that God as the

71. Ugorji, *The Principle of Double Effect*, 107; see also corresponding commentaries in *The Jerome Biblical Commentary*, ed. R. E. Brown et al. (Englewood Cliffs,
N.J.: Prentice Hall, 1974).

72. McCormick, *Notes on Moral Theology, 1965 through 1980*, 767.

greatest good cannot be mingled with any evil whatsoever. Hence, the divine will cannot be turned to evil.[73] Further, willing evil always presupposes some intellectual lack, a lack incompatible with God's intelligence; hence, Aquinas concludes that God cannot will evil. In his *Disputed Questions on Evil (De malo),* Aquinas argues that only a defective good is the cause of evil, and insofar as God is in no way defective, he can in no way be the *per se* cause of evil.[74] God as the greatest good can will *per se* no evil whatsoever and only *permits,* that is foresees but does not intend, certain evils such as sinning in order to preserve some other good that would be impeded were the evil removed—in this example, the good of human freedom.

To my knowledge, only one text of Thomas seems to contradict this view and suggest that God could indeed will non-moral evils, the proportionalist view. In *ST* I, 19, 9, Thomas says:

> [God] in no way wills the evil of sin, which is the privation of right order toward the divine good. The evil of natural defect, or of punishment, He does will, by willing the good to which such evils are attached. Thus in willing justice He wills punishment; and in willing the preservation of the natural order, He wills some things to be naturally corrupted.[75]

Walter interprets this as meaning that God wills non-moral evils *per se* for the sake of a greater good, but does not will moral evils for the sake of the greater good. Hence, God himself gives us a model of proportionate reason in action, though certain differences would have to be acknowledged between God's agency and human agency, such as omniscience.

How might one reconcile these two sets of texts? In the response to the third objection, Thomas himself suggests a possible way.[76] God wills to permit evil to be done, and in this sense God wills evil though it is willing evil not *per se* but only *per accidens.* In other words, God's permission of evil is foreseen, "indirect," or

73. *ScG* I, 95.
74. *De malo* q.3, a.1, ad 14.
75. Translation of this passage is from the Blackfriars (English Dominican Province) edition of the *Summa Theologica.*
76. Cf. Finnis, *Moral Absolutes,* 76

not intended, rather than a means or a choice *per se*.[77] God wills all good in the created order directly, all physical evil in the created order indirectly (i.e., God wills *per accidens* and indirectly physical evil, in the sense that God refers the good to which the physical evil is annexed to the good to which the evil is opposed), and God only wills to permit the existence of all moral evil in the created order without willing it directly or indirectly. One could also add the following argument to others in order to show that it is impossible for God to will pre-moral evil *per se:* God's will has for its object the Divine Essence which is Goodness Itself. But evil does not fall within this Object, for goodness and evil are opposed as contraries. Therefore, God cannot have for the object of His Will evil *per se*. As a result, God cannot be the *per se* cause of pre-moral evil.

At least two counterexamples may be cited against the considerations brought forward thus far concerning God's willing evil. Both of these counterexamples come from Thomas's Christology. It would seem that Christ, on Thomas's account, fully foresaw and indeed willed his own death as a means to our salvation. He willed a non-moral evil (death) for the sake of some greater good (salvation). Secondly, Christ is even said by Thomas to be the judge of the damned. He wills damnation, certainly a great evil, for the sake of some good, namely justice. Insofar as Christ is fully God and fully man, we have evidence that God wills non-moral evil. Insofar as Christians are called to follow Christ, it seems that we have grounds for a Christian proportionalism.

Although at times Thomas speaks ambiguously on this matter, in the final analysis, Christ did not, on Thomas's account, intend or choose his own death as a means or an end. Such an act would be suicide rather than martyrdom. Rather, he willed to allow himself to be killed by others. As Thomas puts it in the *Compendium*: "Christ had it in his power to submit his nature to the destructive cause or to resist that influence, just as he willed.

---

77. On this, see Stephen Brock, *Action and Conduct*.

Thus, Christ died voluntarily, and yet the Jews killed him."[78] Christ thus foresaw and accepted voluntarily his death, but he did not make a choice to or intend to kill himself. Like a martyr, he could have avoided his fate, yet he accepted it as the price for maintaining fidelity. Christ in condemning the damned wills that justice is done, a good that is conceptually distinct from the willing of evil. Such punishment is a restoration of justice, a restoration that *consists in* the deprivation of the wrongdoer's will.[79] As Aquinas says in *De malo:*

[I]t is not necessary that a good which is the accidental cause of evil be a deficient good. And in this way God is the cause of the evil of punishment, for in punishing he does not intend evil to the one punished but the imprinting of the order of his justice on human affairs, on which follows the evil of the one punished, just as the privation of the form of water follows on the form of fire."[80]

This deprivation of the wrongdoer's will is itself a good, namely, the restoration of justice; hence, it can be willed by an all-good God.

The idea that God wills non-moral evils as a means to an end is found not in Thomas, nor in Damascene, nor in Trent. Indeed, all of these authorities deny that God can will any evil *qua* evil (i.e., *per se*), as a means or an end.[81] The idea may be found among manualists such as J. De Vries: "God can not only allow physical evil, but he positively causes it as a means to reach a higher goal."[82] One can find a source of the idea that God intends or positively wills non-moral evil in the manuals.

Another question pertinent to the present discussion is the following: Can God "dispense," so to speak, divine law such as the Decalogue? Thomas raises the question in more than one

78. Thomas Aquinas, *Light of Faith: Compendium of Theology,* trans. Cyril Vollert (Manchester, N.H.: Sophia Institute Press, 1988) 295.

79. *ST* III, 89, 1; *ST* I-II, 87, 3, ad 3.

80. *De malo* q.1, a.3, ad 10.

81. Finnis, *Moral Absolutes,* 74–77.

82. J. De Vries, "Theodizee," in W. Brugger, ed., *Philosophisches Worterbuch* (Freiburg 1967) 381, as cited by Schüller, "Direct Killing/Indirect Killing," 155.

place[83] and gives answers that appear, at first glance, to be contradictory. The best study of Thomas on this topic is Patrick Lee's
"Permanence of the Ten Commandments: St. Thomas and His
Modern Commentators."[84] In this article, Lee both reconciles the
apparently contradictory answers of Aquinas (sometimes appear-
ing in the same work!) and argues, I think soundly, that scholars
such as Dedek and Milhaven have misinterpreted Thomas on the
matter of moral absolutes and dispensations from the commandments.

In *Prima secundae*, 94, 5, Thomas notes that natural law may
be supplemented *(superaddita)* but not reduced *(subtractio)*. The
three cases given here, taking gold from the Egyptians, Hosea
having intercourse with a prostitute, and Abraham (almost)
killing Isaac are treated in three different but similar ways by
Thomas.

One could begin to work toward a resolution of the "despoil-
ing of the Egyptians" by considering the case of a father loaning
a car to a son. If that father were to send his daughter to get the
car, the son having departed already in it, the daughter would
not be stealing the car from the son. Rather, the car belongs to
the father, who can send whomever he wants to retrieve it.

Similarly, in court cases, a judge may allocate property from
one person to another. Clearly, the transfer of the property following such an order is not theft. Thomas holds that God's relationship to property is analogous to the father's or the judge's relationship to property in these examples. It is not that the norm
against theft, taking what belongs to another, admits exception.
What is quite mutable however is what will count as "belonging
to another." Thomas believes that God as a father or judge can
reallocate property among human beings, changing what properly belongs to one to what properly belongs to another.

Similarly, norms against fornication or adultery likewise are

83. *In Sent.* I, d.47, q.1, a.4; *In Sent.* IV, d.33, q.1, a.2; *In Sent.* III, d.37, a.4; *De malo* q.3, a.1, ad 17; *ST* I-II, 100, 8.
84. Patrick Lee, "Permanence of the Ten Commandments: St. Thomas and His Modern Commentators," *Theological Studies* 42 (1981) 422–43.

exceptionless, but what is not immutable is the status of a couple as married or not. In fact, lesser authorities than God can alter this fact, as couples with witnesses do every day. In the case of Hosea, God has commanded or altered the unmarried status of the couple to a married status. No adultery has taken place at God's command, but rather God's command has brought about a marriage between Hosea and the prostitute.

Thomas explains the case of Abraham and Isaac in terms of original sin and the debt of death owed by every person to God because of the Fall. In other words, the killing of the innocent at God's command turns out to be another example of capital punishment. Each person is guilty, as human, of the communal crime against the divine. Abraham can sacrifice Isaac *qua* agent of God, not *qua* individual. God, in punishing human beings with death, does not, as previously noted, intend or choose the evil of death but only the good of justice.[85]

Moral perplexity does not arise from God's commands,[86] but it can arise from human beings. There are, according to Aquinas, two kinds of moral perplexity—*perplexus secundum quid* and *perplexus simpliciter*. *Perplexus secundum quid* arises when an agent, through his or her own fault, arrives in a situation in which he or she can only choose between two wrong alternatives. However, the alternatives may not be equally wrong. If a father of a large family fathers a child with a woman to whom he is not married, he will find himself in *perplexus secundum quid*. Either he must leave his family, marry his mistress, and be a father to his child (thereby ceasing to be a proper father for his other children) or he must leave his new child without a proper father. Either way he does something wrong, but one option is *ceteris paribus* worse than the other.

Perplexus simpliciter, on the other hand, is a perplexity that arises from no fault of the agent's own. Both proportionalism and its alternative reject this possibility, proportionalism through an appeal to the lesser evil or greater good, and the alternative in

85. Ibid.
86. *STI*-II, 79, 2.

part through double-effect reasoning, which helps differentiate cases in which one foresees evil following an act.[87] Indeed, cases of perplexity, whether allegedly *simpliciter* or *secundum quid*, contributed to the genesis of proportionalism. Unfortunately, this genesis did not take into account fully the resources of the natural law tradition and, operating out of a truncated version of this tradition, concluded that there are no non-tautological exceptionless norms.

87. Another aspect of the solution comes from Aquinas's account of practical rationality. See Alasdair MacIntyre, *Whose Justice? Which Rationality?* 186–88.

CONCLUSION

What explains proportionalism? John Finnis and others have suggested that it was the drive to justify contraception that led to proportionalism. This response does not fully answer the question. Even if this were accepted, one has to ask, why *this* justification of contraception instead of another?

Another way to approach the topic is to ask of proportionalism: What are its unexamined presuppositions? Why does it have such force and plausibility for many Catholics, but not a single non-Catholic advocate? Why are some groups of Catholic moral theologians and philosophers, notably the Dominicans, almost uniformly opposed to the movement and others, such as many Jesuits, among its most energetic proponents? Certainly, part of the answer is to be found in the larger ecclesiastical struggles of which the debate about proportionalism is a part. However, another aspect of the answer to these questions is to be found in the predecessor culture of proportionalism, the neoscholasticism that reigned before Vatican II. For the handbooks of neoscholasticism are 'the tradition' against which the advocates of proportionalism rebel.[1]

The Genealogy of Proportionalism

In many ways already detailed, proportionalism can be understood, in part, as an extension of the scholasticism of the

1. Schüller, "Die Quellen der Moralität," 535.

manuals rather than as a recovery of Thomas. Other authors have pointed out the continuity between proportionalism and the scholasticism of the manuals in other respects. Servais Pinkaers sees the treatment of law in proportionalism as an outgrowth of scholastic nominalism.[2] Martin Rhonheimer suggests that proportionalism inherits the manuals' conception of human action.[3] Romanus Cessario argues that both the ethics of the manuals and the ethics of proportionate reason marginalize the virtues and champion a particular understanding of freedom.[4] If James Keenan and Brian V. Johnstone are correct, the account of binding erroneous conscience from which the rightness/goodness distinction developed finds its roots in the neoscholastic rejection of the Thomistic account of such cases as wrong but 'excused' acts.[5] Likewise, Richard McCormick has written: "I would suggest that Paul McKeever has the matter very well in hand when he refers to contemporary Catholic discussions as an 'evolution,' with an organic relation to the past, rather than a 'revolution.'"[6] And again he writes of proportionalism: "Unless I am mistaken, I can detect the general shape of this *Denkform* as early as 1951 in the work of Gerard Kelly. . . . Kelly was not at that time what is now known as a proportionalist. But . . . with a few minor analytic moves he would be."[7] If the authors just cited are correct, there is a great continuity, though certainly not in each and every respect, between the manuals that immediately preceded and served as the textbooks for early revisionists

---

2. Servais Pinckaers, "La question des actes intrinséquement mauvais et le 'proportionalisme,'" *Revue Thomiste* 82 (1982) 181–212, and *Ce qu'on ne peut jamais faire* (Fribourg: Editions Universitaires, 1986).

3. Martin Rhonheimer, "'Ethics of Norms' and the Lost Virtues: Searching the Roots of the Crisis of Ethical Reasoning" *Anthropotes* 9.2 (1993) 233, and "Intrinsically Evil Acts and the Moral Viewpoint: Clarifying a Central Teaching of *Veritatis Splendor*," 38.

4. Romanus Cessario, "Casuistry and Revisionism: Structural Similarities in Method and Content," in *Humanae Vitae: 20 Anni Dopo Atti del II Congresso Internazionale di Teologia Morale* (Rome, 9–12 November 1988) 385–409.

5. James Keenan, "Can a Wrong Action Be Good? The Development of Theological Opinion on Erroneous Conscience," *Église et Théologie* 24 (1993) 205–19; Brian V. Johnstone, "Erroneous Conscience in *Veritatis splendor* and the Theological Tradition," in *The Splendor of Accuracy* ed. Selling and Jans, 114–35.

6. McCormick, *Notes on Moral Theology, 1965 through 1980*, 652.

7. McCormick, "Moral Theology 1940–1989" 9–10.

and the movement that came to be known as proportionalism. Certainly the continuity is not unambiguous. As noted, central aspects of the tradition dating back to patristic authors were jettisoned in favor of novel readings of marginal positions of a rather younger vintage. Proportionalists harnessed the terminology of the moral manuals in service of undermining the conclusions not just of the manuals but of the natural law tradition. Following more than twenty-five years of debate on the matter, John Paul II in 1993 issued the encyclical *Veritatis splendor* on "certain fundamentals of the moral teaching of the Church" that addressed the topic of proportionalism explicitly in its second chapter. He writes: "Such theories however are not faithful to the Church's teaching, when they believe they can justify, as morally good, deliberate choices of kinds of behavior contrary to the commandments of the divine and natural law. These theories cannot claim to be grounded in the Catholic moral tradition."[8]

Proportionalism cannot claim to be grounded in the tradition, save in the most superficial sense, for what was marginal and derivative in this tradition, like double-effect reasoning, replaced what was central and primary, like the biblical tenet that one must not do evil that good may come, a tenet adhered to unto death by the martyrs. Doubtless, a continuity was maintained and indeed sought as much as possible with as much of the natural law tradition as possible. But like a seamless garment, the unraveling of one aspect of this tradition led to the significant changes in the whole. Proportionalism turned out to be much more revolution than evolution.

What difference, if any, does proportionalism's continuity with the manuals make to moral theory? The answer is not entirely clear. For some, the continuity between the manuals and proportionalism serves as an argument against those who consider proportionalism a novelty with no prior precedent. Furthermore, it is argued that this continuity serves as evidence that proportionalism is not a radical shift in Catholic thought but rather part of the authentic development of doctrine. Authentic development, as described by Newman's *Essay on the Development*

---

8. John Paul II, *Veritatis splendor* 76.

of Christian Doctrine, is an organic continuity of principle in logical sequence with previous teaching. Authentic development is not a radical shift or violent rejection of the past but rather a bringing to perfection of what was already present in previous doctrine, if only implicitly. That proportionalism manifests this organic unity with the manual tradition serves as evidence that *this* revision authentically develops received moral doctrine.

For others, the continuity between proportionalism and the scholasticism of the manuals serves precisely the opposite function, namely as *prima facie* evidence against proportionalism. The value of being in continuity with a tradition would seem to depend on the authority of the tradition in question. What then is the authority of the scholasticism of the manuals? It is safe to say that the consensus following the Council is not entirely favorable. At least in part in order to remove the negative connotations of the "scholastic" label, *Revue Néoscolastique* became *Revue philosophique, Skolastik* became *Philosophie und Theologie,* and *The New Scholasticism* became the *American Catholic Philosophical Quarterly.* In Bruno Schüller's words: "In most cases, when used as an evaluative term, 'Scholasticism' stands precisely for what one must totally abandon or, still better, completely forget."[9] If one takes this view of the scholasticism of the manuals, continuity with them might be considered more a liability than an asset.

Indeed, it is strange that the manuals are cited as authorities. As Grisez notes: "[T]he classical moralists were not specialists in ethical theory and it is odd that anyone should rely on their authority in questions of theory while disregarding it in substantive matters to which they gave almost all their attention."[10]

Whatever the merits or weaknesses of this kind of moral theory, it surely has not been completely forgotten. The manuals were, on the contrary, what shaped those involved in the early debate, though in ways sometimes not completely recognized. In this, the words of McCormick are applicable.

9. Schüller, *Wholly Human,* 1.
10. Germain Grisez, "Against Consequentialism," in *Proportionalism For and Against,* ed. C. Kaczor, 292.

Moral analyses often reflect basic assumptions and cultural variables that operate behind them. Karl Rahner, in discussing moral argument, refers to such assumptions as "global prescientific convictions." . . . He was discussing bad moral arguments and explaining how they often trace to such assumptions. Philip Rieff has something very similar in mind when he referred to "reasons" that form the "unwitting" part of a culture and give shape to its habits, customs, policies, and procedures.[11]

From a sociological point of view, those educated in the manuals that followed Gury's model tend to find proportionalism rather plausible. On the other hand, those either lacking training in the manuals or those whose manuals differed radically in organization from Gury's, such as Dominican and some diocesan manuals, tend to find proportionalism rather implausible.[12]

The plausibility of proportionalism arises in part from the shared late-neoscholastic background of its chief protagonists and their audience. Proportionalism arose from, partially rejects, but fully presupposes this background. This can be seen, in part, in the accounts of double-effect reasoning given by Aquinas, later manualists such as Gury, and proportionalists. It is reflected also in the emaciated theory of human action prevalent in many manualists and presupposed by proportionalism. It may be clearly seen in the handling of law in these theories. When virtues dropped out of the manualist account of morals, a new basis for norms was needed in order to justify traditional Catholic teaching. Thus, killing the innocent was said to be wrong from lack of right rather than, as for Thomas, because of its discordance with justice.

What Rahner called the "global prescientific convictions" engendered by the manualists are no longer widely shared. These convictions help, in part, to explain the rapid acceptance of proportionalism in many but not all Catholic circles, and help to explain why proportionalism does not enjoy great popularity among many younger scholars working in the natural law tradition today.

11. McCormick, *Critical Calling*, 51, 212.
12. Salzman, *Deontology and Teleology*, 414–17, provides a short summary of the difference between and relative influence of these two styles of manuals.

BIBLIOGRAPHY

Aertsen, Jan A. "Beauty in the Middle Ages: A Forgotten Transcendental?" *Medieval Philosophy and Theology* 1 (1991): 68–97.

Albertus Magnus. *Super Matthaeum.* Münster: Aschendorff, 1998.

Allsopp, Michael E., and John F. O'Keefe, eds. *Veritatis Splendor: American Responses.* Kansas City: Sheed and Ward, 1995.

Anscombe, Elizabeth. "Modern Moral Philosophy." *Philosophy* 33 (1958): 26–42.

———. *Intention.* Ithaca, N.Y.: Cornell University Press, 1963.

———. "Action, Intention, and Double Effect." *Proceedings of the American Catholic Philosophical Association* 56 (1982): 12–25.

Aristotle. *Nicomachean Ethics.* Translated by Hippocrates G. Apostle. Grinnell, Iowa: The Peripatetic Press, 1984.

———. *Aristotle: Selected Works.* Translated by Hippocrates G. Apostle and Lloyd P. Gerson. Grinnell, Iowa: The Peripatetic Press, 1986.

———. *Nicomachean Ethics.* Translated by Terence Irwin. 2d edition. Indianapolis: Hackett Publishing, 1999.

Augustine. *Confessiones.* Patrologia Latina 32.659–868 (Migne).

———. *Contra Faustum.* Patrologia Latina 42.207–518 (Migne).

———. *Contra mendacium.* Corpus Scriptorum Ecclesiasticorum Latinorum 41.

———. *De moribus ecclesiae catholicae.* Patrologia Latina 32.1300–1377 (Migne).

———. *De vera religione.* Corpus Scriptorum Ecclesiasticorum Latinorum 32.

Aulisio, Mark P. "On the Importance of the Intention/Foresight Distinction." *American Catholic Philosophical Quarterly* 70.2 (1996): 189–205.

Bazán, B. Carlos, Eduardo Andujar, and Leonard G. Sbrocchi, eds. *Moral and Political Philosophy in the Middle Ages: Proceedings of the Ninth International Congress of Medieval Philosophy* vol. II Ottawa: Legas, 1992.

Belmans, Theo G. *Le sens objectif de l'agir humain: Pour relire la moral conjugale de Saint Thomas.* Vatican City: Libertia Editrice Vaticana, 1980.

Bennett, Jonathan Francis. *The Act Itself.* Oxford: Clarendon Press, 1995.

Berlin, Isaiah. *Four Essays on Liberty.* London: Oxford University Press, 1969.

Bourke, Vernon. *Ethics: A Textbook in Moral Philosophy.* New York: Macmillan, 1966.

Bouscaren, T. L. *Ethics of Ectopic Operations.* Milwaukee: The Bruce Publishing Company, 1933.

Boyle, Joseph. "Double Effect and a Certain Type of Embryotomy." *Irish Theological Quarterly* 44 (1977): 303–18.

———. "*Praeter Intentionem* in Aquinas." *The Thomist* 42 (1978): 649–65.

———. "Toward Understanding the Principle of Double Effect." *Ethics* 90 (1980): 527–38.

———. "The Principle of Double Effect: Good Actions Entangled in Evil." In *Moral Theology Today.* St. Louis: John XXIII Center for Bioethics, 1984.

———. "Who's Entitled to Double Effect?" *Journal of Medicine and Philosophy* 16 (1991): 475–94.

Boyle, Joseph, and T. Sullivan. "The Diffusiveness of Intention: A Counter-Example." *Philosophical Studies* 31 (1977): 357–60.

Bratman, Michael. *Intention, Plans, and Practical Reason.* Cambridge: Harvard University Press, 1987.

Brock, Dan W. "Recent Work in Utilitarianism." *American Philosophical Quarterly* 10 (1973): 241–76.

Brock, Stephen. "The Use of *Usus* in Aquinas' Psychology of Action." In *Moral and Political Philosophy in the Middle Ages: Proceedings of the Ninth International Congress of Medieval Philosophy,* vol. II, edited by B. Carlos Bazán, Eduardo Andujar, and Leonard G. Sbrocchi. Ottawa: Legas, 1992.

———. *Action and Conduct: Thomas Aquinas and the Theory of Action.* Edinburgh: T&T Clark, 1998.

Brown, R. E., J. A. Fitzmyer, and Roland Murphy, eds. *The New Jerome Biblical Commentary.* Englewood Cliffs, N.J.: Prentice Hall, 1990.

Burke, Ronald R. "Papal Authority and the Sovereignty of Reason." In *Veritatis Splendor: American Responses,* edited by Michael E. Allsopp and John J. O'Keefe. Kansas City: Sheed and Ward, 1995.

Cahill, Lisa. "Teleology, Utilitarianism, and Christian Ethics." *Theological Studies* 42 (1981): 601–29.

———. "Contemporary Challenge to Exceptionless Moral Norms." In

Moral Theology Today. St. Louis: John XXIII Center for Bioethics, 1984.

Caspi, E., and D. Sherman. "Tubal Abortion and Infundibular Ectopic Pregnancy." *Clinical Obstetrics and Gynecology* 30 (1987): 155–63.

Cavanaugh, Thomas Anthony. *Double Effect Reasoning: A Critique and Defense.* Dissertation. University of Notre Dame, 1995.

———. "The Intended/Foreseen Distinction's Ethical Relevance." *Philosophical Papers* 25.3 (1996): 179–88.

———. "Aquinas's Account of Double Effect." *The Thomist* 61 (1997): 107–21.

Cessario, Romanus. "Casuistry and Revisionism: Structural Similarities in Method and Content." In *Humanae Vitae: 20 Anni Dopo Atti del II Congresso Internazionale di Teologia Morale.* Rome: Città Nuova Editrice, 1988.

———. "Virtue Theory and Human Life Issues." *The Thomist* 53 (April 1989): 173–196.

Charlton, William. *Weakness of the Will.* Oxford: Blackwell, 1988.

Chenu, M.-D. "Le plan de la *Somme théologique* de saint Thomas." *Revue Thomiste* 47 (1939): 93–107.

Childress, James F. "Just-War Theories: The Bases, Interrelations, Priorities, and Functions of Their Criteria." *Theological Studies* 39 (1978): 427–45.

Chisholm, R. "The Structure of Intention." *Journal of Philosophy* 67 (1970): 633–47.

Christie, Dolores L. *Adequately Considered: An American Perspective on Louis Janssens' Personalist Morals.* Leuven: Peeters, 1990.

Composta, Diaro. "Il consequenzialismo: Uno nuova corrente della 'Nuova Morale.'" *Divinitas* 25 (1981): 127–56.

Connery, John. *Abortion: The Development of the Roman Catholic Perspective.* Chicago: Loyola University Press, 1977.

Cornerotte, L. "Loi morale, valeurs humaines et situations de conflit." *Nouvelle revue théologique* 100 (1978): 502–3.

Cunningham, T. P. "The Contumacy Required to Incur Censures." *Irish Theological Quarterly* 4 (1954): 332–56.

Curran, Charles. "Moral Absolutes and Medical Ethics." In *Absolutes in Moral Theology?* Edited by Charles Curran. Washington, D.C.: Corpus Books, 1968.

———. *Directions in Fundamental Moral Theology.* Notre Dame: University of Notre Dame Press, 1985.

———. *Toward an American Catholic Moral Theology.* Notre Dame: University of Notre Dame Press, 1987.

———. "The Manual and Casuistry of Aloysius Sabetti." In *The Context of Casuistry,* edited by James Keenan and Thomas Shannon. Washington, D.C.: Georgetown University Press, 1995.

————. "*Veritatis Splendor:* A Revisionist Perspective." In *Veritatis Splendor: American Responses,* edited by Michael E. Allsopp and John J. O'Keefe. Kansas City: Sheed and Ward, 1995.

————, ed. *Absolutes in Moral Theology?* Washington, D.C.: Corpus Books, 1968.

————, ed. *Moral Theology Challenges for the Future: Essays in Honor of Richard McCormick.* New York: Paulist Press, 1990.

Curran, Charles, and Richard McCormick, eds. *Moral Norms and Catholic Tradition.* New York: Paulist Press, 1979.

Dannen, Fredrick. "The G-Man and the Hit Man." *The New Yorker* (December 16, 1996) 68–81.

DeBlois, Jean. "Ectopic Pregnancy." In *A Primer for Health Care Ethics: Essays for a Pluralistic Society,* edited by J. DeBlois. Washington, D.C: Georgetown University Press, 1996.

De Vries, J. "Theodizee." In *Philosophisches Worterbuch,* edited by W. Brugger. Freiburg, 1967.

Dedek, John F. "Intrinsically Evil Acts: An Historical Study of the Mind of St. Thomas." *The Thomist* 43 (1979): 385–413.

————. "Premarital Sex: The Theological Argument from Peter Lombard to Durand." *Theological Studies* 41 (1980): 643–67.

————. "Intrinsically Evil Acts: The Emergence of a Doctrine." *Recherches de Théologie ancienne et médiéval* 50 (1983): 191–226.

Demmer, Klaus. "Deuten und Wählen: Vorbermerkungen zu einer moraltheologischen Handlungstheorie." *Gregorianum* 62 (1981): 231–75.

Dewan, Lawrence. "'Objectum': Notes on the Invention of a Word." *Archives D'Histoire Doctrinale et Littéraire du Moyen Age* (1982): 37–96.

————. "St. Thomas, James Keenan, and the Will." *Science et Esprit* 47 (1995): 153–76.

Diamond, E. "Moral and Medical Considerations in the Management of Extrauterine Pregnancy." *Linacre Quarterly* 66.3 (1999): 5–15.

Diamond, E., and A. DeCherney. "Surgical Management of Ectopic Pregnancy." *Clinical Obstetrics and Gynecology* 30 (1987): 200–209.

DiNoia, Augustine, and Romanus Cessario, eds. *Veritatis Splendor and the Renewal of Moral Theology.* Chicago: Midwest Theological Forum, 1999.

Dobler, E. *Nemesius von Emesa unde die Psychologie des menschlichen Aktes bei Thomas von Aquin (ST Ia IIa, qq. 6–17): Eine Quellenanalytische Studie.* Lucerne, 1950.

Donagan, Alan. "Thomas Aquinas on Human Action." In *The Cambridge History of Later Medieval Philosophy,* edited by Norman Kretzmann, Anthony Kenny, Jan Pinborg, and Eleanor Stump. Cambridge: Cambridge University Press, 1982.

Finnis, John. *Natural Law and Natural Rights.* Oxford and New York: Oxford University Press, 1980.

———. "The Consistent Ethic—A Philosophical Critique." In *Joseph Bernardin's Consistent Ethic of Life,* edited by Thomas G. Fuechtmann. Kansas City: Sheed and Ward, 1988.

———. *Moral Absolutes: Tradition, Revision, and Truth.* Washington D.C.: The Catholic University of America Press, 1991.

———. *Aquinas: Moral, Political, and Legal Theory.* Oxford: Oxford University, 1998.

Flannery, Kevin. "What Is Included in a Means to an End?" *Gregorianum* 74 (1993): 499–512.

Frankena, William K. *Ethics.* 2d edition. Englewood Cliffs, N.J.: Prentice-Hall, 1973.

———. "McCormick and the Traditional Distinction." In *Doing Evil to Achieve Good,* edited by Richard McCormick and Paul Ramsey. Milwaukee: Marquette University Press, 1978.

Fuchs, Josef. "The Absoluteness of Moral Terms." *Gregorianum* 52 (1971): 415–85. Reprinted in *Moral Norms and Catholic Tradition,* edited by Charles E. Curran and Richard A. McCormick. New York: Paulist Press, 1979.

———. *Christian Ethics in a Secular Arena.* Translated by Bernard Hoose and Brian McNeil. Washington D.C.: Georgetown University Press, 1984.

———. *Für eine menschliche Moral: Grundfragen der theologischen Ethik.* Freiburg, Switzerland: Universitätsverlag 1997 [with appendix of 400+ entry bibliography of Fuch's works].

Gaffney, James. "The Pope on Proportionalism." In *Veritatis Splendor: American Responses,* edited by Michael E. Allsopp and John J. O'Keefe. Kansas City: Sheed and Ward, 1995.

Garcia, J. L. A. "On High Mindedness." *Proceedings of the ACPA* 47 (1989): 98–107.

———. "Motive and Duty." *Idealistic Studies* 20 (1990): 230–37.

———. "The Right and the Good." *Philosophia* 21.3–4 (1992): 235–56.

Grisez, Germain G. "Toward a Consistent Natural-Law Ethics of Killing." *American Journal of Jurisprudence* 15 (1970): 64–96.

———. "Against Consequentialism." *American Journal of Jurisprudence* 23 (1978): 21–72. Reprinted in *Proportionalism For and Against,* edited by Christopher Kaczor. Milwaukee: Marquette University Press, 2000.

Grisez, Germain G., and Joseph Boyle, Jr. *Life and Death with Liberty and Justice.* Notre Dame: University of Notre Dame Press, 1979.

Gula, Richard M. *What Are They Saying about Moral Norms?* New York: Paulist Press, 1982.

Gury, Jean P. *Compendium theologiae moralis.* Rome, 1874.

Hagstrom, H. G., et al. "Prediction of Persistent Ectopic Pregnancy after Salpingostomy." *Obstetrics and Gynecology* 84 (1994): 798–802.

Hallet, Garth. *Greater Good: The Case for Proportionalism.* Washington, D.C.: Georgetown University Press, 1995.

Hanink, James G. "Karol Wojtyla: Personalism, Intransitivity, and Character." *Communio: International Catholic Review* 23 (Summer 1996): 244–51.

Hart, H. L. A. "Intention and Punishment." In *Punishment and Responsibility: Essays in the Philosophy of Law.* New York: Oxford University Press, 1968.

Hoose, Bernard. *Proportionalism: The American Debate and Its European Roots.* Washington, D.C.: Georgetown University Press, 1987.

Iozzio, Mary Jo. *Self-Determination and the Moral Act: A Study of the Contributions of Odon Lottin, O.S.B.* Leuven: Peeters, 1995.

Janssens, Louis. "Norms and Priorities in a Love Ethics." *Louvain Studies* 6 (1976–77): 207–38.

———. "Ontic Evil and Moral Evil." In *Moral Norms and Catholic Tradition,* edited by Charles E. Curran and Richard A. McCormick. New York: Paulist Press, 1979. Reprinted in *Proportionalism For and Against,* edited by Christopher Kaczor. Milwaukee: Marquette University Press, 2000.

———. "St. Thomas Aquinas and the Question of Proportionality." *Louvain Studies* 6.3 (1982): 26–46.

———. "Ontic Good and Evil-Premoral Values and Disvalues." *Louvain Studies* 12.1 (1987): 62–82.

Jensen, Steven John. *Intrinsically Evil Actions According to St. Thomas Aquinas.* Dissertation. University of Notre Dame, 1993.

John Paul II. *Evangelium vitae.* Vatican City: Libreria Editrice Vaticana, 1995.

———. *Veritatis splendor.* Vatican City: Libreria Editrice Vaticana, 1993.

Johnson, Mark. "Proportionalism and a Text of the Young Aquinas: Quodlibetum IX, Q. 7, A. 2." *Theological Studies* 53 (1992): 683–99.

Johnstone, Brian V. "The Meaning of Proportionate Reason in Contemporary Moral Theology." *The Thomist* 49 (1985): 223–47.

———. "Erroneous Conscience in *Veritatis splendor* and the Theological Tradition." In *The Splendor of Accuracy: An Examination of the Assertions Made by Veritatis Splendor,* edited by Joseph Selling and Jan Jans. Grand Rapids, Mich.: William B. Eerdmans Publishing Co., 1994.

Jonsen, Albert, and Stephen Toulmin. *The Abuse of Casuistry: A History of Moral Reasoning.* Berkeley: University of California Press, 1988.

Kaczor, Christopher. "Exceptionless Norms in Aristotle? Thomas Aquinas and 20th-Century Interpreters of the *Nicomachean Ethics.*" *The Thomist* 61 (1997): 33–62.

———. "Review of *Greater Good: The Case for Proportionalism.*" *Review of Metaphysics* L.4 (1997): 898–99.

———. "Review of *Veritatis Splendor: American Responses.*" *Studies in Christian Ethics* 10.2 (1997): 86–87.

———. "MacIntyre and Emotivism: Gaps Between the Meaning and Use of Words." In *Resurrecting the Phoenix,* edited by David Durst. Sophia: EOS Publishing (1998): 38–46.

———. "Faith and Reason and Physician-Assisted Suicide." *Journal of Christian Bioethics* 4.2 (1998): 183–201.

———. "Double-Effect Reasoning: From Jean Pierre Gury to Peter Knauer" *Theological Studies* 59 (June 1998): 297–316.

———. "Is the 'Medical Management' of Ectopic Pregnancy by the Administration of Methotrexate Morally Acceptable?" In *Issues for a Catholic Bioethic,* edited by L. Gormally. London: Linacre Center (1999): 353–58.

———. "Proportionalism and the Pill: How Developments in Theory Lead to Contradictions to Practice." *The Thomist* 63 (1999): 269–81. Reprinted in *Proportionalism For and Against,* edited by Christopher Kaczor. Milwaukee: Marquette University Press, 2000.

———. "Moral Absolutism and Ectopic Pregnancy" *Journal of Medicine and Philosophy* 26.1 (2001): 61–74.

———, ed. *Proportionalism For and Against.* Milwaukee: Marquette University Press, 2000.

Kamm, Francis. "The Doctrine of Double Effect: Reflections on Theoretical and Practical Issues." *Journal of Medicine and Philosophy* 16.5 (October 1991): 571–85.

Kant, Immanuel. *Grundlegung zur Metaphysik der Sitten,* edited by Karl Vorländer. Hamburg: Meiner, 1994.

Keenan, James. *Goodness and Rightness in Thomas Aquinas's Summa theologiae.* Washington, D.C.: Georgetown University Press, 1992.

———. "Can a Wrong Action Be Good? The Development of Theological Opinion on Erroneous Conscience." *Église et Théologie* 24 (1993): 205–19.

———. "The Function of the Principle of Double Effect." *Theological Studies* 54 (1993): 294–315.

Keenan, James, and Thomas Shannon, eds. *The Context of Casuistry.* Washington, D.C.: Georgetown University Press, 1995.

Kelly, G. *Medico-Moral Problems.* St. Louis: Catholic Hospital Association, 1958.

Kiely, Bartholomew M. "The Impracticality of Proportionalism." *Gregorianum* 66 (1985): 655–86.

Knauer, Peter, "The Hermeneutic Function of the Principle of Double Effect." In *Moral Norms and Catholic Tradition,* edited by Charles E. Curran and Richard A. McCormick. New York: Paulist Press, 1979. Reprinted in *Proportionalism For and Against,* edited by Christopher Kaczor. Milwaukee: Marquette University Press, 2000.

———. "Fundamentalethik: teleologische als deontologische Normenbegründung." *Theologie und Philosophie* 55 (1980): 60–74.

———. "A Good End Does Not Justify an Evil Means—Even in Teleological Ethics." In *Personalist Morals: Essays in Honor of Louis Janssens,* edited by Joseph Selling. Leuven: Leuven University Press, 1988.

———. "The Concept of Intention." Lecture at K. U. Leuven, October 7th, 1988.

———. "Zu Grundbegriffen der Enzyklika 'Veritatis Splendor.'" *Stimmen der Zeit* 212 (1994): 14–26.

Langan, John. "Catholic Moral Rationalism and the Philosophical Bases of Moral Theology." *Theological Studies* 50 (1989): 25–43.

Lear, Jonathan. *Aristotle: The Desire to Understand.* Cambridge: Cambridge University Press, 1988.

Lee, Patrick. "Permanence of the Ten Commandments: St. Thomas and His Modern Commentators." *Theological Studies* 42 (1981): 422–43.

Levy, Sanford S. "Richard McCormick and Proportionate Reason." *Journal of Religious Ethics* 13 (1985): 258–78.

Long, Steven. "*Evangelium Vitae,* St. Thomas Aquinas, and the Death Penalty." *The Thomist* 63 (1999): 511–52.

Lustig, B. Andrew. "*Veritatis Splendor*: Some Implications for Bioethics." In *Veritatis Splendor: American Responses,* edited by Michael E. Allsopp and John J. O'Keefe. Kansas City: Sheed and Ward, 1995.

MacIntyre, Alasdair. *After Virtue.* Notre Dame: University of Notre Dame Press, 1984.

———. *Whose Justice? Which Rationality?* Notre Dame: University of Notre Dame Press, 1989.

———. *Dependent Rational Animals: Why Human Beings Need the Virtues.* Chicago: Open Court, 1999.

Maguire, Daniel C. *The Moral Choice.* Garden City, N.Y.: Doubleday, 1978.

———. "Abortion: A Question of Catholic Honesty." *Christian Century* 100 (1983): 803–7.

Mahoney, John. *The Making of Moral Theology.* Oxford: Oxford University Press, 1990.

Mangan, Joseph. "An Historical Analysis of the Principle of Double Effect." *Theological Studies* 10 (1949): 41–61.

Marshner, William H. "Aquinas on the Evaluation of Human Actions." *The Thomist* 59 (1995): 347–70.

Marquis, Donald. "Four Versions of Double Effect." *Journal of Medicine and Philosophy* 16 (1991): 515–44.

Mausbach, Joseph, and Gustav Ermecke. *Katholische Moraltheologie.* Münster, 1954.

May, William E. "Aquinas and Janssens on the Moral Meaning of Human Acts." *The Thomist* 48 (1984): 566–606.

McCormick, Richard A. "Ambiguity in Moral Choice." In *Doing Evil to Achieve Good,* edited by Richard McCormick and Paul Ramsey. Milwaukee: Marquette University Press, 1978.

————. "A Commentary on the Commentaries" in *Doing Evil to Achieve Good,* edited by Richard McCormick and Paul Ramsey. Milwaukee: Marquette University Press, 1978.

————. *Notes on Moral Theology, 1965 through 1980.* Washington, D.C.: University Press of America, 1981.

————. *Notes on Moral Theology, 1981 through 1984.* Washington, D.C.: University Press of America, 1985.

————. "Notes on Moral Theology: 1984." *Theological Studies* 46 (1985): 50–64.

————. "Notes on Moral Theology: 1985." *Theological Studies* 47 (1986): 69–88.

————. *Health Care and Medicine in the Catholic Tradition.* New York: Crossroad Publishing Company, 1987.

————. "Moral Theology 1940–1989: An Overview." *Theological Studies* 50 (1989): 3–24.

————. *The Critical Calling: Reflections on Moral Dilemmas Since Vatican II.* Washington, D.C.: Georgetown University Press, 1989.

————. "*Veritatis Splendor* and Moral Theology." *America* 169.13 (October 1993): 8–11.

————. "Some Early Reactions to *Veritatis splendor.*" *Theological Studies* 55 (1994): 481–506.

McCormick, Richard, and Paul Ramsey, eds. *Doing Evil to Achieve Good: Moral Choice in Conflict Situations.* Chicago: Loyola University Press, 1978.

McInerny, Ralph. *Aquinas on Human Action: A Theory of Practice.* Washington, D.C.: The Catholic University of America Press, 1992.

Merkelbach, Benedict. *Summa Theologiae Moralis,* vol. 1. Paris: Desclée de Brouwer, 1949.

Milhaven, John G. "Moral Absolutes in Thomas Aquinas." In *Absolutes in Moral Theology?* edited by Charles E. Curran. Washington, D.C.: Corpus, 1968.

————. *Toward a New Catholic Morality.* New York: Doubleday, 1972.

Mullady, Brian Thomas. *The Meaning of the Term "Moral" in St. Thomas Aquinas.* Vatican City: Libreria Editrice Vaticana, 1986.

Müller, Gregory. *Die Wahrhaftigkeitspflicht und die Problematik der Lüge.* Freiburg: Verlag Herder, 1962.

Nussbaum, Martha. *The Fragility of Goodness*. New York: Cambridge University Press, 1987.

O'Connell, Timothy. *Principles for a Catholic Morality*. New York: Seabury, 1978.

O'Donnell, Thomas J. *Medicine and Christian Morality*. New York: Alba House, 1976.

Odozor, Paulinus Ikechukwu. *Richard A. McCormick and the Renewal of Moral Theology*. Notre Dame: University of Notre Dame Press, 1995. [Lengthy bibliography of McCormick's work is in the appendix.]

Oelsner, G. "Ectopic Pregnancy in the Remaining Tube and the Management of the Patient with Multiple Ectopic Pregnancies." *Clinical Obstetrics and Gynecology* 30 (1987): 225–29.

Oesterle, J. A. *Ethics: The Introduction to Moral Science*. Englewood Cliffs, N.J.: Prentice Hall, 1957.

Pinckaers, Servais. "La question des actes intrinséquement mauvais et le 'proportionalisme.'" *Revue Thomiste* 82 (1982): 181–212.

———. *Ce qu'on ne peut jamais faire*. Fribourg: Editions Universitaires, 1986.

———. *The Sources of Christian Ethics*. Translated by Sr. Mary Thomas Noble. Washington, D.C.: The Catholic University of America Press, 1995.

Porter, Jean. *The Recovery of Virtue: The Relevance of Aquinas for Christian Ethics*. Louisville: John Knox Press, 1990.

———. "The Moral Act in *Veritatis splendor* and in Aquinas's *Summa theologiae*: A Comparative Analysis." *Veritatis Splendor: American Responses*, edited by Michael E. Allsopp and John J. O'Keefe. Kansas City: Sheed and Ward, 1995.

———. "Recent Studies in Aquinas's Virtue Ethic." *Journal of Religious Ethics* 26.1 (Spring 1998): 191–215.

Quine, W. V. O. *Ontological Relativity and Other Essays*. New York: Columbia University Press, 1969.

———. "Two Dogmas of Empiricism." *Philosophical Review* 60 (1951): 20–43.

Quinn, W. S. "Actions, Intentions, and Consequences: The Doctrine of Double Effect." *Philosophy and Public Affairs* 18 (1989): 334–51.

Ramsey, Boniface. "Two Traditions on Lying and Deception in the Ancient Church." *The Thomist* 49 (1985): 504–33.

Regatillo, E. F., and M. Zalba. *Theologiae Moralis Summa*. Vol. 1. Madrid: Editorial Catolica, 1952.

Rhonheimer, Martin. "'Ethics of Norms' and the Lost Virtues: Searching the Roots of the Crisis of Ethical Reasoning." *Anthropotes* 9.2 (1993): 231–43.

———. "Intrinsically Evil Acts and the Moral Viewpoint: Clarifying a Central Teaching of *Veritatis Splendor*." *The Thomist* 58 (1994): 1–39.

———. "Intentional Actions and the Meaning of Object: A Reply to Richard McCormick." *The Thomist* 59 (1995): 279–311.

———. *Natural Law and Practical Reason: A Thomist View of Moral Autonomy.* Translated by Gerald Malsbary. New York: Fordham University Press, 1999.

Roach, Richard R. "Medicine and Killing: The Catholic View." *Journal of Medicine and Philosophy* 4 (1979): 383–97.

Salzman, Todd. *Deontology and Teleology: An Investigation of the Normative Debate in Roman Catholic Moral Theology.* Leuven: Leuven University Press, 1995.

Schillebeeckx, E. *De Sacramentele Heilseconomie.* Anvers, 1952.

Scholz, Frank. "Problems on Norms Raised by Ethical Borderline Situations: Beginnings of a Solution in Thomas Aquinas and Bonaventure." In *Moral Norms and Catholic Tradition,* edited by Charles E. Curran and Richard A. McCormick. New York: Paulist Press, 1979.

Schüller, Bruno. "Zur Problematik allgemein verbindlicher ethischer Grundsätze." *Theologie und Philosophie* 45 (1970): 1–23.

———. "The Double Effect in Catholic Thought: A Reevaluation." In *Doing Evil to Achieve Good: Moral Choice in Conflict Situations,* edited by Richard McCormick and Paul Ramsey. Chicago: Loyola University Press, 1978.

———. "Direct Killing/Indirect Killing." In *Moral Norms and Catholic Tradition,* edited by Charles E. Curran and Richard A. McCormick. New York: Paulist Press, 1979. Reprinted in *Proportionalism For and Against,* edited by Christopher Kaczor. Milwaukee: Marquette University Press, 2000.

———. "Die Quellen der Moralität: Zur systematischen Ortung eines alten Lehrstücks der Moraltheologie." *Theologie und Philosophie* 59 (1984): 535–59.

———. *Wholly Human: Essays on the Theory and Language of Morality.* Translated by Peter Heinegg. Washington, D.C.: Georgetown University Press, 1986.

Selling, Joseph. "The Problem of Reinterpreting the Principle of Double Effect." *Louvain Studies* 8 (1980): 47–62.

———. "Louis Janssens' Interpretation of Aquinas: A Response to Recent Criticism." *Louvain Studies* 19 (1994): 65–74.

———. "*Evangelium Vitae* and the Question of Infallibility." *Doctrine and Life* 45.5 (1995): 330–39.

———, ed. *Personalist Morals: Essays in Honor of Professor Louis Janssens.* Leuven: Leuven University Press, 1988. [A complete bibliography of Janssens' career may be found as an appendix.]

Smith, Janet E. *Humanae Vitae: A Generation Later.* Washington, D.C.: The Catholic University of America Press, 1991.

————. "Moral Terminology and Proportionalism." In *Recovering Nature: Essays in Natural Philosophy, Ethics, and Metaphysics in Honor of Ralph McInerny*, edited by John P. O'Callaghan and Thomas S. Hibbs. Notre Dame: University of Notre Dame Press, 1999.

Stanke, Gerhard. *Die Lehre von den "Quellen der Moralität" Darstellung und Diskussion der neuscholastischen Aussagen und neuerer Ansätze*. Studien zur Geischichte der katholischen Moraltheologie 26. Regensburg: Friedrich Pustet, 1984.

Steel, Carlos. "Does Evil Have a Cause?" *Review of Metaphysics* 48.2 (1994): 251–73.

Stevens, Clifford. "A Matter of Credibility." In *Veritatis Splendor: American Responses*, edited by Michael E. Allsopp and John J. O'Keefe. Kansas City: Sheed and Ward, 1995.

Sullivan, Joseph. *Special Ethics*. Worcester, Mass.: Holy Cross College Press, 1931.

Sunshine, Edward R. "'The Splendor of Truth' and the Rhetoric of Morality." In *Veritatis Splendor: American Responses*, edited by Michael E. Allsopp and John J. O'Keefe. Kansas City: Sheed and Ward, 1995.

Talvacchia, Kathleen, and Mary Elizabeth Walsh. "The *Splendor of Truth*: A Feminist Critique." In *Veritatis Splendor: American Responses*, edited by Michael E. Allsopp and John J. O'Keefe. Kansas City: Sheed and Ward, 1995.

Tauer, Carol A. "The Tradition of Probabilism and the Moral Status of the Early Embryo." *Theological Studies* 45 (1984): 3–33.

Thomas Aquinas. *Opera omnia*. Rome: Leonine edition, 1882–

————. *Super Evangelium Matthaei*. Paris edition, 1876.

————. *The Summa Theologica of St. Thomas Aquinas*. Literally translated by Fathers of the English Dominican Province. Westminster, Md.: Christian Classics, 1948.

————. *On Truth*. Translated by Robert Mulligan. Chicago: Henry Regnery Company, 1952.

————. *Summa contra Gentiles: Book One*. Translated by Anton C. Pegis. Notre Dame: University of Notre Dame Press, 1975.

————. *Summa contra Gentiles: Book Two*. Translated by James F. Anderson. Notre Dame: University of Notre Dame Press, 1975.

————. *Summa contra Gentiles: Book Three*. Translated by Vernon J. Bourke. Notre Dame: University of Notre Dame Press, 1975.

————. *Summa contra Gentiles: Book Four*. Translated by Charles J. O'Neil. Notre Dame: University of Notre Dame Press, 1975.

————. *Light of Faith: Compendium of Theology*. Translated by Cyril Vollert. Manchester, N.H.: Sophia Institute Press, 1988.

————. *Commentary on the Nicomachean Ethics*. Translated by C. I. Litzinger. Notre Dame: Dumb Ox Books, 1993.

────. *On Evil.* Translated by Jean Oesterle. Notre Dame: University of Notre Dame, 1995.

Torrell, Jean-Pierre. *Saint Thomas Aquinas: The Person and His Work.* Washington D.C.: The Catholic University of America Press, 1996.

Ugorji, L. I. *The Principle of Double Effect: A Critical Appraisal of Its Traditional Understanding and Its Modern Reinterpretation.* Frankfurt am Main: Peter Lang, 1993.

Vacek, Edward. "Proportionalism: One View of the Debate." *Theological Studies* 46 (1985): 287–314. Reprinted in *Proportionalism For and Against,* edited by Christopher Kaczor. Milwaukee: Marquette University Press, 2000.

Wallace, C. J. "Transplantation of Ectopic Pregnancy from Fallopian Tube to Cavity of Uterus." *Surgery, Gynecology, and Obstetrics* 24 (1917): 578–79.

Walter, James J. "Joseph Fletcher and the Ends-Means Problematic." *Heythrop Journal* 17 (1976): 50–63.

────. "Proportionate Reason and Its Three Levels of Inquiry: Structuring the Ongoing Debate." *Louvain Studies* 10 (1984): 30–40. Reprinted in *Proportionalism For and Against,* edited by Christopher Kaczor. Milwaukee: Marquette University Press, 2000.

────. "Proportionalism." In *The Harper Collins Encyclopedia of Catholicism,* edited by Richard McBrien. San Francisco: Harper, 1995.

Weiß, A. M. *Sittlicher Wert und nichtsittliche Werte. Zur Relevanz der Unterscheidung in der moraltheologischen Diskussion um deontologiche Normen.* Freiburg: Universitätsverlag, 1996.

Westberg, Daniel. "Aquinas and the Process of Human Action." In *Moral and Political Philosophy in the Middle Ages: Proceedings of the Ninth International Congress of Medieval Philosophy,* edited by B. Carlos Bazán, Eduardo Andujar, and Leonard G. Sbrocchi. Ottawa: Legas, 1992.

────. *Right Practical Reason: Aristotle, Action, and Prudence in Aquinas.* Oxford: Clarendon Press, 1994.

Williams, Bernard. "Utilitarianism and Moral Self-Indulgence." In *Moral Luck: Philosophical Papers 1973–1980.* Cambridge: Cambridge University Press, 1981.

────, ed. *Utilitarianism and Beyond.* Cambridge: Cambridge University Press, 1982.

Williams, Bernard, and J. J. C. Smart. *Utilitarianism: For and Against.* Cambridge: Cambridge University Press, 1973.

Williams, Glanville. *The Sanctity of Life and the Criminal Law.* London: Faber and Faber, 1958.

Witschen, D. *Gerechtigkeit und teleologische Ethik.* Freiburg: Universitätsverlag, 1992.

Wolbert, Werner. *Vom Nutzen der Gerechtigkeit. Zur Diskussion um Utilitaris-mus und Teleologische Theorie.* Freiburg: Universitätsverlag, 1992.

———. "Die 'in sich schlechten' Handlungen und der Konsequentialis-mus." In *Moraltheologie im Abseits?* edited by Dietmar Mieth. Freiburg/Basel/Vienna: Herder, 1994.

———. "Konsistenzprobleme im Tötungsverbot." *Freiburger Zeitschrift für Philosophy und Theologie* 43 (1996): 199–240.

Zalba, M. *Theologiae Moralis Summa.* Vol. 2. Madrid: La Editorial Catolica, 1957.

INDEX

Abelard, Peter, 18, 65
abortion, 22, 33, 67, 71, 73, 77, 88, 111, 116, 125, 128, 174–75
absolute: moral norms, 3, 16, 20, 101, 121, 184n, 189, 197; exceptionless norms,132, 171–204
adultery, 20, 47, 88, 94, 101, 104, 117, 118, 125, 135, 176–80, 186, 198, 202, 203
amputation, 21, 33, 119, 159–61, 169–70
Aquinas, see "Thomas Aquinas"
Aristotle, 24, 50–52, 60, 134, 138, 142, 144–47, 149–50, 152–55, 160, 178, 184–85
Augustine, 14, 47, 49–50, 75, 123, 159, 189–90, 192–95

Bonaventure, 181n, 190
borderline situations, 181n
Boyle, Joseph, 1, 32, 36n, 62, 66–67, 70, 111
Broad, C. D., 10–11, 175

Cajetan, 77
capital punishment (death penalty), 13, 17, 94, 118, 159, 163, 165–70, 189, 196, 203
Cavanaugh, Thomas, 23, 68n, 107n
character: moral, 49, 65, 67, 69, 74n, 80, 99, 146, 149–51, 198
charity: as giving charity, 65, 81; as

love (see also "love"), 28, 41, 50, 120, 148, 154, 158, 163, 164n, 197
Church, 1, 4, 6, 187, 193, 207
circumstances, 2, 13, 18, 20, 26, 65, 79–82, 89–92, 95, 101–6, 109, 111, 113, 118, 139, 158, 165, 170, 177, 179, 181, 184
commensurate reason, 15–16, 19, 31–33, 68, 79, 121, 160–61
commitments, 57, 59, 66, 68n, 190
conflict situations (war), 2, 17, 22, 33, 56, 71, 73–74, 78, 86–87, 94, 99,124,128–29, 130n, 139, 159, 163–65, 168, 170, 187, 189, 190, 196
Connery, John, 77n, 119
conscience, 36, 45, 94, 173, 206
consequence(s), 1–3, 10, 12–13, 20, 28, 33, 38, 41, 43, 61–62, 63n, 67, 70, 72–73, 77, 79, 85, 89–90, 94–96, 110, 112, 121, 123, 126, 138, 151, 159, 194, 196
consequentialism, 12, 85, 89n, 125, 131–32
contraception (birth control), 4, 101, 205
craniotomy, 1, 111–12, 114
Curran, Charles, 3, 12, 18

Damascene, John, 45, 55, 201
Decalogue, 172–73, 181, 184, 201–2

225

deceiving, 20, 99, 190, 193
Dedek, John, 92, 198, 202
deliberation, 38, 55–56, 66, 78, 107, 109–11, 113–16, 117. *See also* "practical reasoning."
deontological & deontology, 9–13, 129, 131, 175–76
desire, 63, 73, 75, 78, 137
deter(rent), 131, 140, 165–67
direct/indirect, within double effect, 3, 14, 17, 32, 68–69, 160n, 189, 195
disproportionate, 34
doing evil to achieve good, 33, 75, 141–70, 188
Donagan, Alan, 4, 57, 63–64
double effect, 1–3, 8, 10, 21, 22, 23–44, 70, 77, 111, 120, 204, 207, 209

ectopic pregnancy, 21, 84, 113, 114n, 115–16
Ermecke, Gustav, 28–29, 32, 41
euthanasia, 3, 101, 110
evil: moral, 2, 15–16, 19–20, 31, 33, 69, 74, 79, 94, 117n, 122–23, 131, 135, 137, 178, 193, 200; non–moral, 158, 200, 201; pre-moral, 3, 10, 15–16, 20–21, 30–31, 33, 37, 39, 69, 82–83, 99, 100n, 101, 117–18, 121–22, 124–25, 130, 132–39, 144, 147, 150, 158, 160, 186, 193

faith, 5, 8, 172, 188, 194
feeling(s), 108, 136–37
Finnis, John, 1, 55n, 62, 111, 132, 159, 162, 179, 195, 198, 205
fontes moralitatis, 80
Ford, John C.,
foreseen consequences, 38–39, 43, 55, 64, 68–70, 72, 79, 95, 194
fornication, 64, 104, 118, 202
Frankena, William, 4, 122
Fuchs, Josef, 10, 16, 19, 30, 39, 82–83, 122, 132, 133n, 144, 151, 160, 182, 184

genocide, 177
God: as end, 45–46, 48–50, 53, 75, 134, 148, 154, 156–57, 192; with relation to moral norms, 4, 8, 17–18, 52, 64, 68, 74, 132n,

139, 172–74, 181–82, 184, 189–90, 197–203
Gorman, Michael, ix
grace, 35, 46, 48–49, 172, 174
Grisez, Germain, 1, 6, 62, 66–67, 111, 170n, 208
Gury, J. P., 23–24, 27–30, 34–39, 41, 43–35, 76–78, 120, 173, 209

Hallet, Garth, 2, 11, 13, 20, 33, 64n, 132n, 198
Hauerwas, Stanley, 4
Hoose, Bernard, 179n
Humanae Vitae, 4, 88n, 102n, 206n
human nature, 172
hysterectomy, 111–12

infallibility, 5, 181n
injury, intentional causing of, 26, 62, 64, 103n, 129, 154, 160n, 161, 196–97
intention: in general, 2, 14, 19, 25–26, 31–32, 37–39, 50, 54–70, 72, 79–81, 87, 88n, 89, 94–99, 102, 106–14, 116, 118–19, 129, 151, 164, 170n, 190, 191n, 193, 196; proximate, 26, 96–97; remote, 26, 81, 96–98
intercourse: extramarital, *see* "adultery;" forced (*see also* "rape"), 47, 99–101, 103, 178; premarital, *see* "fornication"
intrinsically evil acts, 3, 11, 14, 17–19, 21, 69–70, 76n, 78, 92, 99–100, 118, 177, 179, 198

Janssens, 24, 30, 34–35, 39, 44, 54, 73n, 76n, 100–101, 117n, 121–23, 124n, 125n, 133, 136, 137n, 160, 183n, 184n
John Paul II, 1, 169n, 196, 207
justice: in general, 24–25, 28, 35, 41, 47, 85, 100, 120, 143, 153–56, 158, 163–67, 169–70, 172–73, 179, 182, 186, 196, 199, 200–203, 209; commutative, 24–25, 35, 154–56, 158, 163–65, 170; distributive, 24, 154–56, 165, 170; retributive (*see also* "punishment"), 156n, 165n, 166, 167n, 169

Kaczor, Christopher, 4n, 16n, 21n,

68n, 73n, 179n, 180n, 185n, 208n, 215–18, 221, 223
Kelly, Gerard, 28, 41, 206
Knauer, ix, 2, 6, 15–16n, 22, 24, 30–35, 37–39, 42–45, 68–69, 74, 79, 85, 86, 88n, 101n, 120–21, 123–28, 132n, 135, 160

lesser evil, 12, 43, 187–88, 203
love, 9, 45, 50, 76n, 100n, 101n, 150, 156–58, 176, 192. See also "charity."
lying, 14–17, 20, 118, 130n, 159, 178, 188–96

McCormick, Richard, 2–3, 4n, 6–8, 11, 14, 17–18, 20, 22, 30, 32–33n, 54, 69, 71–72, 74, 76n, 78, 85–88, 95–99, 117n, 119–22, 124n–25, 128–30, 134, 137, 159n–61, 174n, 177, 179n, 186, 190n, 197n–98, 206, 208–9
MacIntyre, Alasdair, 60n–61n, 84, 127, 147–48, 152, 155n, 168, 180, 193, 204
Maguire, Daniel, 3, 37, 174
Mahoney, John, 8, 50n, 53–54, 173–74
Mangan, Joseph, 36–37
martyr(dom), 68, 193, 195, 200–201
Mausbach, Joseph, 28–29, 32, 41
maximize value, 34, 43, 127, 131–32
May, William, 31, 85n, 198
means, 3, 21, 16, 28–29, 31–32, 38–40, 43, 48, 55–56, 58–60, 62, 66–69, 71–78, 80, 83–84, 87–90, 96–99, 106–9, 112, 114–15, 117, 120–21, 124–25, 129, 147–48, 158, 164, 183, 200–201
merit, 12, 64–65, 155, 173, 175
Merkelbach, Benedict, 29
Milhaven, John G., 18n, 198, 202
minimize disvalue, 34, 43, 131–32, 139
moral norms, 6, 10, 72, 171, 175–77, 182–83, 188, 191, 195. See also "absolute."
murder, 17, 19–20, 62, 90, 94, 101, 105, 117–18, 125, 135, 166, 176, 177, 179–82, 186, 189, 197–98

natural law, 5, 7–9, 45, 76, 168, 174, 181, 202, 204, 207, 209
negative norms/precepts, 3, 171, 183–84, 186
New Testament, 20

O'Connell, Timothy, 5, 76, 168
Old Testament, 197
organ: removal of diseased, 33n, 71n, 98n, 112, 160–61, 167–69, 189; transplant of, 97–98, 103, 159, 162, 170

pain, causing/relieving, 15–16, 20–21, 70, 102n, 110, 122, 130, 159, 162–63, 170, 184
Paul, St., 20–21
Pius XII, 196
Porter, Jean, ix, 4, 45n, 64n, 82n, 105
practical reasoning, 32, 38–39, 69, 72–73, 100, 118–19, 139–41, 146, 150, 153, 156, 158, 171, 184. See also "deliberation."
providence, 46, 132n
prudence, 135, 146–47, 149, 153, 172
punishment, 101–2, 130–31, 148, 155–56, 165–67, 169, 199, 201. See also "justice: retributive."

Quay, Paul, 137

Rahner, Karl, 5, 178n, 209
Ramsey, Paul, 4, 122
rape, 19, 85, 100–101. See also "intercourse: forced."
Regatillo, E. F., 29, 32
responsibility, 48, 67, 167
revelation, 5, 172

salpingectomy, 21, 113–14, 116n
salpingostomy, 21–22
Scholz, Franz, 125n, 181n, 182n
Schüller, Bruno, 3, 9–11, 17, 20, 30, 33, 85, 103, 124, 160, 175, 176, 190, 208
self defense, 3, 17, 19, 21–26, 28, 33, 35–36, 39–40, 64, 87, 94, 96–97, 101, 120, 125–26, 130n, 156, 159, 163–64, 170, 188–89
side effects, 113, 116n, 126. See also

"consequences;" "foreseen consequences;" and "intention."
slavery, 177
steal(ing), see "theft"
suicide, 17, 48, 68, 70, 109, 111,
   197, 200
Sullivan, Joseph, 29

technical finality, 134
teleological & teleology, 9–14, 18,
   22, 71–73, 117n, 119, 121, 131,
   142, 152, 175, 186–89, 191, 195,
   197
Ten Commandments, see "Decalogue"
theft, 20, 57–58, 81, 88, 94, 99–100,
   103–6, 117, 177, 186, 198, 202
Thomas Aquinas, 2, 5, 8–9, 19,
   22–28, 34–70, 74–75, 77–83,
   88–89, 91–95, 97–98, 100,
   103–4, 106–7, 109, 117, 120,
   122–26, 132, 134–36, 138–44,
   146–47, 151–59, 161–76,

178–79, 181–85, 189–90,
   192–204, 209
Thomas More, 194–95
Trent, Council of, 201

Utilitarian(ism), 7, 8, 12, 133–34

Vacek, Edward V., 4, 73, 133–34
value: moral, 2, 122n, 132n; non-
   moral, 14, 40, 132n; pre-moral,
   2–3, 82, 134, 136–37, 144
virtue, 15, 28, 41, 45, 47–52, 54–55,
   120, 132, 134–35, 140, 142–54,
   156, 158, 171–73, 185, 192, 196,
   206, 209

Walter, James, ix, 2–3, 121, 124,
   126, 178, 198–99
Williams, Bernard, 12, 70, 182, 195
Williams, Glanville, 62

Zalba, M., 29, 32